Student Solutions Manual

Statistics
for Managers

Student Solutions Manual

David M. Levine
Baruch College

Mark L. Berenson

David Stephan
Baruch College

Statistics for Managers

USING MICROSOFT® EXCEL

SECOND EDITION

Prentice Hall, Upper Saddle River, New Jersey 07458

Acquisitions editor: *Thomas R. Tucker*
Associate editor: *Kristen R. Imperatore*
Project editor: *Joan Waxman*
Manufacturer: *Bawden Printing*

Printed in the United States of America

10   9   8   7   6   5

ISBN 0-13-020331-9

Prentice-Hall International (UK) Limited, *London*
Prentice-Hall of Australia Pty. Limited, *Sydney*
Prentice-Hall Canada Inc., *Toronto*
Prentice-Hall Hispanoamericana, S.A., *Mexico*
Prentice-Hall of India Private Limited, *New Delhi*
Prentice-Hall of Japan, Inc., *Tokyo*
Prentice-Hall Asia Pte. Ltd., *Singapore*
Editora Prentice-Hall do Brasil, Ltda., *Rio de Janeiro*

Table of Contents

Note to Students

The *Student's Solutions Manual* contains the solutions to even-numbered End-of-Section Problems and Chapter Review Problems in each chapter of the text. Bulleted problems that appear in the text along with the answers in the back are again referenced as such here.

The *Student's Solutions Manual* contains many step-by-step, detailed solutions to problems in order to facilitate understanding. In addition, Microsoft Excel output is provided for a variety of problems throughout the text.

Other useful information can also be found on the following World Wide Web page

http://www.prenhall.com/Levine

CHAPTER 1

1.2   Three sizes of soft drink are classified into distinct categories—small, medium, and large—in which order is implied.

•1.4   (a)   discrete numerical   (g)   categorical
        (b)   categorical   (h)   discrete numerical
        (c)   discrete numerical   (i)   continuous numerical
        (d)   continuous numerical   (j)   categorical
        (e)   categorical   (k)   categorical
        (f)   continuous numerical

1.6   (a)   categorical   (e)   discrete numerical
        (b)   continuous numerical   (f)   discrete numerical
        (c)   continuous numerical   (g)   categorical
        (d)   categorical   (h)   categorical

1.8   (a)   categorical   (i)   continuous numerical *
        (b)   categorical   (j)   continuous numerical *
        (c)   continuous numerical   (k)   categorical
        (d)   continuous numerical *   (l)   discrete numerical
        (e)   categorical   (m)   continuous numerical *
        (f)   categorical   (n)   continuous numerical
        (g)   discrete numerical **   (o)   categorical
        (h)   discrete numerical   (p)   continuous numerical *

        *Some researchers consider money as a discrete numerical variable because it can be "counted."
        **Some researchers would "measure" the time since starting the job and consider this a
            continuous numerical variable.

1.10   While it is theoretically true that ties cannot occur with continuous data, the grossness of the measuring instruments used often leads to the reporting of ties in practical applications. Hence two students may both score 90 on an exam—not because they possess identical ability but rather because the grossness of the scoring method used failed to detect a difference between them.

1.12   (a) 001   (b) 040   (c) 902

•1.14   (a)   Row 29: 12 47 83 76 22 99 65 93 10 65 83 61 36 98 89 58 86 92 71
                Note: All sequences above 93 and all repeating sequences are discarded.
        (b)   Row 29: 12 47 83 76 22 99 65 93 10 65 83 61 36 98 89 58 86
                Note: All sequences above 93 are discarded. Elements 65 and 83 are repeated.

1

1.16 This is a random sample because the selection is based on chance. It is not a simple random sample because A is more likely to be selected than B or C.

•1.18 (a) Since a complete roster of full-time students exists, a simple random sample of 200 students could be taken. If student satisfaction with the quality of campus life randomly fluctuates across the student body, a systematic 1-in-20 sample could also be taken from the population frame. If student satisfaction with the quality of life may differ by gender and by experience/class level, a stratified sample using eight strata, female freshmen through female seniors and male freshmen through male seniors, could be selected. If student satisfaction with the quality of life is thought to fluctuate as much within clusters as between them, a cluster sample could be taken.

(b) A simple random sample is one of the simplest to select. The population frame is the registrar's file of 4,000 student names.

(c) A systematic sample is easier to select by hand from the registrar's records than a simple random sample, since an initial person at random is selected and then every 20th person thereafter would be sampled. The systematic sample would have the additional benefit that the alphabetic distribution of sampled students' names would be more comparable to the alphabetic distribution of student names in the campus population.

(d) If rosters by gender and class designations are readily available, a stratified sample should be taken. Since student satisfaction with the quality of life may indeed differ by gender and class level, the use of a stratified sampling design will not only ensure all strata are represented in the sample, it will generate a more representative sample and produce estimates of the population parameter that have greater precision.

(e) If all 4,000 full-time students reside in one of 20 on-campus residence halls which fully integrate students by gender and by class, a cluster sample should be taken. A cluster could be defined as an entire residence hall, and the students of a single randomly selected residence hall could be sampled. Since the dormitories are fully integrated by floor, a cluster could alternatively be defined as one floor of one of the 20 dormitories. Four floors could be randomly sampled to produce the required 200 student sample. Selection of an entire dormitory may make distribution and collection of the survey easier to accomplish. In contrast, if there is some variable other than gender or class that differs across dormitories, sampling by floor may produce a more representative sample.

1.20 (a) The proposed sample design is a nonprobability quota sample. Since the invoices are already separated into strata, a stratified sample should be used to reduce selection bias and improve generalizability of results.

(b) Sampling 4% of the invoices in each of the four strata would produce a sample with the same number of units.

(c) The proposed sample design is not a simple random sample because all invoices do not have an equal chance of being selected.

1.22   Before accepting the results of a survey of college students, you might want to know, for example:
Who funded the survey? Why was it conducted?
What was the population from which the sample was selected?
What sampling design was used?
What mode of response was used: a personal interview, a telephone interview, or a mail
    survey? Were interviewers trained? Were survey questions field-tested?
What questions were asked? Were they clear, accurate, unbiased, valid?
What operational definition of "the most 'in' clothing" was used?
What was the response rate?

1.24   A population contains all the items whereas a sample contains only a portion of the items in the population.

1.26   Descriptive methods deal with the collection, presentation, summarization, and analysis of data whereas inferential methods deal with decisions arising from the projection of sample information to the characteristics of a population.

1.48   (a)   Population: Actual voters
        (b)   Sample: "Exit" poll enables an estimate based on actual voters
        (c)   This is superior to a prior telephone poll of registered voters because not all registered voters will actually vote.

1.50   (a)   Population: Cat owners
        (b)   Sample frame: Households in the United States
        (d)   (1)   categorical   (3)   numerical
               (2)   categorical   (4)   categorical

CHAPTER 2

•2.2   Stem-and-leaf of Finance Scores

5	34
6	9
7	4
8	0
9	38

$n = 7$

2.4   Stem-and-leaf of Organizational Behavior Scores

6	38
7	66
8	77
9	5

$n = 7$

2.6   Ordered array: 50 74 74 76 81 89 92

2.8   (a)   Ordered array: 3 4 5 6 7 7 9 10 10 10
                                    11 11 12 15 18 18 21 26 33 37

           (b)   Stem-and-leaf of Monthly Billing Records

0	3456778
10	000112588
20	16
30	37

$n = 20$

           (c)   Amounts owed on monthly billing records are concentrated between $10 and $19.

•2.10   (a)   Ordered array: 4 5 5 6 6 6 6 7 7 7 7 7 7 8 8
                                    8 8 8 8 8 8 8 9 9 9 9 9 9 9 10 10
                                    10 10 10 10 10 10 11 11 12 12 13 13 14 15 15
                                    15 16 16 18 23

           (b)   Stem-and-leaf of Book Values

0	4556666777777888888888999999
1	00000001122334555668
2	3

$n = 50$

           (c)   Book values on the New York Stock Exchange are more likely to be low, since they are concentrated below $10. Better than half of the stocks sampled had book values below $10.
           (d)   You are much more likely to find a New York stock with a book value below $10 than above $20. In fact, 28 of the 50 stocks sampled had book values below $10, compared to one stock with a book value above $20.

2.12   (a)   Ordered array: 170 170 170 180 180 190 190 200 200 210 220
                                                  220 250 250 265 270 300 300 320 340 350 450

(b)   Stem-and-leaf of VCR Model Prices

	A	B	C	D	E	F
1				**Stem-and-Leaf Display**		
2				**for Price ($)**		
3				**Stem unit:**	**100**	
4						
5	Statistics			1	7 7 7 8 8 9 9	
6	Sample Size	22		2	0 0 1 2 2 5 5 6 7	
7	Mean	245.2273		3	0 0 2 4 5	
8	Median	220		4	5	
9	Std. Deviation	73.26529				
10	Minimum	170				
11	Maximum	450				

(c)   While you can find VCR models priced from $170 to $450, you are more likely to find models priced under $200 than over $300.

(d)   Nine of the 22 models are priced from $200 through $290, which is the greatest concentration of VCR model prices.

2.14   (a)   Width of interval $\cong \dfrac{247,000 - 62,000}{5} = 37,000 \cong 40,000$

                   Annual Salaries   Midpoint

Annual Salaries	Midpoint
$60,000 up to $100,000	$80,000
$100,000 up to $140,000	$120,000
$140,000 up to $180,000	$160,000
$180,000 up to $220,000	$200,000
$220,000 up to $260,000	$240,000

(b)   Width of interval $\cong \dfrac{247,000 - 62,000}{6} = 30,833.3\overline{3} \cong 35,000$

                   Annual Salaries   Midpoint

Annual Salaries	Midpoint
$60,000 up to $95,000	$77,500
$95,000 up to $130,000	$112,500
$130,000 up to $165,000	$147,500
$165,000 up to $200,000	$182,500
$200,000 up to $235,000	$217,500
$235,000 up to $270,000	$252,500

2.14
Cont.

(c) Width of interval $\cong \dfrac{247,000 - 62,000}{7} \cong 26,430 \cong 30,000$

Annual Salaries	Midpoint
$50,000 up to $80,000	$65,000
$80,000 up to $110,000	$95,000
$110,000 up to $140,000	$125,000
$140,000 up to $170,000	$155,000
$170,000 up to $200,000	$185,000
$200,000 up to $230,000	$215,000
$230,000 up to $260,000	$245,000

(d) Width of interval $\cong \dfrac{247,000 - 62,000}{8} \cong 23,125 \cong 25,000$

Annual Salaries	Midpoint
$50,000 up to $75,000	$62,500
$75,000 up to $100,000	$87,500
$100,000 up to $125,000	$112,500
$125,000 up to $150,000	$137,500
$150,000 up to $175,000	$162,500
$175,000 up to $200,000	$187,500
$200,000 up to $225,000	$212,500
$225,000 up to $250,000	$237,500

2.16   (a)   The value appearing in a relative frequency distribution for a class containing 12 out of a total of 40 observations is 12/40 or 0.3.
(b)   The value appearing in a percentage distribution for a class containing 12 out of a total of 40 observations is 12/40 • 100% or 30%.

2.18   (a)   The percentage polygon is plotted at the class midpoints from a frequency distribution.
(b)   The histogram is plotted at the class boundaries from a frequency distribution.
(c)   The histogram contains a series of vertical rectangular bars.
(d)   The percentage polygon is formed by connecting a set of consecutive plotted points.
(e)   The percentage polygon is used for comparing two or more sets of data that have been tallied into corresponding frequency distributions.

•2.20   In constructing an ogive, the vertical axis must show the true zero or "origin" so as not to distort or otherwise misrepresent the character of the data.

2.22   (a)   4%   (b) 36%   (c) 32%   (d) 16 (e) 100%

2.24   (a)

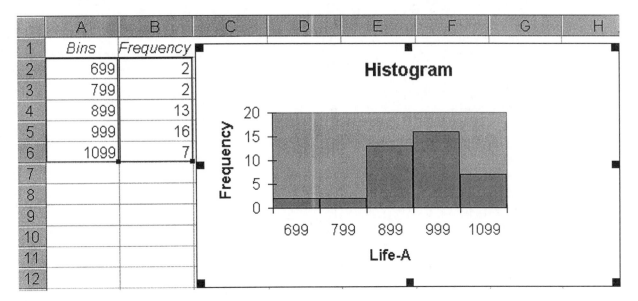

	A	B
1	Bins	Frequency
2	699	2
3	799	2
4	899	13
5	999	16
6	1099	7

(b)

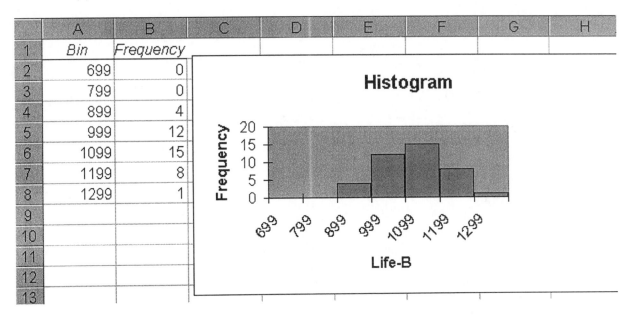

	A	B
1	Bin	Frequency
2	699	0
3	799	0
4	899	4
5	999	12
6	1099	15
7	1199	8
8	1299	1

2.24
cont.

(c)

Bulb Life (hrs)	Frequency, Mfgr A	Frequency, Mfgr B
650 – 699	2	0
700 – 749	1	0
750 – 799	1	0
800 – 849	4	2
850 – 899	9	2
900 – 949	11	6
950 – 999	5	6
1000 – 1049	4	10
1050 – 1099	3	5
1100 – 1149	0	4
1150 – 1199	0	4
1200 – 1249	0	1

(d)

Bulb Life (hrs)	Percentage, Mfgr A	Percentage, Mfgr B
650 – 749	7.5%	0.0%
750 – 849	12.5	5.0
850 – 949	50.0	20.0
950 – 1049	22.5	40.0
1050 – 1149	7.5	22.5
1150 – 1249	0.0	12.5

(g)

Bulb Life (hrs)	Frequency Less Than, Mfgr A	Frequency Less Than, Mfgr B
650 – 749	3	0
750 – 849	8	2
850 – 949	28	10
950 – 1049	37	26
1050 – 1149	40	35
1150 – 1249	40	40

(h)

Bulb Life (hrs)	Percentage Less Than, Mfgr A	Percentage Less Than, Mfgr B
650 – 749	7.5%	0.0%
750 – 849	20.0	5.0
850 – 949	70.0	25.0
950 – 1049	92.5	65.0
1050 – 1149	100.0	87.5
1150 – 1249	100.0	100.0

(j)   Manufacturer B produces bulbs with longer lives than Manufacturer A. The cumulative percentage for Manufacturer B shows 65% of their bulbs lasted 1049 hours or less contrasted with 70% of Manufacturer A's bulbs which lasted 949 hours or less. None of Manufacturer A's bulbs lasted more than 1149 hours, but 12.5% of Manufacturer B's bulbs lasted between 1150 and 1249 hours. At the same time, 7.5% of Manufacturer A's bulbs lasted less than 750 hours, while all of Manufacturer B's bulbs lasted at least 750 hours.

2.26   (a)

Book Values	Frequency	Percentage
0 – 4	1	2%
5 – 9	27	54
10 – 14	15	30
15 – 19	6	12
20 – 24	1	2

(b)

Book Values	Frequency Less Than	Percentage Less Than
0 – 4	1	2%
5 – 9	28	56
10 – 14	43	86
15 – 19	49	98
20 – 24	50	100

(f)   Better than half of the book values for the sampled stocks on the New York Stock Exchange had book values between $5 and $9.

2.28   (a)   Stem-and-leaf of Amount of Soft Drink

1.8H	9
1.9L	03444
1.9H	555666677788899999
2.0L	00111111111222223334
2.0H	556678
2.1L	0

$n = 50$

Note: 1.8H are the "high 1.8s" such as 1.85, 1.86, 1.87, 1.88, or 1.89. 1.9L are the "low 1.9s" such as 1.90, 1.91, 1.92, 1.93, or 1.94. 1.9H are the "high 1.9s" such as 1.95, 1.96, 1.97, 1.98, or 1.99.

(b)

Amount of Soft Drink	Frequency	Percentage
1.85 – 1.89	1	2%
1.90 – 1.94	5	10
1.95 – 1.99	18	36
2.00 – 2.04	19	38
2.05 – 2.09	6	12
2.10 – 2.14	1	2

(c)

Amount of Soft Drink	Frequency Less Than	Percentage Less Than
1.85 – 1.89	1	2%
1.90 – 1.94	6	12
1.95 – 1.99	24	48
2.00 – 2.04	43	86
2.05 – 2.09	49	98
2.10 – 2.14	50	100

2.28
cont.

(g) The amount of soft drink filled in the two liter bottles is most concentrated in two intervals on either side of the two-liter mark, from 1.95 to 1.99 and from 2.00 to 2.04 liters. Almost three-fourths of the 50 bottles sampled contained between 1.95 liters and 2.04 liters.

(h) You would predict that the amount of soft drink filled in the next bottle will be between 1.95 liters and 2.04 liters because 74% of the bottles sampled fell within those bounds. If the prediction is for a specific value, you would predict 2.00 liters because it is the midpoint of the combined interval.

2.32

(d) The bar chart does not facilitate comparison of the size of the various categories to the whole. The multiple divisions present in the pie chart are in some instances narrow and difficult to discern. The Pareto diagram is preferable here because it builds on the strength of the bar chart and conveys the relative sense of importance in sales of various food product groups through the cumulative polygon.

(e) Grocery, soy foods, and dairy represent 27.4% of the sales of organic foods purchased from natural food stores in the U.S. during 1995, while Produce represented an additional 21.5% of sales. Together they represent nearly 50% of the sales for that year.

•2.34

(e) Highway transportation accounted for better than half of the oil consumption in the United States in 1995.

2.36

(b) The number one area for residential water consumption in a suburban area during a recent summer was lawn watering, accounting for better than one-third of all water consumed by households that summer. When bathing/showering and toilet usage were added, better than 80% of all water consumed was accounted for. The suburban water district should target those three areas in developing a water reduction plan.

2.38

(b) Restaurants make up almost 24% of the commercial properties in the Times Square area of New York City. Quick-service (food) outlets and vacant stores made up additional 13.3% and 11% of the commercial properties, respectively.

(c) Restaurant-goers will find ample choice among the 232 food establishments serving this 32-block region of New York City, 149 of which afford a full dining experience and the remaining 83 provide quick food service.

•2.42

(a) Table based on column percentages

Financial Conditions	H.S. Degree or Lower	Education Level Some College	College Degree or Higher	Totals
Worse off now	21.2%	24.4%	8.6%	18.5%
No difference	24.2%	45.6%	14.8%	26.0%
Better off now	54.7%	30.0%	76.7%	55.5%
Totals	100%	100%	100%	100%

(c) Financial conditions were rated as better now than before by a majority of the groups with the lowest and highest education levels. But the largest segment of the group with some college rated their financial conditions as no different now than before.

2.44   (d) The row percentages allow us to block the effect of disproportionate group size and show us that the pattern for day and evening tests among the nonconforming group is very different from the pattern for day and evening tests among the conforming group. Where 40% of the nonconforming group was tested during the day, 68% of the conforming group was tested during the day.

(e) The director of the lab may be able to cut the number of nonconforming tests by reducing the number of tests run in the evening, when there is a higher percent of tests run improperly.

•2.64   (f) There is a great deal of variation in the number of days it took to resolve customer complaints. Better than one-quarter of all complaints were resolved in less than 20 days, over half within 30 days. But the amount of time to resolution ranged from one day to 165 days, with over 40% of the complaints requiring more than 30 days to settle and 20% requiring more than 60 days to settle.

(g) You should tell the president of the company that over half of the complaints are resolved within a month, but point out that some complaints take as long as three or four months to settle.

2.66   (a)   (1)   Ordered arrays:

Weight:	5	6	6	6	6	6	7	7	7	7	7	10
	10	10	11	12	12	15	17	17	18	19	20	21
	21	22	22	22	24	25	26	26	27	29	29	29
	30	31	31	47								

Cost:	0.52	0.62	0.64	0.64	0.69	0.71	0.72	0.72	0.73	0.75	0.77
	0.80	0.80	0.81	0.81	0.83	0.85	0.87	0.90	0.90	0.92	1.00
	1.11	1.11	1.13	1.14	1.15	1.23	1.23	1.28	1.46	1.49	1.50
	1.51	1.51	1.52	1.53	1.54	1.71	1.90				

Calories:	264	275	288	296	299	305	309	312	313	316	322
	323	327	332	333	337	338	347	348	349	350	353
	357	358	360	361	364	365	367	370	372	381	382
	387	390	393	394	409	436	442				

Fat:	3	4	7	7	7	9	9	9	10	10	10	11
	11	12	12	13	13	13	14	14	14	15	15	16
	16	16	17	17	17	18	19	19	20	20	20	21
	21	22	25	26								

2.66
cont.

(2)   Stem-and-leaf for Weight   Stem-and-leaf for Calories
0   56666677777   Hundreds   Tens
1   00012257789   2H   67899
2   01122245667999   3L   001112223333444
3   011   3H   55556666677888999
4   7   4L   034
      $n = 40$ $n = 40$

      Stem-and-leaf for Cost   Stem-and-leaf for Fat
0.5   2   0L   34
0.6   2449   0H   777999
0.7   122357   1L   0001122333444
0.8   0011357   1H   55666777899
0.9   002   2L   000112
1.0   0   2H   56
1.1   11345 $n = 40$
1.2   338   *Note*: L is "low" and H is "high"
1.3   to create more stems.
1.4   69
1.5   011234
1.6
1.7   1
1.8
1.9   0
      $n = 40$

(b)   Ordered arrays by pizza type:

Weight:									
Type 1:	21	25	26	29	31	31	47		
Type 2:	6	6	6	7	7	7	10	10	17	17
	19	21	22	24	26	29	29		
Type 3:	5	6	6	7	7	10	11	12	12	15
	18	20	22	22	27	30			

Cost:									
Type 1:	1.23	1.23	1.28	1.51	1.51	1.53	1.90		
Type 2:	0.52	0.64	0.69	0.72	0.72	0.75	0.80	0.81	0.85
	0.90	0.90	0.92	1.00	1.15	1.49	1.50	1.54	
Type 3:	0.62	0.64	0.71	0.73	0.77	0.80	0.81	0.83	0.87
	1.11	1.11	1.13	1.14	1.46	1.52	1.71		

Calories:									
Type 1:	305	309	313	327	338	349	382		
Type 2:	275	288	296	299	316	322	323	332	333
	337	347	350	353	357	358	364	393	
Type 3:	264	312	348	360	361	365	367	370	372
	381	387	390	394	409	436	442		

Fat:									
Type 1:	9	9	10	11	13	14	16		
Type 2:	4	7	7	9	10	10	12	12	13	13
	14	14	16	16	17	17	19		
Type 3:	3	7	11	15	15	17	18	19	20	20
	20	21	21	22	25	26			

(c)-(d)

Weight	Frequency	Percentage	Frequency Less Than	Percentage Less Than
0 up to 10	11	27.5%	11	27.5%
10 up to 20	11	27.5	22	55.0
20 up to 30	14	35.0	36	90.0
30 up to 40	3	7.5	39	97.5
40 up to 50	1	2.5	40	100.0

Cost	Frequency	Percentage	Frequency Less Than	Percentage Less Than
0.50 up to 0.75	9	22.5%	9	22.5%
0.75 up to 1.00	12	30.0	21	52.5
1.00 up to 1.25	8	20.0	29	72.5
1.25 up to 1.50	3	7.5	32	80.0
1.50 up to 1.75	7	17.5	39	97.5
1.75 up to 2.00	1	2.5	40	100.0

Calories	Frequency	Percentage	Frequency Less Than	Percentage Less Than
250 up to 280	2	5.0%	2	5.0%
280 up to 310	5	12.5	7	17.5
310 up to 340	10	25.0	17	42.5
340 up to 370	12	30.0	29	72.5
370 up to 400	8	20.0	37	92.5
400 up to 430	1	2.5	38	95.0
430 up to 460	2	5.0	40	100.0

(h)   The typical weight for a slice of pizza is between 10 and 20 ounces, where the cumulative percentage shows 55% of the sample is less than or equal to 20 ounces.

(i)   The typical cost for a slice of pizza is between $.75 and $1.00, since that is both the most frequently occurring interval and better than 50% of the sample is less than or equal to $1.00.

(j)   The typical caloric content for a slice of pizza is between 340 and 370 calories, since that is the most frequently occurring interval and better than 70% of the sample is less than or equal to 370 calories.

(k)   Based on the results of the pairwise scatter diagrams prepared for part (g), calories and fat seem to be related. Other variables do not show any particular pattern in the scatter plot, but the graph of calories and fat has a positive slope because it rises from left to right, showing that as one variable increases, the other tends to also increase. The data points are tightly distributed within the cloud of points, indicating that the relationship between calories and fat content is strong.

2.68   (a)

Number of Calls	Frequency	Percentage
2650-2850	1	3.33%
2850-3050	1	3.33
3050-3250	16	53.33
3250-3450	9	30.00
3450-3650	2	6.67
3650-3850	1	3.33

(f)   There is very little variation in the daily number of calls over the 30 day period sampled.

2.70   (c)

Amount	Percentage Less Than, March	Percentage Less Than, April
$0 up to $2,000	12%	20%
$2,000 up to $4,000	38	48
$4,000 up to $6,000	72	74
$6,000 up to $8,000	92	94
$8,000 up to $10,000	100	94
$10,000 up to $12,000	100	100

(d)

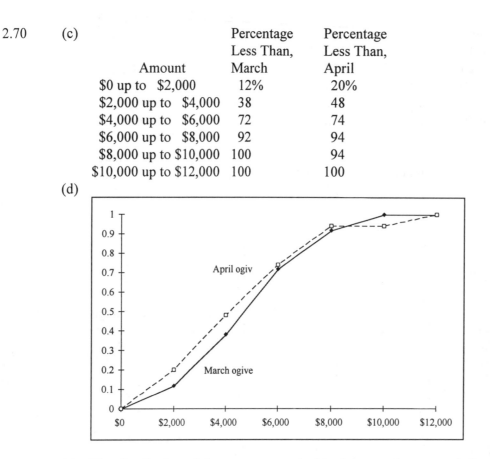

(e)   The distribution of the accounts receivable does not change much from March to April.

2.72   (e)   Two of the 30 NFL teams account for over 30% of the sales of licensed products, and six of the 30 NFL teams account for over 50% of the sales of licensed products. So a relatively few number of NFL teams account for a majority of the sales of licensed products. Clothing and hats account for 50% of the sales of licensed products. Retail licensing and sponsorships account for more than 70% of the reported revenues.

2.74   (b)   A first-time buyer of computer equipment is more than twice as likely to make a purchase from a consumer electronics store or mass merchant as is a repeat buyer. A repeat buyer is at least

14

CHAPTER 3

•3.2 (a) Mean = 7   Midrange = (3 + 12)/2 = 7.5
           Median = 7   Midhinge = (4 + 9)/2 = 6.5
           Mode = 7
       (b) Range = 9   Variance = 10.8
           Interquartile range = 5   Standard deviation = 3.286
           Coefficient of variation = (3.286/7)•100% = 46.94%
       (c) Since the mean equals the median, the distribution is symmetrical.

3.4   (a) Mean = 2   Midrange = (– 8 + 9)/2 = 0.5
           Median = 7   Midhinge = (– 6.5 + 8)/2 = 0.75
           Mode = 7
       (b) Range = 17   Variance = 62
           Interquartile range = 14.5   Standard deviation = 7.874
           Coefficient of variation = (7.874/2)•100% = 393.7%
       (c) Since the mean is less than the median, the distribution is left-skewed.

•3.6 (a)

	Set 1	Set 2
Mean	4	14
Median	3	13
Mode	2	12
Midrange	6	16
Midhinge	3.5	13.5

   (b)-(c) The data values in Set 2 are each 10 more than the corresponding values in Set 1.
            The measures of central tendency for Set 2 are all 10 more than the comparable statistics for
            Set 1.
       (d)

	Set 1	Set 2
Range	8	8
Interquartile range	3	3
Variance	8.33*	8.33*
Standard deviation	2.89*	2.89*
Coefficient of variation	72.17%	20.62%

            *Note: Slight differences are due to rounding.
       (e) Since the mean is greater than the median for each data set, the distributions are both right-
            skewed.
       (f) Because the data values in Set 2 are each 10 more than the corresponding values in Set 1, the
            measures of spread among the data values remain the same across the two sets, with the
            exception of the coefficient of variation. The coefficients of variation are different because the
            sample standard deviation is divided by the set's mean; in the case of Set 2, the mean is 10
            more than the mean for Set 1, resulting in a larger denominator and a smaller coefficient. Set 2
            is a reflection of Set 1 simply shifted up the scale 10 units, so the distributions are also
            reflections of each other.

(g)   Generally stated, when a second data set is an additive shift from an original set:
        • the measures of central tendency for the second set are equal to the comparable measures for the original set plus the value, or distance, of the shift;
        • the measures of spread for the second set are equal to the corresponding measures for the original set, with the exception of the coefficient of variation;
        • the shape of the second distribution will be a reflection of the shape of the original distribution.

3.8   (a)

	Bad Data	Good Data
Mean	20	15
Median	15	15
Midrange	37	15

The midrange is drastically affected by the error. But the mean is only moderately altered and the median remains unchanged.

(b)

	Bad Data	Good Data
Range	48	4
Interquartile range	3	2.5
Variance	238.25	2.00
Standard deviation	15.435	1.414
Coefficient of variation	77.18%	9.43%

(c)-(d) The interquartile range is the only measure of variation that is not significantly altered by the error in one of the price-to-earnings ratios reported on the American Stock Exchange. In comparison to what they should be, the range is 12 times bigger, the variance is better than 119 times bigger, the standard deviation almost 11 (or the square root of 119) times bigger, and the coefficient of variation over 8 times bigger.

(e)   The distribution of the bad data set is right-skewed since the mean is greater than the median. But the distribution of the good data set is symmetrical since the mean and the median are equal.

3.10   (a)

	A	B	C
1	Rent ($)		
2		Center City	Outlying Area
3	Mean	1016.5	718.4
4	Standard Error	29.916272	19.37937047
5	Median	982.5	725
6	Mode	#N/A	725
7	Standard Deviation	94.6035588	61.28295032
8	Sample Variance	8949.83333	3755.6
9	Kurtosis	3.82059257	3.088218812
10	Skewness	2.02510267	-1.335483061
11	Range	307	225
12	Minimum	940	575
13	Maximum	1247	800
14	Sum	10165	7184
15	Count	10	10

  (b)   Rental prices for unfurnished studio apartments in the center of a large city are much higher than in an outlying part of the city. The lowest rent found in the sample of central city rents ($940) was higher than the highest rent found in sample of rents for the outlying area ($800). All measures of central tendency are higher for the sample taken in the center of the city than the sample taken from the outlying area.

3.12   (a)

(1) Mean = 7.11   (7) Range = 6.67
(2) Median = 6.68   (8) Interquartile range = 3.09
(3) Midrange = 7.155   (9) Variance = 4.336
(4) Q_1 = 5.64   (10) Standard deviation = 2.082
(5) Q_3 = 8.73   (11) Coefficient of variation = 29.27%
(6) Midhinge = 7.185

  (b)   Since the mean is greater than the median, the distribution is right-skewed.

  (c)   The mean and median are both well over 5 minutes and the distribution is right-skewed, meaning that there are more unusually high observations than low. Further, 13 of the 15 bank customers sampled (or 86.7%) had wait times in excess of 5 minutes. So, the customer is more likely to experience a wait time in excess of 5 minutes. The manager overstated the bank's service record in responding that the customer would "almost certainly" not wait longer than 5 minutes for service.

3.12
cont.   (e)   The sample reported in Problem 3.11 above was taken from a bank located in a commercial district of a city and was taken between 12 and 1 p.m. The sample reported in this problem was taken from a bank located in a residential area and was taken on Friday evening between 5 and 7 p.m. Customer service needs are likely to be quite different between the two locales, which may influence the length of time required to serve each customer. Differences in time of day and day of week may also influence the mix of customer service needs. Additional information on what week and what month the samples were taken would be useful, as would the customer base and the number of employees for each branch.

3.14   (a)   Mean = 18.46   Midrange = 21.70
                Median = 18.20   Midhinge = 18.05
        (b)   (4,500)(18.46) = 83,070
        (d)   The town council was interested in residential water use, not commercial.
        (e)   Range = 21   Standard deviation = 5.20
                Interquartile range = 6.90   Coefficient of variation = 28.2%
                Variance = 27.00
        (f)   The majority of the data fall within 5.20 thousand gallons on either side of the mean.
        (g)   Since the mean is only slightly larger than the median, the distribution is approximately symmetrical.

•3.16   (a)   Five-number summary: 3 4 7 9 12
        (b)
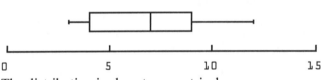
                The distribution is almost symmetrical.
        (c)   The data set is almost symmetrical since the median line almost divides the box in half.

3.18   (a)   Five-number summary: − 8 − 6.5 7 8 9
        (b)
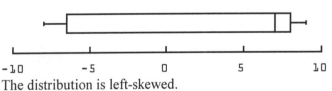
                The distribution is left-skewed.
        (c)   The box-and-whisker plot shows a longer left box from Q_1 to Q_2 than from Q_2 to Q_3, visually confirming our conclusion that the data are left-skewed.

•3.20   (a)   Five-number summary: 264 307.5 451 553.5 1,049
        (b)
                The distribution is right-skewed.

18

•3.20
cont. (c)   Because the data set is small, one very large value (1,049) skews the distribution to the right.

3.22 (a)

	A	B	C
1	Box-and-whisker Plot		
2			
3	Five-number Summary		
4		Center City	Outlying Area
5	Minimum	940	575
6	First Quartile	967.5	696.75
7	Median	982.5	725
8	Third Quartile	999.75	748.75
9	Maximum	1247	800

(b)

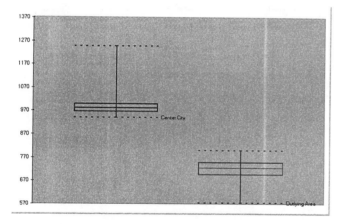

Monthly rental prices in the center of a large city are right-skewed and, because the data set is small, are affected by two extreme outlying values.
Outlying Area:

Monthly rental prices in the area outlying from a large city are left-skewed, affected by one unusually small value.

3.24 (a)   Five-number summary: 11.2 14.6 18.2 21.5 32.2
     (b)

```
      ┌──┬────┐
 ├────┤  │    ├───┤        *

 └──────┴──────────┴────────────┴─────┘
 10       20         30          40
```
The distribution is right-skewed.

19

3.24
cont.   (c)   The answer above differs from the answer given in Problem 3.13(g), where we concluded that the distribution was approximately symmetrical. The box-and-whisker plot identifies 32.2 as a very large value well beyond the other values in the set. Notice that the box and whisker below the median are longer than the box and whisker above the median, which mean that the values in the second quartile are relatively further away from the median than the values in the third quartile. Normally that would indicate a distribution is left-skewed. In this instance, however, the existence of one very large value (32.2) draws the mean (18.46) to the right of the median (18.20), resulting in a right-skewed distribution.

3.26   (a)   Mean = 6   Midrange = (3 + 9)/2 = 6
               Median = 6   Midhinge = (5 + 7)/2 = 6
               Mode = 6

        (b)   Range = 6   Standard deviation, $\sigma = 1.67$
               Interquartile range = 2   Coefficient of variation = 27.89%
               Variance, $\sigma^2 = 2.8$

        (c)

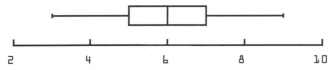

               This distribution is symmetrical. Supporting evidence may include a box-and-whisker plot, as indicated above, or a statement that the mean, median, mode, midrange, and midhinge are all equal to the same value, 6.

        (d)   Measures of central tendency for Problem 3.25(a) are all close to 6, but, unlike those in this problem, do vary from 5.5 (midhinge) to 8 (mode).

        (e)   Measures of variation for Problem 3.25(b) are all larger than comparable measures for this problem, a reflection of the fact that the data values in this problem are more similar than the data values in Problem 3.25.

3.28   (a)   (1) 67%   (2) 90%-95%   (3) 100%

        (b)   (1) Not calculable   (2) 75%   (3) 88.89%

        (c)   Solving for k,

               $$1 - \frac{1}{k^2} = 0.9375$$

               $$\underline{-1 \qquad = -1}$$

               $$-\frac{1}{k^2} = -0.0625$$

               $$k^2 = 16$$

               $$k = \pm 4 \text{ units of } \sigma \text{ above and below } \mu$$

3.28 (c)
Cont.

Since the population standard deviation is given as 6.75% and the mean is 28.20%, at least 93.75% of the one year returns will fall between the following bounds:

Lower bound: 28.20% – 4(6.75%) =   1.20%
Upper bound: 28.20% + 4(6.75%) =   55.20%

3.42 (a)   Mean = 15.33   Median = 16   Standard deviation = 3.674
     (b)   These data are approximately normally distributed, given the mean and median are roughly equivalent.
     (c) $460,000.

3.44 (a)

	A	B	C	D
1		Price($)	Cup Fills	Carafe Price($)
2				
3	Mean	44.52632	9.894736842	13.63157895
4	Standard Error	5.50458	0.237490989	1.915175662
5	Median	40	9.5	11
6	Mode	20	11	9
7	Standard Deviation	23.99391	1.035199221	8.348057168
8	Sample Variance	575.7076	1.071637427	69.69005848
9	Kurtosis	-0.43167	-1.647823665	12.01241645
10	Skewness	0.821537	0.020349441	3.221077289
11	Range	70	3	38
12	Minimum	20	8.5	7
13	Maximum	90	11.5	45
14	Sum	846	188	259
15	Count	19	19	19

3.44
cont.

(b)

	Price	Cups	Carafe
Mean	44.53	9.89	13.63
Median	40	9.5	11
Mode	20	11	9
Midrange	55	10	26
Midhinge	41	10	12.5

(c)

Basic Function		**Programmable**	
Stem-and-leaf for Price		Stem-and-leaf for Price	
2	000025	3	07
3	0	4	00
4		5	
5	002	6	5
6	0	7	
7		8	
8	5	9	00
	$n = 12$		$n = 7$

Stem-and-leaf for Cups		Stem-and-leaf for Cups	
Ones	Tenths	Ones	Tenths
8	555	8	
9	0005	9	055
10	55	10	5
11	005	11	000
	$n = 12$		$n = 7$

Stem-and-leaf for Carafe		Stem-and-leaf for Carafe	
0	78999	0	9
1	012467	1	01246
2		2	0
3			$n = 7$
4	5		
	$n = 19$		

(d)

	Basic Function			**Programmable**		
	Price	Cups	Carafe	Price	Cups	Carafe
Mean	37.83	9.71	13.92	56	10.21	13.14
Median	27.5	9.25	10.5	40	10.5	12
Mode	20	8.5, 9	9	40, 90	11	none
Midrange	52.5	10	26	60	10	14.5
Midhinge	36	9.75	12.5	63.5	10.25	13

(e)

	Price	Cups	Carafe
Range	70	3	38
Interquartile range	38	2	7
Variance	575.71	1.07	69.69
Standard deviation	23.99	1.04	8.35
Coefficient of variation	53.89%	10.46%	61.24%

3.44 (f)
cont.

Basic Function

	Price	Cups	Carafe
Range	65	3	38
Interquartile range	32	2.5	7
Variance	451.06	1.25	105.72
Standard deviation	21.24	1.12	10.28
Coefficient of variation	56.14%	11.51%	73.88%

Programmable

	Price	Cups	Carafe
Range	60	2	11
Interquartile range	53	1.5	6
Variance	657	0.74	14.81
Standard deviation	25.63	0.86	3.85
Coefficient of variation	45.77%	8.41%	29.28%

(g) **Price:** Since the mean is greater than the median price for coffee makers, the distribution of prices is right-skewed.

Cup capacity: Although the mean cup capacity (9.89) is just slightly higher than the median capacity (9.5), the distance from the first quartile to the median is one third of the distance from the median to the third quartile. The distribution is right-skewed.

Carafe replacement cost: The distribution of carafe replacement costs is right-skewed.

(i) Box-and-whisker plot for **Prices**

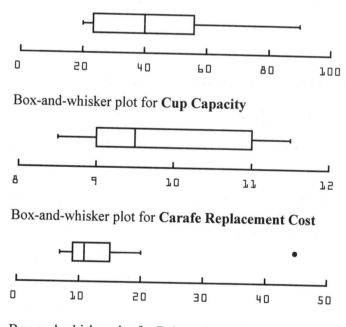

Box-and-whisker plot for **Cup Capacity**

Box-and-whisker plot for **Carafe Replacement Cost**

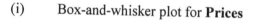

(j) Box-and-whisker plot for **Prices, Basic Function**

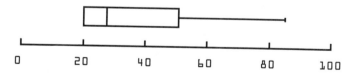

Box-and-whisker plot for **Prices, Programmable**

Box-and-whisker plot for **Cup Capacity, Basic Function**

Box-and-whisker plot for **Cup Capacity, Programmable**

Box-and-whisker plot for **Carafe Replacement Cost, Basic Function**

Box-and-whisker plot for **Carafe Replacement Cost, Programmable**

(k)   For programmable coffee makers, the upper half of the distribution of prices is more dispersed and the cup capacity tends to be higher on average. The extreme value ($45) greatly affects the mean carafe replacement cost for basic coffee makers.

•3.46 (a)

	A	B	C
1	*Time*		
2		Office I	Office II
3	Mean	2.214	2.0115
4	Standard Error	0.384165	0.422998
5	Median	1.54	1.505
6	Mode	1.48	3.75
7	Standard Deviation	1.718039	1.891706
8	Sample Variance	2.951657	3.57855
9	Kurtosis	0.285677	2.405845
10	Skewness	1.126671	1.466424
11	Range	5.8	7.47
12	Minimum	0.52	0.08
13	Maximum	6.32	7.55
14	Sum	44.28	40.23
15	Count	20	20

(b)

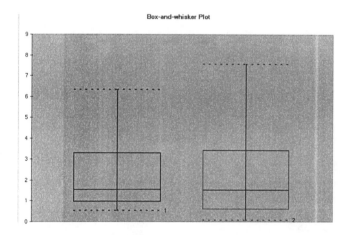

Box-and-whisker Plot

(c)   Times to clear problems at both central offices are right-skewed.

(d)   Times to clear problems for Office I are less dispersed about the mean than times to clear problems for Office II, even though the average for Office I times is higher (2.214) than that for Office II (2.012).

(e)   If the value 7.55 were incorrectly recorded as 27.55, the mean would be one minute higher (from 2.012 to 3.012) and the standard deviation would be over 3 times as large (from 1.892 to 5.936).

25

3.48 (a) (1) Mean   43.889
           (2) Median   45
           (3) Midrange   54
           (4) Q_1 18
           (5) Q_3 63
           (6) Midhinge   40.5
           (7) Range   76
           (8) Interquartile range   45
           (9) Variance   639.256
           (10) Standard deviation   25.284
           (11) Coefficient of variation   57.61%

     (b) Box-and-whisker plot for Bank Processing Times

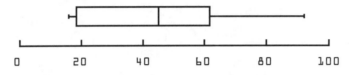

     (c) Although the whisker covering the upper-most quartile of data is significantly longer
          than the whisker covering the lowest quartile of data, the distribution is left-skewed.
          Supporting evidence includes that the distance from the first quartile to the median is
          much longer (27 units) than the distance from the median to the third quartile (18 units),
          and the mean is to the right of the median.

     (d) The customer should be told that the typical approval process takes between 18 and 63
          days, with the average around 45 days. No policy has required longer than 92 days for
          approval.

CHAPTER 4

4.2   (a)   Simple events include selecting a red ball or selecting a white ball.
         (b)   Selecting a white ball

•4.4   (a) $40/100 = 2/5 = 0.4$ (g) $\dfrac{40}{100}+\dfrac{35}{100}-\dfrac{10}{100}=\dfrac{65}{100}=\dfrac{13}{20}=0.65$

         (b) $35/100 = 7/20 = 0.35$

         (c) $60/100 = 3/5 = 0.6$ (h) $\dfrac{40}{100}+\dfrac{65}{100}-\dfrac{30}{100}=\dfrac{75}{100}=\dfrac{3}{4}=0.75$

         (d) $10/100 = 1/10 = 0.1$

         (e) $30/100 = 3/10 = 0.3$ (i) $\dfrac{60}{100}+\dfrac{65}{100}-\dfrac{35}{100}=\dfrac{90}{100}=\dfrac{9}{10}=0.9$

         (f) $35/100 = 7/20 = 0.35$

4.6   (a)   Mutually exclusive, not collectively exhaustive
         (b)   Not mutually exclusive, not collectively exhaustive
         (c)   Mutually exclusive, not collectively exhaustive
         (d)   Mutually exclusive, collectively exhaustive
         (e)   Mutually exclusive, collectively exhaustive

•4.8   (a)   Since simple events have only one criterion specified, an example could be any one of the following:
             (1) Having a bank credit card,
             (2) Not having a bank credit card,
             (3) Having a travel/entertainment credit card,
             (4) Not having a travel/entertainment credit card.
         (b)   Since joint events specify two criteria simultaneously, an example could be any one of the following:
             (1) Having a bank credit card and not having a travel/entertainment credit card,
             (2) Not having a bank credit card and not having a travel/entertainment credit card,
             (3) Having a bank credit card and having a travel/entertainment credit card,
             (4) Not having a bank credit card and having a travel/entertainment credit card.
         (c)   "Not having a bank credit card" is the complement of having a bank credit card, since it involves all events other than having a bank credit card.
         (d)   Having a bank credit card and having a travel/entertainment credit card is a joint event because two criteria are specified simultaneously.
         (e) P(has a bank credit card) $= 120/200 = 3/5 = 0.6$
         (f) P(has a travel/entertainment credit card) $= 75/200 = 3/8 = 0.375$
         (g) P(has a bank credit card *and* a travel/entertainment credit card)
             $= 60/200 = 3/10 = 0.3$
         (h) P(does not have a bank credit card *and* does not have a travel/entertainment credit card)
             $= 65/200 = 13/40 = 0.325$
         (i) P(has a bank credit card *or* has a travel/entertainment credit card)
             $= \dfrac{120}{200}+\dfrac{75}{200}-\dfrac{60}{200}=\dfrac{135}{200}=\dfrac{27}{40}=0.675$

(j)   P(does not have a bank credit card *or* has a travel/entertainment credit card)

$$= \frac{80}{200} + \frac{75}{200} - \frac{15}{200} = \frac{140}{200} = \frac{7}{10} = 0.7$$

•4.10 (a)   Enjoy Clothes

Shopping	Male	Female	Total
Yes	136	224	360
No	104	36	140
Total	240	260	500

(b)   Since simple events have only one criterion specified, an example could be any one of the following:

(1) Being a male,
(2) Being a female,
(3) Enjoying clothes shopping,
(4) Not enjoying clothes shopping.

(c)   Since joint events specify two criteria simultaneously, an example could be any one of the following:

(1) Being a male and enjoying clothes shopping,
(2) Being a male and not enjoying clothes shopping,
(3) Being a female and enjoying clothes shopping,
(4) Being a female and not enjoying clothes shopping.

(d)   "Not enjoying clothes shopping" is the complement of "enjoying shopping for clothes," since it involves all events other than enjoying clothes shopping.

(e) P(male) = 240/500 = 12/25 = 0.48
(f) P(enjoys clothes shopping) = 360/500 = 18/25 = 0.72
(g) P(female *and* enjoys clothes shopping) = 224/500 = 56/125 = 0.448
(h) P(male *and* does not enjoy clothes shopping) = 104/500 = 26/125 = 0.208
(i) P(female *or* enjoys clothes shopping) = 396/500 = 99/125 = 0.792
(j) P(male *or* does not enjoy clothes shopping) = 276/500 = 69/125 = 0.552
(k) P(male *or* female) = 500/500 = 1.00

4.12   (a)   Needs Warranty-

Related Repair	U.S.	Non-U.S.	Total
Yes	0.025	0.015	0.04
No	0.575	0.385	0.96
Total	0.600	0.400	1.00

(b)   Since simple events have only one criterion specified, an example could be any one of the following:

(1) Needing warranty-related repair,
(2) Not needing warranty-related repair,
(3) Manufacturer based in U.S.,
(4) Manufacturer not based in U.S.

(c)   Since joint events specify two criteria simultaneously, an example could be any one of the following:

(1) Needing warranty-related repair and manufacturer based in U.S.,
(2) Needing warranty-related repair and manufacturer not based in U.S.,
(3) Not needing warranty-related repair and manufacturer based in U.S.,
(4) Not needing warranty-related repair and manufacturer not based in U.S.

4.12   (d)   "Not manufactured by an American-based company" is the complement of
cont.   "manufactured by an American-based company," since it involves all events other than
               the occurrence of vehicles manufactured by an American-based company.
    (e) P(needs warranty repair) = 0.04
    (f) P(manufacturer not based in U.S.) = 0.40
    (g) P(needs warranty repair and manufacturer based in U.S.) = 0.025
    (h) P(does not need warranty repair and manufacturer not based in U.S.) = 0.385
    (i) P(needs warranty repair or manufacturer based in U.S.) = 0.615
    (j) P(needs warranty repair or manufacturer not based in U.S.) = 0.425
    (k) P(needs or does not need warranty repair) = 1.00

• 4.14   (a) $P(A \mid B) = 10/35 = 2/7 = 0.2857$
    (b) $P(A \mid B') = 30/65 = 6/13 = 0.4615$
    (c) $P(A' \mid B') = 35/65 = 7/13 = 0.5385$
    (d)   Since $P(A \mid B) = 0.2857$ and $P(A) = 0.40$, events A and B are not statistically independent.

4.16 $P(A \text{ and } B) = P(A)\,P(B) = 0.3 \bullet 0.4 = 0.12$

•4.18   (a) P(has travel/entertainment credit card | has bank credit card) = 60/120 = 1/2 = 0.5
    (b) P(has bank credit card | does not have travel/entertainment credit card)
        = 60/125 = 12/25 = 0.48
    (c)   Since P(has travel/entertainment credit card | has bank credit card) = 60/120 or 0.5 and
P(has travel/entertainment credit card) = 75/200 or 0.375, the two events are not statistically
independent.

•4.20   (a) P(does not enjoy clothes shopping | female) = 36/260 = 9/65 = 0.1385
    (b) P(male | enjoys clothes shopping) = 136/360 = 17/45 = 0.378
    (c)   Since P(male | enjoys clothes shopping) = 0.378 and P(male) = 240/500 or 0.48, the two
events are not statistically independent.

4.22   (a) P(needs warranty repair | manufacturer based in U.S.) = 0.025/0.6 = 0.0417
    (b) P(needs warranty repair | manufacturer not based in U.S.) = 0.015/0.4
        = 0.0375
    (c)   Since P(needs warranty repair | manufacturer based in U.S.) = 0.0417 and P(needs
warranty repair) = 0.04, the two events are not statistically independent.

4.24   (a) $P(\text{both queens}) = \dfrac{4}{52} \cdot \dfrac{3}{51} = \dfrac{12}{2{,}652} = \dfrac{1}{221} = 0.0045$

    (b) $P(\text{10 followed by 5 or 6}) = \dfrac{4}{52} \cdot \dfrac{8}{51} = \dfrac{32}{2{,}652} = \dfrac{8}{663} = 0.012$

    (c) $P(\text{both queens}) = \dfrac{4}{52} \cdot \dfrac{4}{52} = \dfrac{16}{2{,}704} = \dfrac{1}{169} = 0.0059$

    (d) $P(\text{blackjack}) = \dfrac{16}{52} \cdot \dfrac{4}{51} + \dfrac{4}{52} \cdot \dfrac{16}{51} = \dfrac{128}{2{,}652} = \dfrac{32}{663} = 0.0483$

•4.26

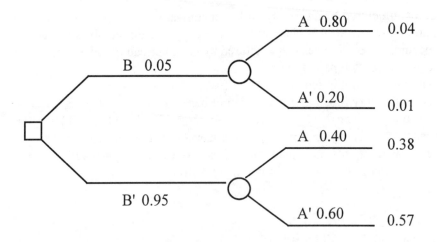

$$P(B \mid A) = \frac{P(A \mid B) \cdot P(B)}{P(A \mid B) \cdot P(B) + P(A \mid B') \cdot P(B')}$$

$$= \frac{0.8 \cdot 0.05}{0.8 \cdot 0.05 + 0.4 \cdot 0.95} = \frac{0.04}{0.42} = \mathbf{0.095}$$

4.28   (a) D = has disease and T = test positive

$$P(D \mid T) = \frac{P(T \mid D) \cdot P(D)}{P(T \mid D) \cdot P(D) + P(T \mid D') \cdot P(D')}$$

$$= \frac{0.9 \cdot 0.03}{0.9 \cdot 0.03 + 0.01 \cdot 0.97} = \frac{0.027}{0.0367} = \mathbf{0.736}$$

(b)

$$P(D' \mid T') = \frac{P(T' \mid D') \cdot P(D')}{P(T' \mid D') \cdot P(D') + P(T' \mid D) \cdot P(D)}$$

$$= \frac{0.99 \cdot 0.97}{0.99 \cdot 0.97 + 0.01 \cdot 0.03} = \frac{0.9603}{0.9633} = \mathbf{0.997}$$

4.30   (a) B = Base Construction Co. enters a bid
O = Olive Construction Co. wins the contract

$$P(B \mid O) = \frac{P(O \mid B) \cdot P(B)}{P(O \mid B') \cdot P(B') + P(O \mid B) \cdot P(B)}$$

$$= \frac{0.5 \cdot 0.3}{0.5 \cdot 0.3 + 0.25 \cdot 0.7} = \frac{0.15}{0.325} = \mathbf{0.4615}$$

(b) $P(O) = 0.175 + 0.15 = 0.325$

•4.32   (a) P(A rating | issued by city) = 0.35/0.56 = 0.625
       (b) P(issued by city) = 0.5(0.7) + 0.6(0.2) + 0.9(0.1) = 0.56
       (c) P(issued by suburb) = 0.4(0.7) + 0.2(0.2) + 0.05(0.1) = 0.325

4.34   (a)   Distribution C   Distribution D

X	P(X)	X*P(X)	X		P(X)	X*P(X)
0	0.20	0.00	0		0.10	0.00
1	0.20	0.20	1		0.20	0.20
2	0.20	0.40	2		0.40	0.80
3	0.20	0.60	3		0.20	0.60
4	0.20	0.80	4		0.10	0.40
	1.00	2.00 $\mu = 2.00$			1.00	2.00 $\mu = 2.00$

(b)   Distribution C

X	$(X-\mu)^2$	P(X)	$(X-\mu)^2 * P(X)$
0	$(-1)^2$	0.20	0.80
1	$(0)^2$	0.20	0.20
2	$(1)^2$	0.20	0.00
3	$(2)^2$	0.20	0.20
4	$(3)^2$	0.20	0.80
		$\sigma^2=$	2.00

$$\sigma = \sqrt{\Sigma(X-\mu)^2 \cdot P(X)} = \sqrt{2.00} = 1.414$$

Distribution D

X	$(X-\mu)^2$	P(X)	$(X-\mu)^2 * P(X)$
0	$(-3)^2$	0.10	0.40
1	$(-2)^2$	0.20	0.20
2	$(-1)^2$	0.40	0.00
3	$(0)^2$	0.20	0.20
4	$(1)^2$	0.10	0.40
		$\sigma^2=$	1.20

$$\sigma = \sqrt{\Sigma(X-\mu)^2 \cdot P(X)} = \sqrt{1.20} = 1.095$$

(c)   Distribution C is uniform and symmetric; D is unimodal and symmetric.

•4.36   (a)-(b)

X	P(x)	X*P(X)	$(X-\mu_X)^2$	$(X-\mu_X)^2 * P(X)$
0	0.10	0.00	4	0.40
1	0.20	0.20	1	0.20
2	0.45	0.90	0	0.00
3	0.15	0.45	1	0.15
4	0.05	0.20	4	0.20
5	0.05	0.25	9	0.45
	(a) Mean =	2.00	variance =	1.40
			(b) Stdev =	1.18321596
6	0.01	0.06	15.5236	0.155236
	(a) Mean =	2.06	variance =	1.558836
			(b) Stdev =	1.248534

31

4.38   (a)

X	P(X)
$-1	21/36
$+1	15/36

(b)

X	P(X)
$-1	21/36
$+1	15/36

(c)

X	P(X)
$-1	30/36
$+4	6/36

    (d) $ – 0.167 for each method of play

4.40

	Mean	Standard Deviation
(a)	0.40	0.60
(b)	1.60	0.980
(c)	4.00	0.894
(d)	1.50	0.866

4.42   (a)

	A	B	C	D	E	F	G
1	Warranty Repair						
2							
3	Sample size	3					
4	Probability of success	0.05					
5	Mean	0.15					
6	Variance	0.1425					
7	Standard deviation	0.377492					
8							
9	Binomial Probabilities Table						
10		X	P(X)	P(<=X)	P(<X)	P(>X)	P(>=X)
11		0	0.857375	0.857375	0	0.142625	1
12		1	0.135375	0.99275	0.857375	0.00725	0.142625
13		2	0.007125	0.999875	0.99275	0.000125	0.00725
14		3	0.000125	1	0.999875	0	0.000125

    (b)   Two assumptions: (1) Independence of the cars, (2) Only two outcomes - car needs repair or car does not need repair.

    (c)   Mean: $\mu = 0.15$ Standard deviation: $\sigma = 0.377$

    (d)   If $p = 0.10$ and $n = 3$,

        (1) $P(X = 0) = 0.7290$

        (2) $P(X \geq 1) = 1 - P(X = 0) = 1 - 0.7290 = 0.2710$

        (3) $P(X > 1) = P(X = 2) + P(X = 3) = 0.0270 + 0.0010 = 0.0280$

            Mean: $\mu = 0.30$ Standard deviation: $\sigma = 0.520$

•4.44　(a)

	A	B	C	D	E	F	G
1	Troubles in Residential Service						
2							
3	Sample size	5					
4	Probability of success	0.7					
5	Mean	3.5					
6	Variance	1.05					
7	Standard deviation	1.024695					
8							
9	Binomial Probabilities Table						
10		X	P(X)	P(<=X)	P(<X)	P(>X)	P(>=X)
11		0	0.00243	0.00243	0	0.99757	1
12		1	0.02835	0.03078	0.00243	0.96922	0.99757
13		2	0.1323	0.16308	0.03078	0.83692	0.96922
14		3	0.3087	0.47178	0.16308	0.52822	0.83692
15		4	0.36015	0.83193	0.47178	0.16807	0.52822
16		5	0.16807	1	0.83193	0	0.16807

(b)　Two assumptions: (1) Independence of the repairs, (2) Only two outcomes - repair accomplished same day or repair not accomplished same day.

(c)　Mean: $\mu = 3.5$　Standard deviation: $\sigma = 1.0247$

(d)　If $p = 0.8$ and $n = 5$,

　　　(1)　$P(X = 5) = 0.3277$

　　　(2)　$P(X \geq 3)$　　　$= P(X = 3) + P(X = 4) + P(X = 5)$
　　　　　　$= 0.2048 + 0.4096 + 0.3277 = 0.9421$

　　　(3)　$P(X < 2) = P(X = 0) + P(X = 1) = 0.0003 + 0.0064 = 0.0067$
　　　　　　Mean: $\mu = 4$　Standard deviation: $\sigma = 0.894$

(e)　The larger p is, the more likely it is that troubles reported on a given day will be repaired on the same day, and the less likely it is that troubles reported on a given day will not be repaired on the same day.

•4.46　(a)　Using the equation, if $\lambda = 2.5$, $P(X = 2) = \dfrac{e^{-2.5} \cdot (2.5)^2}{2!} = 0.2565$

　　　(b)　If $\lambda = 8.0$, $P(X = 8) = 0.1396$

　　　(c)　If $\lambda = 0.5$, $P(X = 1) = 0.3033$

　　　(d)　If $\lambda = 3.7$, $P(X = 0) = 0.0247$

　　　(e)　If $\lambda = 4.4$, $P(X = 7) = 0.0778$

•4.48

	X	P(X)	P(<=X)	P(<X)	P(>X)	P(>=X)
1	Insurance Claims					
2						
3	Average/Expected number of successes:			3.1		
4						
5	Poisson Probabilities Table					
6	X	P(X)	P(<=X)	P(<X)	P(>X)	P(>=X)
7	0	0.045049	0.045049	0.000000	0.954951	1.000000
8	1	0.139653	0.184702	0.045049	0.815298	0.954951
9	2	0.216461	0.401163	0.184702	0.598837	0.815298
10	3	0.223677	0.624840	0.401163	0.375160	0.598837
11	4	0.173350	0.798189	0.624840	0.201811	0.375160
12	5	0.107477	0.905666	0.798189	0.094334	0.201811
13	6	0.055530	0.961196	0.905666	0.038804	0.094334
14	7	0.024592	0.985787	0.961196	0.014213	0.038804
15	8	0.009529	0.995317	0.985787	0.004683	0.014213
16	9	0.003282	0.998599	0.995317	0.001401	0.004683
17	10	0.001018	0.999617	0.998599	0.000383	0.001401
18	11	0.000287	0.999903	0.999617	0.000097	0.000383
19	12	0.000074	0.999977	0.999903	0.000023	0.000097

•4.50   (a) – (d)

	X	P(X)	P(<=X)	P(<X)	P(>X)	P(>=X)
1	Chocolate Chip Cookies					
2						
3	Average/Expected number of successes:			6		
4						
5	Poisson Probabilities Table					
6	X	P(X)	P(<=X)	P(<X)	P(>X)	P(>=X)
7	0	0.002479	0.002479	0.000000	0.997521	1.000000
8	1	0.014873	0.017351	0.002479	0.982649	0.997521
9	2	0.044618	0.061969	0.017351	0.938031	0.982649
10	3	0.089235	0.151204	0.061969	0.848796	0.938031
11	4	0.133853	0.285057	0.151204	0.714943	0.848796
12	5	0.160623	0.445680	0.285057	0.554320	0.714943
13	6	0.160623	0.606303	0.445680	0.393697	0.554320
14	7	0.137677	0.743980	0.606303	0.256020	0.393697
15	8	0.103258	0.847237	0.743980	0.152763	0.256020
16	9	0.068838	0.916076	0.847237	0.083924	0.152763
17	10	0.041303	0.957379	0.916076	0.042621	0.083924
18	11	0.022529	0.979908	0.957379	0.020092	0.042621
19	12	0.011264	0.991173	0.979908	0.008827	0.020092
20	13	0.005199	0.996372	0.991173	0.003628	0.008827
21	14	0.002228	0.998600	0.996372	0.001400	0.003628
22	15	0.000891	0.999491	0.998600	0.000509	0.001400
23	16	0.000334	0.999825	0.999491	0.000175	0.000509
24	17	0.000118	0.999943	0.999825	0.000057	0.000175

(e)   If $\lambda = 5.0$,

    (a) $P(X < 5) = 0.2650$
    (b) $P(X = 5) = 0.1755$
    (c) $P(X \geq 5) = 0.7350$
    (d) $P(X = 4) + P(X = 5) = 0.3510$

4.52   (a) If $\lambda = 9.0$, $P(X = 7) = 0.1171$

        (b) $P(7 \leq X \leq 9) = 0.1171 + 0.1318 + 0.1318 = 0.3807$

        (c) $P(X < 5) = 0.0001 + 0.0011 + 0.0050 + 0.0150 + 0.0337 = 0.0549$

•4.54   (a) $P(X = 3) = \dfrac{\binom{5}{3} \cdot \binom{10-5}{4-3}}{\binom{10}{4}} = \dfrac{\dfrac{5 \cdot 4 \cdot 3!}{3! 2 \cdot 1} \cdot \dfrac{5 \cdot 4!}{4! 1!}}{\dfrac{10 \cdot 9 \cdot 8 \cdot 7 \cdot 6!}{6! 4 \cdot 3 \cdot 2 \cdot 1}} = \dfrac{5}{3 \cdot 7} = 0.2381$

        (b) $P(X = 1) = \dfrac{\binom{3}{1} \cdot \binom{6-3}{4-1}}{\binom{6}{4}} = \dfrac{\dfrac{3 \cdot 2!}{2! 1} \cdot \dfrac{3!}{3! 0!}}{\dfrac{6 \cdot 5 \cdot 4!}{4! 2 \cdot 1}} = \dfrac{1}{5} = 0.2$

        (c) $P(X = 0) = \dfrac{\binom{3}{0} \cdot \binom{12-3}{5-0}}{\binom{12}{5}} = \dfrac{\dfrac{3!}{3! 0!} \cdot \dfrac{9 \cdot 8 \cdot 7 \cdot 6 \cdot 5!}{5! 4 \cdot 3 \cdot 2 \cdot 1}}{\dfrac{12 \cdot 11 \cdot 10 \cdot 9 \cdot 8 \cdot 7!}{7! 5 \cdot 4 \cdot 3 \cdot 2 \cdot 1}} = \dfrac{7}{44} = 0.1591$

        (d) $P(X = 3) = \dfrac{\binom{3}{3} \cdot \binom{7-0}{3-3}}{\binom{10}{3}} = \dfrac{\dfrac{3!}{3! 0!} \cdot \dfrac{7!}{7! 0!}}{\dfrac{10 \cdot 9 \cdot 8 \cdot 7!}{7! 3 \cdot 2 \cdot 1}} = \dfrac{1}{120} = 0.0083$

•4.56   (a) (1)   If $n = 6$, $A = 25$, and $N = 100$, $P(X \geq 2) = 1 - [P(X = 0) + P(X = 1)]$
                          $= 1 - [0.1689 + 0.3620] = 0.4691$

              (2)   If $n = 6$, $A = 30$, and $N = 100$, $P(X \geq 2) = 1 - [P(X = 0) + P(X = 1)]$
                          $= 1 - [0.1100 + 0.3046] = 0.5854$

              (3)   If $n = 6$, $A = 5$, and $N = 100$, $P(X \geq 2) = 1 - [P(X = 0) + P(X = 1)]$
                          $= 1 - [0.7291 + 0.2430] = 0.0279$

              (4)   If $n = 6$, $A = 10$, and $N = 100$, $P(X \geq 2) = 1 - [P(X = 0) + P(X = 1)]$
                          $= 1 - [0.5223 + 0.3687] = 0.1090$

        (b) The probability that the entire group will be audited is very sensitive to the true number of improper returns in the population. If the true number is very low ($A = 5$), the probability is very low (0.0279). When the true number is increased by a factor of six ($A = 30$), the probability the group will be audited increases by a factor of almost 21 (0.5854).

4.58　(a)

	A	B	C
1	Defective Radios		
2			
3	Sample size	8	
4	No. of successes in population	12	
5	Population size	48	
6			
7	Hypergeometric Probabilities Table		
8		X	P(x)
9		0	0.080192
10		1	0.265463
11		2	0.340677
12		3	0.219792
13		4	0.077271
14		5	0.014986
15		6	0.001543
16		7	7.56E-05
17		8	1.31E-06

(b)　(1)　If $n = 6$, $A = 12$, and $N = 48$, $P(X = 8) = 7.5296 \times 10^{-5} \cong .000075$

　　　(2)　If $n = 6$, $A = 12$, and $N = 48$, $P(X = 0) = 0.1587$

　　　(3)　If $n = 6$, $A = 12$, and $N = 48$, $P(X \geq 1) = 1 - 0.1587 = 0.8413$

4.60　(a)

	A	B	C
1	Defective Disks		
2			
3	Sample size	4	
4	No. of successes in population	5	
5	Population size	15	
6			
7	Hypergeometric Probabilities Table		
8		X	P(x)
9		0	0.153846
10		1	0.43956
11		2	0.32967
12		3	0.07326
13		4	0.003663

(b)　$\mu = n \cdot p = 4 \cdot (0.333) = 1.33$

4.62　(a)　$E(X) = (0.2)(\$ - 100) + (0.4)(\$50) + (0.3)(\$ 200) + (0.1)(\$300) = \$90$

　　　(b)　$E(Y) = (0.2)(\$50) + (0.4)(\$30) + (0.3)(\$ 20) + (0.1)(\$20) = \$30$

(c)
$$\sigma_X = \sqrt{(0.2)(-100 - 90)^2 + (0.4)(50 - 90)^2 + (0.3)(200 - 90)^2 + (0.1)(300 - 90)^2}$$
$$= \sqrt{15900} = 126.10$$

(d)
$$\sigma_Y = \sqrt{(0.2)(50 - 30)^2 + (0.4)(30 - 30)^2 + (0.3)(20 - 30)^2 + (0.1)(20 - 30)^2}$$
$$= \sqrt{120} = 10.95$$

4.62
cont.

(e) σ_{XY} $= (0.2)(-100 - 90)(50 - 30) + (0.4)(50 - 90)(30 - 30)$
$+ (0.3)(200 - 90)(20 - 30) + (0.1)(300 - 90)(20 - 30) = -1300$

(f) $E(X + Y) = E(X) + E(Y) = \$90 + \$30 = \$120$

(g) $\sigma_{X+Y} = \sqrt{15900 + 120 + 2(-1300)} = \sqrt{13420} = 115.85$

4.64 (a) – (e)

	A	B	C	D
1	Covariance Analysis			
2				
3	Probabilities & Outcomes:	P	X	Y
4	Cool Weather	0.4	50	30
5	Warm Weather	0.6	60	90
6				
7	Statistics			
8	E(X)	56		
9	E(Y)	66		
10	Variance(X)	24		
11	Standard Deviation(X)	4.898979		
12	Variance(Y)	864		
13	Standard Deviation(Y)	29.39388		
14	Covariance(XY)	144		

(f) On the analysis of the expected return alone, you should sell ice cream. But there is more variability in the profits, so there is higher risk with selling ice cream. Both products generate more profits in warmer weather than in cool, but ice cream profits increase more in warm weather.

•4.66 (a) – (e)

	A	B	C	D
1	Covariance Analysis			
2			Stock	
3	Probabilities & Outcomes:	P	X	Y
4		0.1	-100	50
5		0.3	0	100
6		0.3	80	-20
7		0.3	150	100
8				
9	Statistics			
10	E(X)	59		
11	E(Y)	59		
12	Variance(X)	6189		
13	Standard Deviation(X)	78.6702		
14	Variance(Y)	2889		
15	Standard Deviation(Y)	53.74942		
16	Covariance(XY)	39		
17	Variance(X+Y)	9156		
18	Standard Deviation(X+Y)	95.68699		
19				
20	Portfolio Management			
21	Weight Assigned to X	0.1		
22	Weight Assigned to Y	0.9		
23	Portfolio Expected Return	59		
24	Portfolio Risk	49.08156		

(f) Stock Y gives the investor a lower standard deviation while yielding the same expected return as investing in stock X, so the investor should select stock Y.

•4.66 (g) (1) $E(P) = \$59$ $\sigma_P = 49.01$
cont.   (2) $E(P) = \$59$ $\sigma_P = 44.41$
      (3) $E(P) = \$59$ $\sigma_P = 47.64$
      (4) $E(P) = \$59$ $\sigma_P = 57.38$
      (5) $E(P) = \$59$ $\sigma_P = 71.01$

(h) Based on the results of (g), you should recommend a portfolio with 30% stock X and 70% stock Y because it has the same expected return as other portfolios ($59) but has the smallest portfolio risk ($44.41).

•4.68 (a) $E(X) = \$77$ (b) $E(Y) = \$97$
    (c) $\sigma_X = 39.76$ (d) $\sigma_Y = 108.95$
    (e) $\sigma_{XY} = 4161$
    (f) Stock Y gives the investor a higher expected return than stock X, but also has a standard deviation better than 2.5 times higher than that for stock X. An investor should carefully weigh the increased risk.
    (g) (1) $E(P) = \$95$ $\sigma_P = 101.88$
      (2) $E(P) = \$91$ $\sigma_P = 87.79$
      (3) $E(P) = \$87$ $\sigma_P = 73.78$
      (4) $E(P) = \$83$ $\sigma_P = 59.92$
      (5) $E(P) = \$79$ $\sigma_P = 46.35$
    (h) Based on the results of (g), an investor should recognize that as the expected return increases, so does the portfolio risk.

•4.84 (a) Since simple events have only one criterion specified, an example could be any one of the following:
      (1) Being filled by machine I,
      (2) Being filled by machine II,
      (3) Being a conforming bottle,
      (4) Being a nonconforming bottle.
    (b) Since joint events specify two criteria simultaneously, an example could be any one of the following:
      (1) Being filled by machine I and being a conforming bottle,
      (2) Being filled by machine I and being a nonconforming bottle,
      (3) Being filled by machine II and being a conforming bottle,
      (4) Being filled by machine II and being a nonconforming bottle.
    (c) (1) $P(\text{nonconforming bottle}) = 0.01 + 0.025 = 0.035$
      (2) $P(\text{machine II}) = 0.5$
      (3) $P(\text{machine I } and \text{ conforming bottle}) = 0.49$
      (4) $P(\text{machine II } and \text{ conforming bottle}) = 0.475$
      (5) $P(\text{machine I } or \text{ conforming bottle}) = 0.5 + 0.475 = 0.975$
    (d) $P(\text{nonconforming} \mid \text{machine II}) = 0.02$
    (e) $P(\text{machine II} \mid \text{nonconforming}) = 0.01/0.035 = 0.2857$
    (f) The conditions are switched. Part (d) answers $P(A|B)$ and part (e) answers $P(B|A)$.

4.86 (a) Since simple events have only one criterion specified, an example could be high interest in finance.
    (b) Since joint events specify two criteria simultaneously, an example could be average interest in finance and high ability in mathematics.

4.86   (c)   High interest in finance and high mathematics ability is a joint event because two criteria
cont.   are specified simultaneously.

(d)   (1) P(high ability, mathematics) = 50/200 = 1/4 = 0.25

       (2) P(average interest, finance) = 70/200 = 0.14

       (3) P(low ability, mathematics) = 80/200 = 2/5 = 0.4

       (4) P(high interest, finance) = 40/200 = 1/5 = 0.2

       (5) P(low interest, finance *and* low ability, mathematics) = 60/200 = 0.3

       (6) P(high interest, finance *and* high ability, mathematics) = 25/200= 0.125

       (7) P(low interest, finance *or* low ability, mathematics) = 110/200= 0.55

       (8) P(high interest, finance *or* low ability, mathematics) = 65/200= 0.325

       (9) P(low, average, *or* high ability, mathematics) = 1.0. These events are mutually
           exclusive because each individual has only one ability level in mathematics.
           These events are collectively exhaustive because one of the three must occur;
           that is, every individual has some ability level in mathematics.

(e) P(high interest, finance | high ability, mathematics) = 25/50 = 1/2 = 0.5

(f) P(high ability, mathematics | high interest, finance) = 25/40 = 5/8 = 0.625

(g)   The conditions are switched. Part (e) answers $P(F|M)$ and part (f) answers $P(M|F)$.

(h)   Since P(high ability, mathematics | high interest, finance) = 0.625 and P(high ability,
      mathematics) = 0.25, the two events are not statistically independent.

4.88   (a)   If $p = 0.04$ and $n = 20$, $P(X = 1) = 0.3683$

       (b) $P(X \geq 2) = 1 - [P(X = 0) + P(X = 1)] = 1 - [0.4420 + 0.3683] = 0.1897$

4.90   (a)   If $p = 0.10$ and $n = 15$, $P(X = 1) = 0.3432$

       (b) $P(X \geq 2) = 1 - [P(X = 0) + P(X = 1)] = 0.4510$

4.92   (a)   (1)   If $p = 0.90$ and $n = 10$, $P(X = 9) = 0.3874$

           (2) $P(X \geq 9) = P(X = 9) + P(X = 10) = 0.3874 + 0.3487 = 0.7361$

           (3) $P(X \leq 9) = 1 - P(X = 10) = 1 - 0.3487 = 0.6513$

           (4) $P(X > 9) = P(X = 10) = 0.3487$

           (5) $P(X < 9) = 1 - P(X \geq 9) = 1 - 0.7361 = 0.2639$

       (b)   Mean: $\mu = 10 \cdot (0.90) = 9.0$

       (c)   (1)   If $p = 0.95$ and $n = 10$, $P(X = 9) = 0.3151$

           (2) $P(X \geq 9) = P(X = 9) + P(X = 10) = 0.3151 + 0.5987 = 0.9138$

           (3) $P(X \leq 9) = 1 - P(X = 10) = 1 - 0.5987 = 0.4013$

           (4) $P(X > 9) = P(X = 10) = 0.5987$

           (5) $P(X < 9) = 1 - P(X \geq 9) = 1 - 0.9139 = 0.0862$

4.94   (a) $P(X = 0) = (0.98)^{10} = 0.8171$

       (b) $P(X = 1) = 10(0.98)^9 (0.02)^1 = 0.1667$

       (c) $P(X \geq 2) = 1 - P(X = 0) - P(X = 1) = 0.0162$

       (d)   (a) $P(X = 0) = (0.99)^{10} = 0.9044$

           (b) $P(X = 1) = 10(0.99)^9 (0.01)^1 = 0.0914$

           (c) $P(X \geq 2) = 1 - P(X = 0) - P(X = 1) = 0.0043$

CHAPTER 5

5.2 (a) Opportunity loss table:
Profit of

Event	Optimum Action	Optimum Action	Alternative Courses of Action	
			A	B
1	A	50	50 – 50 = 0	50 – 10 = 40
2	A	300	300 – 300 = 0	300 – 100 = 200
3	A	500	500 – 500 = 0	500 – 200 = 300

(b)

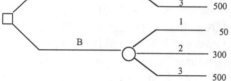

•5.4 (a)-(b) Payoff table: Action

Event	Company A		Company B	
1	$10,000 + $2•1,000 =	$12,000	$2,000 + $4•1,000 =	$6,000
2	$10,000 + $2•2,000 =	$14,000	$2,000 + $4•2,000 =	$10,000
3	$10,000 + $2•5,000 =	$20,000	$2,000 + $4•5,000 =	$22,000
4	$10,000 + $2•10,000 =	$30,000	$2,000 + $4•10,000 =	$42,000
5	$10,000 + $2•50,000 =	$110,000	$2,000 + $4•50,000 =	$202,000

(d) Opportunity loss table:

Profit of

Event	Optimum Action	Optimum Action	Alternative Courses of Action	
			A	B
1	A	12,000	0	6,000
2	A	14,000	0	4,000
3	B	22,000	2,000	0
4	B	42,000	12,000	0
5	B	202,000	92,000	0

•5.6 (a) $EMV_A = 50(0.5) + 200(0.5) = 125$ $EMV_B = 100(0.5) + 125(0.5) = 112.50$

(b) $EOL_A = 50(0.5) + 0(0.5) = 25$ $EOL_B = 0(0.5) + 75(0.5) = 37.50$

(c) Perfect information would correctly forecast which event, 1 or 2, will occur. The value of perfect information is the increase in the expected value if you knew which of the events 1 or 2 would occur prior to making a decision between actions. It allows us to select the optimum action given a correct forecast.

EMV with perfect information = 100 (0.5) + 200 (0.5) = 150

$EVPI = EMV$ with perfect information – $EMV_A = 150 – 125 = 25$

(d) Based on (a) and (b) above, select action A because it has a higher expected monetary value (a) and a lower opportunity loss (b) than action B.

•5.6
cont.

(e) $\sigma_A^2 = (50 - 125)^2 (0.5) + (200 - 125)^2 (0.5) = 5625$ $\sigma_A = 75$

$CV_A = \dfrac{75}{125} \cdot 100\% = 60\%$

$\sigma_B^2 = (100 - 112.5)^2 (0.5) + (125 - 112.5)^2 (0.5) = 156.25$ $\sigma_B = 12.5$

$CV_B = \dfrac{12.5}{112.5} \cdot 100\% = 11.11\%$

(f)   Return to risk ratio for $A = \dfrac{125}{75} = 1.667$

              Return to risk ratio for $B = \dfrac{112.5}{12.5} = 9.0$

(g)   Based on (e) and (f), select action B because it has a lower coefficient of variation and a higher return to risk ratio.

(h)   The best decision depends on the decision criteria. In this case, expected monetary value leads to a different decision than the return to risk ratio.

5.8   (a)   Rate of return $= \dfrac{\$100}{\$1,000} \cdot 100\% = 10\%$

              (b) $CV = \dfrac{\$25}{\$100} \cdot 100\% = 25\%$

              (c)   Return to risk ratio $= \dfrac{\$100}{\$25} = 4.0$

5.10   Select portfolio A because it has a higher expected monetary value while it has the same standard deviation as portfolio B.

•5.12   (a), (b)

	A	B	C	D
1	Vendor Decision			
2				
3	Probabilities & Payoff Table:			
4		P	Soft Drinks	Ice Cream
5	Cool Weather	0.4	50	30
6	Warm Weather	0.6	60	90
7				
8	Statistics	Soft Drinks	Ice Cream	
9	Expected Monetary Value	56	66	
10	Variance	24	864	
11	Standard Deviation	4.8989795	29.393877	
12	Coefficient of Variation	0.0874818	0.4453618	
13	Return to risk ratio	11.430952	2.2453656	
14				
15	Expected Opportunity Loss	18	8	
16			EVPI	

41

•5.12 (d)   Based on (a) and (b), choose to sell ice cream because you will earn a higher
cont.   expected monetary value and incur a lower opportunity cost than choosing to sell soft
drinks.

(e) $CV(\text{Soft drinks}) = \dfrac{4.899}{56} \cdot 100\% = 8.748\%$

      $CV(\text{Ice cream}) = \dfrac{29.394}{66} \cdot 100\% = 44.536\%$

(f)   Return to risk ratio for soft drinks = 11.431
      Return to risk ratio for ice cream = 2.245

5.14 (a) $EMV_A = 500(0.3) + 1,000(0.5) + 2,000(0.2) = 1,050$
         $EMV_B = -2,000(0.3) + 2,000(0.5) + 5,000(0.2) = 1,400$
         $EMV_C = -7,000(0.3) - 1,000(0.5) + 20,000(0.2) = 1,400$

(b) $\sigma_A^2 = (500 - 1,050)^2 (0.3) + (1,000 - 1,050)^2 (0.5) + (2,000 - 1,050)^2 (0.2) \quad = 272,500$
    $\sigma_A = 522.02$
    $\sigma_B^2 = (-2,000 - 1,400)^2 (0.3) + (2,000 - 1,400)^2 (0.5) + (5,000 - 1,400)^2 (0.2) = 6,240,000$
    $\sigma_B = 2,498.00$
    $\sigma_C^2 = (-7,000 - 1,400)^2 (0.3) + (-1,000 - 1,400)^2 (0.5)$
          $+ (20,000 - 1,400)^2 (0.2) = 93,240,000$
    $\sigma_C = 9656.09$

(c)

		Profit of			
	Optimum	Optimum	Alternative Courses of Action		
Event	Action	Action	A	B	C
1	A	500	0	2,500	7,500
2	B	2,000	1,000	0	3,000
3	C	20,000	18,000	15,000	0

$EOL_A = 0(0.3) + 1,000(0.5) + 18,000(0.2) = 4,100$
$EOL_B = 2,500(0.3) + 0(0.5) + 15,000(0.2) = 3,750$
$EOL_C = 7,500(0.3) + 3,000(0.5) + 0(0.2) = 3,750$

(d) EMV with perfect information $= 500(0.3) + 2,000(0.5) + 20,000(0.2) = 5,150$
    $EVPI = EMV$ with perfect information $- EMV_{B \, or \, C} = 5,150 - 1,400 = 3,750$
    The investor should not be willing to pay more than \$3,750 for a perfect forecast.

(e) $CV_A = \dfrac{522.02}{1050} \cdot 100\% = 49.72\%$ $CV_B = \dfrac{2498.00}{1400} \cdot 100\% = 178.43\%$

                    $CV_C = \dfrac{9656.09}{1400} \cdot 100\% = 689.72\%$

(f) Return to risk ratio for $A = \dfrac{1050}{522.02} = 2.01$

   Return to risk ratio for $B = \dfrac{1400}{2498} = 0.56$

   Return to risk ratio for $B = \dfrac{1400}{9656.09} = 0.14$

(g)-(h) Actions B and C optimize the expected monetary value, but action A minimizes the
        coefficient of variation and maximizes the investor's return to risk.

(i)

	(1) 0.1, 0.6, 0.3	(2) 0.1, 0.3, 0.6	(3) 0.4, 0.4, 0.2	(4) 0.6, 0.3, 0.1
(a) Max EMV	C: 4,700	C: 11,000	A or B: 800	A: 800
(b) $\sigma_{\text{Max } EMV}$	σ_C: 10,169	σ_C: 11,145	σ_A: 548 σ_B: 2,683	σ_A: 458
(c) Min EOL & (d) $EVPI$	C: 2,550	C: 1,650	A: 4,000 or B: 4,000	A: 2,100
(e) Min CV	A: 40.99%	A: 36.64%	A: 54.77%	A: 57.28%
(f) Max Return to risk	A: 2.4398	A: 2.7294	A: 1.8257	A: 1.7457
(g) Choice on (e), (f)	Choose A	Choose A	Choose A	Choose A
(h) Compare (a) and (g)	Different: (a) C (g) A	Different: (a) C (g) A	Different: (a) A or B (g) A	Same: A

•5.16 (a) $EMV_A = 12{,}000(0.45) + 14{,}000(0.2) + 20{,}000(0.15) + 30{,}000(0.1)$
                $+ 110{,}000(0.1) = 25{,}200$
        $EMV_B = 6{,}000(0.45) + 10{,}000(0.2) + 22{,}000(0.15) + 42{,}000(0.1)$
                $+ 202{,}000(0.1) = 32{,}400$

(b) $EOL_A = 0(0.45) + 0(0.2) + 2{,}000(0.15) + 12{,}000(0.1) + 92{,}000(0.1)$
               $= 10{,}700$
        $EOL_B = 6{,}000(0.45) + 4{,}000(0.2) + 0(0.15) + 0(0.1) + 0(0.1)$
               $= 3{,}500$

(c) EMV with perfect information $= 12{,}000(0.45) + 14{,}000(0.2) + 22{,}000(0.15)$
                $+ 42{,}000(0.1) + 202{,}000(0.1) = 35{,}900$
     $EVPI = EMV$, perfect information $- EMV_B = 35{,}900 - 32{,}400 = 3{,}500$
     The author should not be willing to pay more than \$3,500 for a perfect forecast.

(d)   Sign with company B to maximize the expected monetary value (\$32,400) and minimize the expected opportunity loss (\$3,500).

(e) $CV_A = \dfrac{28{,}792}{25{,}200} \cdot 100\% = 114.25\%$ $CV_B = \dfrac{57{,}583}{32{,}400} \cdot 100\% = 177.73\%$

(f) Return to risk ratio for $A = \dfrac{25{,}200}{28{,}792} = 0.8752$

     Return to risk ratio for $B = \dfrac{32{,}400}{57{,}583} = 0.5627$

(g)   Signing with company A will minimize the author's risk and yield the higher return to risk.

(h)   Company B has a higher EMV than A, but choosing company B also entails more risk and has a lower return to risk ratio than A.

•5.16 (i)   Payoff table:

	Pr	A	B
Event 1	0.3	12,000	6,000
Event 2	0.2	14,000	10,000
Event 3	0.2	20,000	22,000
Event 4	0.1	30,000	42,000
Event 5	0.2	110,000	202,000
	EMV	35,400	52,800
	σ	37,673	75,346
	CV	106.42%	142.70%
	Return to risk	0.9397	0.7008

Opportunity loss table:

	Pr	A	B
Event 1	0.3	0	6,000
Event 2	0.2	0	4,000
Event 3	0.2	2,000	0
Event 4	0.1	12,000	0
Event 5	0.2	92,000	0
	EOL	20,000	2,600

The author's decision is not affected by the changed probabilities.

5.18 (a) $P(E_1 \mid F) = \dfrac{P(F \mid E_1) \cdot P(E_1)}{P(F \mid E_1) \cdot P(E_1) + P(F \mid E_2) \cdot P(E_2)} = \dfrac{0.6(0.5)}{0.6(0.5) + 0.4(0.5)} = 0.6$

$P(E_2 \mid F) = 1 - P(E_1 \mid F) = 1 - 0.6 = 0.4$

(b) $EMV_A = (0.6)(50) + (0.4)(200) = 110$
$EMV_B = (0.6)(100) + (0.4)(125) = 110$

(c) $EOL_A = (0.6)(50) + (0.4)(0) = 30$
$EOL_B = (0.6)(0) + (0.4)(75) = 30$

(d) $EVPI = (0.6)(100) + (0.4)(200) = 140$

(e)   Both have the same EMV.

(f) $\sigma_A^2 = (0.6)(60)^2 + (0.4)(90)^2 = 5400$ $\sigma_A = 73.4847$
$\sigma_B^2 = (0.6)(10)^2 + (0.4)(15)^2 = 150$ $\sigma_B = 12.2474$

$CV_A = \dfrac{73.4847}{110} \cdot 100\% = 66.8\%$ $CV_B = \dfrac{12.2474}{110} \cdot 100\% = 11.1\%$

(g) Return to risk ratio for $A = \dfrac{110}{73.4847} = 1.497$

Return to risk ratio for $B = \dfrac{110}{12.2474} = 8.981$

(h)   Action B has a better return to risk ratio.
(i)   Both have the same EMV, but action B has a better return to risk ratio.

•5.20
$$P(\text{forecast cool} \mid \text{cool weather}) = 0.80$$
$$P(\text{forecast warm} \mid \text{warm weather}) = 0.70$$

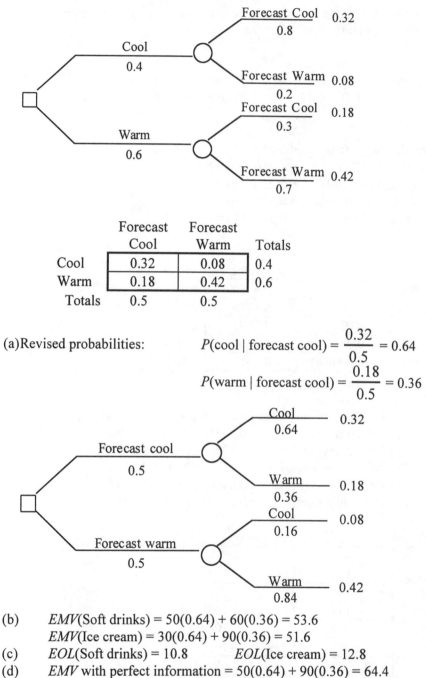

	Forecast Cool	Forecast Warm	Totals
Cool	0.32	0.08	0.4
Warm	0.18	0.42	0.6
Totals	0.5	0.5	

(a) Revised probabilities:

$$P(\text{cool} \mid \text{forecast cool}) = \frac{0.32}{0.5} = 0.64$$

$$P(\text{warm} \mid \text{forecast cool}) = \frac{0.18}{0.5} = 0.36$$

(b) $EMV(\text{Soft drinks}) = 50(0.64) + 60(0.36) = 53.6$
         $EMV(\text{Ice cream}) = 30(0.64) + 90(0.36) = 51.6$
(c) $EOL(\text{Soft drinks}) = 10.8$ $EOL(\text{Ice cream}) = 12.8$
(d) EMV with perfect information $= 50(0.64) + 90(0.36) = 64.4$
         $EVPI = EMV$, perfect information $- EMV_A = 64.4 - 53.6 = 10.8$
         The vendor should not be willing to pay more than $10.80 for a perfect forecast
         of the weather.
(e)   The vendor should sell soft drinks to maximize value and minimize loss.
(f) $CV(\text{Soft drinks}) = \dfrac{4.8}{53.6} \cdot 100\% = 8.96\%$

         $CV(\text{Ice cream}) = \dfrac{28.8}{51.6} \cdot 100\% = 55.81\%$

(g)   Return to risk ratio for soft drinks = 11.6667
         Return to risk ratio for ice cream = 1.7917

(h)   Based on these revised probabilities, the vendor's decision changes because of the increased likelihood of cool weather given a forecast for cool. Under these conditions, she should sell soft drinks to maximize the expected monetary value and minimize her expected opportunity loss.

5.22   (a) $P(\text{favorable} \mid 1{,}000) = 0.01$ $P(\text{favorable} \mid 2{,}000) = 0.01$
$P(\text{favorable} \mid 5{,}000) = 0.25$ $P(\text{favorable} \mid 10{,}000) = 0.60$
$P(\text{favorable} \mid 50{,}000) = 0.99$

$P(\text{favorable and } 1{,}000)$ $= 0.01(0.45) = 0.0045$
$P(\text{favorable and } 2{,}000)$ $= 0.01(0.20) = 0.0020$
$P(\text{favorable and } 5{,}000)$ $= 0.25(0.15) = 0.0375$
$P(\text{favorable and } 10{,}000)$ $= 0.60(0.10) = 0.0600$
$P(\text{favorable and } 50{,}000)$ $= 0.99(0.10) = 0.0990$

Joint probability table:

	Favorable	Unfavorable	Totals
1,000	0.0045	0.4455	0.45
2,000	0.0020	0.1980	0.20
5,000	0.0375	0.1125	0.15
10,000	0.0600	0.0400	0.10
50,000	0.0990	0.0010	0.10
Totals	0.2030	0.7970	

Given an unfavorable review, the revised conditional probabilities are:
$P(1{,}000 \mid \text{unfavorable})$ $= 0.4455/0.7970 = 0.5590$
$P(2{,}000 \mid \text{unfavorable})$ $= 0.1980/0.7970 = 0.2484$
$P(5{,}000 \mid \text{unfavorable})$ $= 0.1125/0.7970 = 0.1412$
$P(10{,}000 \mid \text{unfavorable})$ $= 0.0400/0.7970 = 0.0502$
$P(50{,}000 \mid \text{unfavorable})$ $= 0.0010/0.7970 = 0.0013$

(b)   Payoff table, given unfavorable review:

	Pr	A	B
1,000	0.5590	12,000	6,000
2,000	0.2484	14,000	10,000
5,000	0.1412	20,000	22,000
10,000	0.0502	30,000	42,000
50,000	0.0013	110,000	202,000
	EMV	14,658.60	11,315.4
	σ^2	31,719,333.50	92,268,770.36
	σ	5,631.99	9,605.66
	CV	38.42%	84.89%
	Return to risk	2.6027	1.1780

Opportunity loss table:

	Pr	A	B
Event 1	0.5590	0	6,000
Event 2	0.2484	0	4,000
Event 3	0.1412	2,000	0
Event 4	0.0502	12,000	0
Event 5	0.0013	92,000	0
	EOL	1,004.40	4,347.60

(c) The author's decision is affected by the changed probabilities. Under the new circumstances, signing with company A maximizes the expected monetary value ($14,658.60), minimizes the expected opportunity loss ($1,004.40), minimizes risk with a smaller coefficient of variation and yields a higher return to risk than choosing company B.

5.36 (a), (c), (g), (h)   Payoff table:

	Pr	A: Buy 6,000	B: Buy 8,000	C: Buy 10,000	D: Buy 12,000
Sell 6,000	0.1	2,100	1,400	700	0
Sell 8,000	0.5	2,100	2,800	2,100	1,400
Sell 10,000	0.3	2,100	2,800	3,500	2,800
Sell 12,000	0.1	2,100	2,800	3,500	4,200
	EMV	2,100	2,660	2,520	1,960
	σ	0	420	896	1,120
	CV	0	15.79%	35.57%	57.14%
	Return to risk	undefined	6.3333	2.8111	1.7500

(d) Opportunity loss table:

	Pr	A: Buy 6,000	B: Buy 8,000	C: Buy 10,000	D: Buy 12,000
Sell 6,000	0.1	0	700	1,400	2,100
Sell 8,000	0.5	700	0	700	1,400
Sell 10,000	0.3	1,400	700	0	700
Sell 12,000	0.1	2,100	1,400	700	0
	EOL	980	420	560	1,120

(e) EVPI = $420. The management of Shop-Quick Supermarkets should not be willing to pay more than $420 for a perfect forecast.

(f) To maximize the expected monetary value and minimize expected opportunity loss, the management should buy 8,000 loaves.

(i) Action B (buying 8,000 loaves) maximizes the return to risk and, while buying 6,000 loaves reduces the coefficient of variation to zero, action B has a smaller coefficient of variation than C or D.

5.36
cont. (k) Payoff table:

	Pr	*A*: Buy 6,000	*B*: Buy 8,000	*C*: Buy 10,000	*D:* Buy 12,000
Sell 6,000	0.3	2,100	1,400	700	0
Sell 8,000	0.4	2,100	2,800	2,100	1,400
Sell 10,000	0.2	2,100	2,800	3,500	2,800
Sell 12,000	0.1	2,100	2,800	3,500	4,200
	EMV	2,100	2,380	2,100	1,540
	σ	0	642	1,084	1,321
	CV	0	26.96%	51.64%	85.76%
	Return to risk	undefined	3.7097	1.9365	1.1660

Opportunity loss table:

	Pr	*A*: Buy 6,000	*B*: Buy 8,000	*C*: Buy 10,000	*D:* Buy 12,000
Sell 6,000	0.3	0	700	1,400	2,100
Sell 8,000	0.4	700	0	700	1,400
Sell 10,000	0.2	1,400	700	0	700
Sell 12,000	0.1	2,100	1,400	700	0
	EOL	700	490	770	1,330

The management's decision is not affected by the changed probabilities.

•5.38 (c), (e), (f) Payoff table:

	Pr	New	Old
Weak	0.3	− 4,000,000	0
Moderate	0.6	1,000,000	0
Strong	0.1	5,000,000	0
	EMV	− 100,000	0
	σ	2,808,914	0
	CV	− 2,808.94%	undefined
	Return to risk	− 0.0356	undefined

(b), (d) Opportunity loss table:

	Pr	New	Old
Weak	0.3	4,000,000	0
Moderate	0.6	0	1,000,000
Strong	0.1	0	5,000,000
	EOL	1,200,000	1,100,000

EVPI = $1,100,000. The product manager should not be willing to pay more than $1,100,000 for a perfect forecast.

•5.38 (g) The product manager should continue to use the old packaging to maximize
cont. expected monetary value and to minimize expected opportunity loss and risk.

(h) Payoff table:

	Pr	New	Old
Weak	0.6	− 4,000,000	0
Moderate	0.3	1,000,000	0
Strong	0.1	5,000,000	0
	EMV	1,600,000	0
	σ	3,136,877	0
	CV	− 196.05%	undefined
	Return to risk	− 0.5101	undefined

Opportunity loss table:

	Pr	New	Old
Weak	0.6	4,000,000	0
Moderate	0.3	0	1,000,000
Strong	0.1	0	5,000,000
	EOL	2,400,000	800,000

$EVPI$ = $800,000. The product manager should not be willing to pay more than $800,000 for a perfect forecast.

(i) The product manager should use the new packaging to maximize expected monetary value and to minimize expected opportunity loss and risk.

(j) P(Sales decreased | weak response) = 0.6
P(Sales stayed same | weak response) = 0.3
P(Sales increased | weak response) = 0.1
P(Sales decreased | moderate response) = 0.2
P(Sales stayed same | moderate response) = 0.4
P(Sales increased | moderate response) = 0.4
P(Sales decreased | strong response) = 0.05
P(Sales stayed same | strong response) = 0.35
P(Sales increased | strong response) = 0.6

P(Sales decreased *and* weak response) = 0.6(0.3) = 0.18
P(Sales stayed same *and* weak response) = 0.3(0.3) = 0.09
P(Sales increased *and* weak response) = 0.1(0.3) = 0.03
P(Sales decreased *and* moderate response) = 0.2(0.6) = 0.12
P(Sales stayed same *and* moderate response) = 0.4(0.6) = 0.24
P(Sales increased *and* moderate response) = 0.4(0.6) = 0.24
P(Sales decreased *and* strong response) = 0.05(0.1) = 0.005
P(Sales stayed same *and* strong response) = 0.35(0.1) = 0.035
P(Sales increased *and* strong response) = 0.6(0.1) = 0.06

Joint probability table:

	Pr	Sales Decrease	Sales Stay Same	Sales Increase
Weak	0.3	0.180	0.090	0.030
Moderate	0.6	0.120	0.240	0.240
Strong	0.1	0.005	0.035	0.060
Total		0.305	0.365	0.330

(j) Given the sales stayed the same, the revised conditional probabilities are:

$$P(\text{weak response} \mid \text{sales stayed same}) = \frac{.09}{.365} = 0.2466$$

$$P(\text{moderate response} \mid \text{sales stayed same}) = \frac{.24}{.365} = 0.6575$$

$$P(\text{strong response} \mid \text{sales stayed same}) = \frac{.035}{.365} = 0.0959$$

(k) Payoff table:

	Pr	New	Old
Weak	0.2466	− 4,000,000	0
Moderate	0.6575	1,000,000	0
Strong	0.0959	5,000,000	0
	EMV	150,685	0
	σ	2,641,457	0
	CV	1752.97%	undefined
	Return to risk	0.0570	undefined

Opportunity loss table:

	Pr	New	Old
Weak	0.2466	4,000,000	0
Moderate	0.6575	0	1,000,000
Strong	0.0959	0	5,000,000
	EOL	986,301	1,136,986

EVPI = $986,301. The product manager should not be willing to pay more than $986,301 for a perfect forecast.

The product manager should use the new packaging to maximize expected monetary value and to minimize expected opportunity loss and risk.

(l) Given the sales decreased, the revised conditional probabilities are:

$$P(\text{weak response} \mid \text{sales decreased}) = \frac{.18}{.305} = 0.5902$$

$$P(\text{moderate response} \mid \text{sales decreased}) = \frac{.12}{.305} = 0.3934$$

$$P(\text{strong response} \mid \text{sales decreased}) = \frac{.005}{.305} = 0.0164$$

•5.38 (m)
cont.

Payoff table:

	Pr	New	Old
Weak	0.5902	− 4,000,000	0
Moderate	0.3934	1,000,000	0
Strong	0.0164	5,000,000	0
EMV		− 1,885,246	0
σ		2,586,842	0
CV		− 137.22%	undefined
Return to risk		− 0.7288	undefined

Opportunity loss table:

	Pr	New	Old
Weak	0.5902	4,000,000	0
Moderate	0.3934	0	1,000,000
Strong	0.0164	0	5,000,000
EOL		2,360,656	475,410

EVPI = $475,410. The product manager should not be willing to pay more than $475,410 for a perfect forecast.

The product manager should continue to use the old packaging to maximize expected monetary value.

•5.40 (c), (e), (f)

Payoff table:*

	Pr	A: Do Not Call Mechanic	B: Call Mechanic
Very low	0.25	20	100
Low	0.25	100	100
Moderate	0.25	200	100
High	0.25	400	100
EMV		180	100
σ		142	0
CV		78.96%	0
Return to risk		1.2665	undefined

*Note: The payoff here is cost and not profit. The opportunity cost is therefore calculated as the difference between the payoff and the minimum in the same row.

(b), (d)

Opportunity loss table:

	Pr	A: Do Not Call Mechanic	B: Call Mechanic
Very low	0.25	0	80
Low	0.25	0	0
Moderate	0.25	100	0
High	0.25	300	0
EOL		100	20

(g) We want to minimize the expected monetary value because it is a cost. To minimize the expected monetary value, call the mechanic.

cont. (h) Given 2 successes out of 15, the binomial probabilities and their related revised conditional probabilities are:

	Pr	Binomial Probabilities	Revised Conditional Probabilities
Very low	0.01	0.0092	0.0092/0.6418 = 0.0143
Low	0.05	0.1348	0.1348/0.6418 = 0.2100
Moderate	0.10	0.2669	0.2669/0.6418 = 0.4159
High	0.20	0.2309	0.2309/0.6418 = 0.3598
		0.6418	

(i)

Payoff table:

	Pr	A: Do Not Call Mechanic	B: Call Mechanic
Very low	0.0144	20	100
Low	0.2100	100	100
Moderate	0.4159	200	100
High	0.3598	400	100
EMV		248	100
σ		121	0
CV		48.68%	0
Return to risk		2.0544	undefined

Opportunity loss table:

	Pr	A: Do Not Call Mechanic	B: Call Mechanic
Very low	0.0144	0	80
Low	0.2100	0	0
Moderate	0.4159	100	0
High	0.3598	300	0
EOL		149.52	1.15

We want to minimize the expected monetary value because it is a cost. To minimize expected monetary value, call the mechanic.

CHAPTER 6

6.2   (a) $P(Z > 1.34) = 0.5 - 0.4099 = 0.0901$

       (b) $P(Z < 1.17) = 0.5 + 0.3790 = 0.8790$

       (c) $P(0 < Z < 1.17) = 0.3790$

       (d) $P(Z < -1.17) = 0.5 - 0.3790 = 0.1210$

       (e) $P(-1.17 < Z < 1.34) = 0.3790 + 0.4099 = 0.7889$

       (f) $P(-1.17 < Z < -0.50) = 0.3790 - 0.1915 = 0.1875$

6.4   (a) $P(-2.00 < Z < 2.00) = P(-2.00 < Z < 0) + P(0 < Z < 2.00)$

             $= 0.4772 + 0.4772 = 0.9544$

       (b) $P(-3.00 < Z < 3.00) = P(-3.00 < Z < 0) + P(0 < Z < 3.00)$

             $= 0.49865 + 0.49865 = 0.9973$

6.6   (a)   (1) $P(X > 43) = P(Z > -1.75) = 0.4599 + 0.5 = 0.9599$

              (2) $P(X < 42) = P(Z < -2.00) = 0.5 - 0.4772 = 0.0228$

              (3) $P(42 < X < 48) = P(-2.00 < Z < -0.50) = 0.4772 - 0.1915 = 0.2857$

              (4) $P(X > 57.5) = P(Z > 1.88) = 0.5 - 0.4699 = 0.0301$

              (5) $P(X < 40) = P(Z < -2.50) = 0.5 - 0.4938 = 0.0062$

                     $P(X > 55) = P(Z > 1.25) = 0.5 - 0.3944 = 0.1056$

                     $P(X < 40) + P(X > 55) = 0.0062 + 0.1056 = 0.1118$

       (b) $P(X < A) = 0.05$, so $P(A < X < 0) = 0.45$ and $P(-1.645 < Z < 0) = 0.45$

$$Z = -1.645 = \frac{X - 50}{4} \qquad\qquad X = 50 - 1.645(4) = 43.42$$

       (c) $P(-A < X < A) = 0.60$

            $P(-0.84 < Z < 0) = 0.30$ and $P(0 < Z < 0.84) = 0.30$

$$Z = -0.84 = \frac{X_{\text{lower}} - 50}{4} \qquad\qquad Z = +0.84 = \frac{X_{\text{upper}} - 50}{4}$$

            $X_{\text{lower}} = 50 - 0.84(4) = 46.64$ and $X_{\text{upper}} = 50 + 0.84(4) = 53.36$

       (d) $P(X > A) = 0.85$, so $P(A < X < 0) = 0.35$

$$P(-1.04 < Z < 0) = 0.35 \qquad\qquad Z = -1.35 = \frac{X - 50}{4}$$

            $X = 50 - 1.35(4) = 44.60$

•6.8   (a) $P(34 < X < 50) = P(-1.33 < Z < 0) = 0.4082$

       (b) $P(34 < X < 38) = P(-1.33 < Z < -1.00) = 0.4082 - 0.3413 = 0.0669$

       (c) $P(X < 30) + P(X > 60) = P(Z < -1.67) + P(Z > 0.83)$

             $= (0.5 - 0.4525) + (0.5 - 0.2967) = 0.2508$

       (d) $1000(1 - 0.2508) = 749.2$ trucks

     (e) $P(X > A) = 0.80$ $P(-0.84 < Z < 0) \cong 0.30$ $Z = -0.84 = \dfrac{X - 50}{12}$

            $X = 50 - 0.84(12) = 39.92$ thousand miles or 39,920 miles

•6.8 (f) The larger standard deviation makes the Z-values smaller.
cont.
(a) $P(34 < X < 50) = P(-1.60 < Z < 0) = 0.4452$

(b) $P(34 < X < 38) = P(-1.60 < Z < -1.20) = 0.4452 - 0.3849$
$= 0.0603$

(c) $P(X < 30) + P(X > 60) = P(Z < -2.00) + P(Z > 1.00)$
$= (0.5 - 0.4772) + (0.5 - 0.3413) = 0.1815$

(d) $1000(1 - 0.1815) = 818.5$ trucks

(e) $X = 50 - 0.84(10) = 41.6$ thousand miles or 41,600 miles

6.10 (a) $P(X < 91) = P(Z < 2.25) = 0.4878 + 0.5 = 0.9878$

(b) $P(65 < X < 89) = P(-1.00 < Z < 2.00) = 0.3413 + 0.4772 = 0.8185$

(c) $P(81 < X < 89) = P(1.00 < Z < 2.00) = 0.4772 - 0.3413 = 0.1359$

(d) $P(X > A) = 0.05 \quad P(0 < Z < 1.645) = 0.4500$
$$Z = 1.645 = \frac{X - 73}{8} \qquad X = 73 + 1.645(8) = 86.16\%$$

(e) Option 1: $P(X > A) = 0.10 \quad P(0 < Z < 1.28) \cong 0.4000$
$$Z = \frac{81 - 73}{8} = 1.00$$

Since your score of 81% on this exam represents a Z-score of 1.00, which is below the minimum Z-score of 1.28, you will not earn an "A" grade on the exam under this grading option.
$$\text{Option 2: } Z = \frac{68 - 62}{3} = 2.00$$

Since your score of 68% on this exam represents a Z-score of 2.00, which is well above the minimum Z-score of 1.28, you will earn an "A" grade on the exam under this grading option. You should prefer Option 2.

•6.12 (a) $P(X < 35) = P(Z < -1.00) = 0.5 - 0.3414 = 0.1587$

(b) $P(28 < X < 32) = P(-2.40 < Z < -1.60) = 0.4918 - 0.4452 = 0.0466$

(c) $P(35 < X < 48) = P(-1.00 < Z < 1.60) = 0.3413 + 0.4452 = 0.7865$

(d) $\quad P(X > A) = 0.10 \qquad\qquad P(0 < Z < 1.28) \cong 0.4000$
$X = 40 + 1.28(5) = 46.40$ hours

(e) $Q_2 = 40$

(f) $Q_1 = 40 - 0.67(5) = 36.65 \qquad Q_3 = 40 + 0.67(5) = 43.35$
Interquartile range $= Q_3 - Q_1 = 43.35 - 36.65 = 6.7$ hours

(g) The larger standard deviation cuts the prior Z-values in half.

(a) $P(X < 35) = P(Z < -0.50) = 0.5 - 0.1915 = 0.3085$

(b) $P(28 < X < 32) = P(-1.20 < Z < -0.80) = 0.3849 - 0.2881 = 0.0968$

(c) $P(35 < X < 48) = P(-0.50 < Z < 0.80) = 0.1915 + 0.2881 = 0.4796$

(d) $X = 40 + 1.28(10) = 52.80$ hours

(e) $Q_2 = 40$

(f) $Q_1 = 40 - 0.67(10) = 33.30 \qquad Q_3 = 40 + 0.67(10) = 46.70$
Interquartile range $= Q_3 - Q_1 = 46.70 - 33.30 = 13.4$ hours

6.14 With 19 observations, the 18th largest observation covers an area under the normal curve of .90. The corresponding Z-value is +1.28. The largest observation covers an area under the normal curve of .95. The corresponding Z-value is either + 1.645, + 1.64, or + 1.65 depending on the "rule" used for this selection.

•6.16 Area under normal curve covered: 0.1429 0.2857 0.4286 0.5714 0.7143 0.8571
Standardized normal quantile value: -1.07 -0.57 -0.18 $+0.18$ $+0.57$ $+1.07$

6.18 (a) $\overline{X} = \$40.71$ $S = \$9.45$
Five-number summary $23.84 $32.10 $42.70 $48.31 $54.58
Because the mean is slightly less than the median, the distribution is slightly left-skewed.

(b)

The Normal Probability Plot

Z-value	$	Z-value	$
-1.82	23.84	0.04	44.24
-1.48	24.21	0.13	44.84
-1.26	25.93	0.22	45.32
-1.09	27.28	0.35	45.93
-0.94	28.73	0.35	45.93
-0.82	30.84	0.50	46.58
-0.70	31.15	0.60	47.36
-0.60	34.96	0.70	48.62
-0.50	35.56	0.82	49.92
-0.40	37.19	0.94	50.66
-0.31	38.58	1.09	50.97
-0.22	38.94	1.26	52.62
-0.13	40.22	1.48	53.81
-0.04	41.16	1.82	54.58

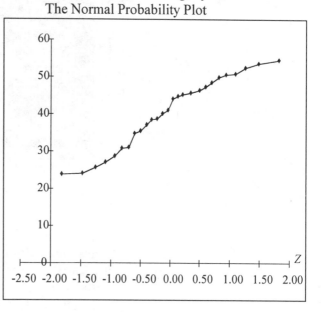

•6.20 (a) Office I: $\overline{X} = 2.214$ $S = 1.718$
Five-number summary 0.52 0.93 1.54 3.93 6.32
The distribution is right-skewed.

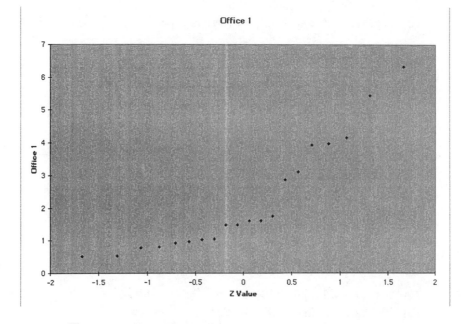

Office II: $\overline{X} = 2.011$ $S = 1.892$
Five-number summary 0.08 0.60 1.505 3.75 7.55
The distribution is right-skewed.

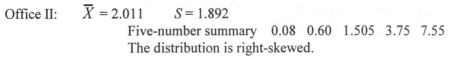

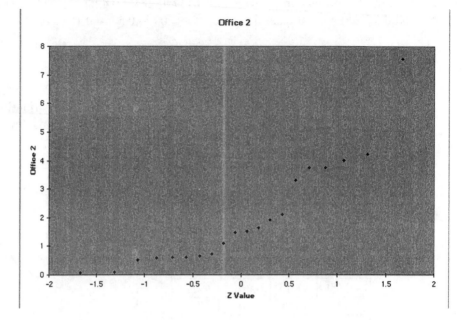

Office 2

•6.22 (a) $P(\text{arrival time} \leq 0.1) = 1 - e^{-\lambda x} = 1 - e^{-(10)(0.1)} = 0.6321$
(b) $P(\text{arrival time} > 0.1) = 1 - P(\text{arrival time} \leq 0.1) = 1 - 0.6321 = 0.3679$
(c) $P(0.1 < \text{arrival time} < 0.2) = P(\text{arrival time} < 0.2) - P(\text{arrival time} < 0.1)$
$= 0.8647 - 0.6321 = 0.2326$
(d) $P(\text{arrival time} < 0.1) + P(\text{arrival time} > 0.2) = 0.6321 + 0.1353 = 0.7674$

6.24 (a) $P(\text{arrival time} \leq 0.4) = 1 - e^{-(20)(0.4)} = 0.9997$
(b) $P(\text{arrival time} > 0.4) = 1 - P(\text{arrival time} \leq 0.4) = 1 - 0.9997 = 0.0003$
(c) $P(0.4 < \text{arrival time} < 0.5) = P(\text{arrival time} < 0.5) - P(\text{arrival time} < 0.4)$
$= 0.99995 - 0.9997 = 0.00025$
(d) $P(\text{arrival time} < 0.4) + P(\text{arrival time} > 0.5) = 0.9997 + 0.000045 = 0.999745$

•6.26 (a)

	A	B
1	Fast Food Arrivals	
2		
3	Mean	2
4	X Value	1
5	P(<=X}	0.864665

(b) $P(\text{arrival time} \leq 5) = 0.99996$
(c) If $\lambda = 1$, $P(\text{arrival time} \leq 1) = 0.6321$,
$P(\text{arrival time} \leq 5) = 0.9933$

6.28 (a) $P(\text{arrival time} \leq 10) = 1 - e^{-(0.1)(10)} = 0.6321$
(b) $P(\text{arrival time} \leq 5) = 0.3935$
(c) $P(\text{arrival time} \leq 1) = 0.0952$

•6.30　(a)　$P(\overline{X} < 95) = P(Z < -2.50) = 0.5 - 0.4938 = 0.0062$
　　　(b)　$P(95 < \overline{X} < 97.5) = P(-2.50 < Z < -1.25) = 0.4938 - 0.3944 = 0.0994$
　　　(c)　$P(\overline{X} > 102.2) = P(Z > 1.10) = 0.5 - 0.3643 = 0.1357$
　　　(d)　$P(99 < \overline{X} < 101) = P(-0.50 < Z < 0.50) = 0.1915 + 0.1915 = 0.3830$
　　　(e)　$P(\overline{X} > A) = P(Z > -0.39) = 0.65$　　　　　　$\overline{X} = 100 - 0.39(\dfrac{10}{\sqrt{25}}) = 99.22$

　　　(f)　(a)　$P(\overline{X} < 95) = P(Z < -2.00) = 0.5 - 0.4772 = 0.0228$
　　　　　　(b)　$P(95 < \overline{X} < 97.5) = P(-2.00 < Z < -1.00)$
　　　　　　　　$= 0.4772 - 0.3413 = 0.1359$
　　　　　　(c)　$P(\overline{X} > 102.2) = P(Z > 0.88) = 0.5 - 0.3106 = 0.1894$
　　　　　　(d)　$P(99 < \overline{X} < 101) = P(-0.40 < Z < 0.40)$
　　　　　　　　$= 0.1554 + 0.1554 = 0.3108$

　　　　　　(e)　$P(\overline{X} > A) = P(Z > -0.39) = 0.65$　　$\overline{X} = 100 - 0.39(\dfrac{10}{\sqrt{16}}) = 99.025$

6.32

　　　(a)　For samples of 25 travel expense vouchers for a university in an academic year, the sampling distribution of sample means is the distribution of means from all possible samples of 25 vouchers that could occur.

　　　(b)　For samples of 25 absentee records in 1997 for employees of a large manufacturing company, the sampling distribution of sample means is the distribution of means from all possible samples of 25 records that could occur.

　　　(c)　For samples of 25 sales of unleaded gasoline at service stations located in a particular county, the sampling distribution of sample means is the distribution of means from all possible samples of 25 sales that could occur.

•6.34　(a)　$P(1.28 < X < 1.30) = P(-0.50 < Z < 0) = 0.1915$
　　　(b)　$P(1.31 < X < 1.33) = P(0.25 < Z < 0.75) = 0.2734 - 0.0987 = 0.1747$
　　　(c)　$P(-A < X < A) = P(0.84 < Z < 0.84) = 0.60$
　　　　　$X = 1.30 - 0.84(0.04) = 1.2664 \quad X = 1.30 + 0.84(0.04) = 1.3336$
　　　(d)　　　　(1)　$\mu_{\overline{X}} = 1.30$　　　　$\sigma_{\overline{X}} = 0.01$
　　　　　(2)　Because the population diameter of Ping-Pong balls is approximately normally distributed, the sampling distribution of samples of 16 will also be approximately normally distributed.
　　　　　(3)　$P(1.28 < \overline{X} < 1.30) = P(-2.00 < Z < 0) = 0.4772$
　　　　　(4)　$P(1.31 < \overline{X} < 1.33) = P(1.00 < Z < 3.00) = 0.49865 - 0.3413 = 0.15735$
　　　　　(5)　$P(-A < \overline{X} < A) = P(0.84 < Z < 0.84) = 0.60$
　　　　　　　Lower bound: $\overline{X} = 1.30 - 0.84(0.01) = 1.2916$
　　　　　　　Upper bound: $\overline{X} = 1.30 + 0.84(0.01) = 1.3084$
　　(e)-(f)　When samples of size 16 are taken rather than individual values (samples of $n = 1$), more values lie closer to the mean and fewer values lie farther away from the mean with the increased sample size. This occurs because the standard deviation of the sampling distribution, the standard error, is given by:

$$\sigma_{\overline{X}} = \frac{\sigma}{\sqrt{n}}$$

As n increases, the value of the denominator increases, resulting in a smaller value of the overall fraction. The standard error for the distribution of sample means of size 16 is 1/4 of the population standard deviation of individual values and means that the sampling distribution is more concentrated around the population mean.

•6.34 (g) They are equally likely to occur (probability = 0.1587) since as n increases, more sample
cont. means will be closer to the mean of the distribution.

6.36 (a) $P(\overline{X} > 3) = P(Z > -1.00) = 0.3413 + 0.5 = 0.8413$
   (b) $P(\overline{X} < A) = P(Z < 1.04) = 0.85$ $\overline{X} = 3.10 + 1.04(0.1) = 3.204$
   (c) To be able to use the standard normal distribution as an approximation for the area under the curve, we must assume that the population is symmetrically distributed such that the central limit theorem will likely hold for samples of $n = 16$.
   (d) $P(\overline{X} < A) = P(Z < 1.04) = 0.85$ $\overline{X} = 3.10 + 1.04(0.05) = 3.152$
   (e) To be able to use the standard normal distribution as an approximation for the area under the curve, we must assume that the central limit theorem will hold for samples of $n = 64$.
   (f) For $n = 1$, $P(X < 2) = P(Z < -2.75) = 0.5 - 0.4970 = 0.0030$
   For $n = 16$, $P(\overline{X} > 3.4) = P(Z > 3.00) = 0.5 - 0.49865 = 0.00135$
   For $n = 100$, $P(\overline{X} < 2.9) = P(Z < -4.00) =$ virtually zero
   It is more likely to have an individual service time below 2 minutes.

6.38 (a)(1) $P(5 < \overline{X} < 5.5) = P(0 < Z < 1.67) = 0.4525$
   (2) $P(4.2 < \overline{X} < 4.5) = P(-2.67 < Z < -1.67)$
   $= 0.4962 - 0.4525 = 0.0437$
   (3) $P(\overline{X} < 4.6) = P(Z < -1.33) = 0.5 - 0.4082 = 0.0918$

   (b) $P(-1.96 < Z < 1.96) = 0.95$
   $\overline{X} = 5 - 1.96(0.3) = 4.412$ $\overline{X} = 5 + 1.96(0.3) = 5.588$

   (c)(a) (1) $P(5 < \overline{X} < 5.5) = P(0 < Z < 2.50) = 0.4938$
   (2) $P(4.2 < \overline{X} < 4.5) = P(-4.00 < Z < -2.50)$
   $= 0.5 - 0.4938 = 0.0062$
   (3) $P(\overline{X} < 4.6) = P(Z < -2.00) = 0.5 - 0.4772 = 0.0228$
   (b) $P(-1.96 < Z < 1.96) = 0.95$
   $\overline{X} = 5 - 1.96(0.2) = 4.608$ $\overline{X} = 5 + 1.96(0.2) = 5.392$

6.40 (a) $p_s = 15/50 = 0.30$ (b) $\sigma_{p_s} = \sqrt{\dfrac{0.40(0.60)}{50}} = 0.0693$

•6.42 (a) $P(0.09 < p_s < 0.10) = P(-0.67 < Z < 0) = 0.2486$
   (b) $P(p_s < 0.08) = P(-1.33 < Z) = 0.5 - 0.4082 = 0.0918$
   (c) Decreasing the sample size by a factor of 4 increases the standard error by a factor of 2.
   (a) $P(0.09 < p_s < 0.10) = P(-0.33 < Z < 0) = 0.1293$
   (b) $P(p_s < 0.08) = P(Z < -0.67) = 0.5 - 0.2486 = 0.2514$
   (d) If $n = 100$, $P(p_s > 0.13) = P(Z > 1.00) = 0.5 - 0.3413 = 0.1587$
   If $n = 400$, $P(p_s > 0.105) = P(Z > 0.33) = 0.5 - 0.1293 = 0.3707$
   It is more likely that a percent defective above 10.5% occur among samples of size 400.

6.44   (a) $P(0.20 < p_s < 0.30) = P(-2.18 < Z < 0) = 0.4854$

       (b) $P(-1.96 < Z < 1.96) = 0.95$

             $p_s = .30 - 1.96(0.0458) = 0.2102$ $p_s = .30 + 1.96(0.0458) = 0.3898$

6.46   (a) $P(0.93 < p_s < 0.95) = P(0 < Z < 1.75) = 0.4599$

       (b) $P(p_s > 0.95) = P(Z > 1.75) = 0.5 - 0.4599 = 0.0401$

       (c)   (a) $P(0.93 < p_s < 0.95) = P(0 < Z < 2.48) = 0.4934$

              (b) $P(p_s > 0.95) = P(Z > 2.48) = 0.5 - 0.4934 = 0.0066$

       (d)   If $n = 500$, $P(p_s > 0.95) = P(Z > 1.75) = 0.5 - 0.4599 = 0.0401$

             If $n = 1000$, $P(p_s < 0.90) = P(Z < -3.72) = 0.5 - 0.4999 = 0.0001$

             More than 95% in a sample of 500 is more likely than less than 90% in a sample of 1000.

6.48   If $N = 400$ and $n = 100$, fpc = 0.8671.

      If $N = 900$ and $n = 200$, fpc = 0.8824.

      The finite population correction done for a population of 400 sampling 100 has a greater effect in reducing the standard error.

•6.50 $P(1.31 < \overline{X} < 1.33) = P(1.04 < Z < 3.12) = 0.4991 - 0.3508 = 0.1483$

where $Z = \dfrac{1.31 - 1.30}{\dfrac{0.04}{\sqrt{16}} \cdot \sqrt{\dfrac{200 - 16}{200 - 1}}} = 1.04$ and $Z = \dfrac{1.33 - 1.30}{\dfrac{0.04}{\sqrt{16}} \cdot \sqrt{\dfrac{200 - 16}{200 - 1}}} = 3.12$

•6.52   (a) $P(0.09 < p_s < 0.10) = P(-0.69 < Z < 0) = 0.2549$

where $Z = \dfrac{0.09 - 0.10}{\sqrt{\dfrac{0.1(0.9)}{400}} \cdot \sqrt{\dfrac{5000 - 400}{5000 - 1}}} = -0.69$

       (b) $P(p_s < 0.08) = P(Z < -1.39) = 0.5 - 0.4177 = 0.0823$

where $Z = \dfrac{0.08 - 0.10}{\sqrt{\dfrac{0.1(0.9)}{400}} \cdot \sqrt{\dfrac{5000 - 400}{5000 - 1}}} = -1.39$

6.68   (a) $P(0.75 < X < 0.753) = P(-0.75 < Z < 0) = 0.2734$

       (b) $P(0.74 < X < 0.75) = P(-3.25 < Z < -0.75) = 0.49942 - 0.2734 = 0.2260$

       (c) $P(X > 0.76) = P(Z > 1.75) = 0.5 - 0.4599 = 0.0401$

       (d) $P(X < 0.74) = P(Z < -3.25) = 0.5 - 0.49942 = 0.00058$

       (e) $P(X < A) = P(Z < -1.48) = 0.07\ X = 0.753 - 1.48(0.004) = 0.7471$

6.70   (a) $P(X > 5) = P(Z > 2.00) = 0.5 - 0.4772 = 0.0228$

         (b) $P(X > 5) = P(Z > 2.00) = 0.0228$

         (c)   Although the mean processing time is reduced from 3 days to 2, the increased standard deviation offsets any increase, resulting in the same calculated value of Z.

         (d)   The city agency would do better reducing the average to 2 days since the proportion of free permits would be 0.00135 instead of 0.0038.

6.72   (a) $P(100 < X < 115) = P(0 < Z < 0.75) = 0.2734$

         (b) $P(X > 90) = P(Z > -0.50) = 0.5 + 0.1915 = 0.6915$

         (c) $P(X > A) = P(Z > -1.28) = 0.90$ $X = 100 - 1.28(20) = 74.40$ hours

         (d) $Q_1 = 100 - 0.67(20) = 86.60$ $Q_3 = 100 + 0.67(20) = 113.40$

                Interquartile range $= Q_3 - Q_1 = 113.40 - 86.60 = 26.80$

         (e)(1) $P(100 < \overline{X} < 115) = P(0 < Z < 3.00) = 0.49865$

           (2) $P(\overline{X} > 90) = P(Z > -2.00) = 0.5 + 0.4772 = 0.9772$

           (3) $P(-A < \overline{X} < A) = P(-1.645 < Z < 1.645) = 0.90$

                $\overline{X} = 100 - 1.645(5) = 91.775$ $\overline{X} = 100 + 1.645(5) = 108.225$

         (f)   The central limit theorem is not necessary because the population is normally distributed. So the sampling distribution of the mean will also be normally distributed regardless of the sample size.

•6.74   (a)   (1) $P(10 < X < 12.5) = P(0 < Z < 1.00) = 0.3413$

                (2) $P(7.5 < X < 10) = P(-1.00 < Z < 0) = 0.3413$

                (3) $P(7.5 < X < 12.5) = 0.3413 + 0.3413 = 0.6826$

                (4) $P(X > 7.5) = P(Z > -1.00) = 0.5 + 0.3413 = 0.8413$

                (5) $P(X < 7.5) = 1 - P(X > 7.5) = 1 - 0.8413 = 0.1587$

                (6) $P(12.5 < X < 14.3) = P(1.00 < Z < 1.72) = 0.4573 + 0.3413 = 0.1160$

         (b) $P(X > A) = P(Z > 0) = 0.50$ $X = 10$ million dollars

         (c) $P(X > A) = P(Z > -1.28) = 0.90$ $X = 10 - 1.28(2.5) = 6.8$ million dollars

         (d) $Q_1 = 10 - 0.67(2.5) = 8.325$ $Q_3 = 10 + 0.67(2.5) = 11.675$

                Interquartile range $= Q_3 - Q_1 = 11.675 - 8.325 = 3.35$ million dollars

CHAPTER 7

7.2 $\overline{X} \pm Z \cdot \dfrac{\sigma}{\sqrt{n}} = 125 \pm 2.58 \cdot \dfrac{24}{\sqrt{36}}$ $114.68 \le \mu \le 135.32$

7.4   Since the results of only one sample are used to indicate whether something has gone wrong in the production process, the manufacturer can never know with 100% certainty that the specific interval obtained from the sample includes the true population mean. In order to have every possible interval estimate of the true mean, the entire population (sample size N) would have to be selected.

7.6   Approximately 5% of the intervals will not include the true population mean somewhere in the interval. Since the true population mean is not known, we do not know for certain whether it is in the one interval we have developed, between 10.99408 and 11.00192 inches.

7.8   (a)

	A	B
1	Light Bulbs	
2		
3	Population Standard Deviation	100
4	Sample Mean	350
5	Sample Size	64
6	Confidence Level	95%
7	Standard Error of the Mean	12.5
8	Z Value	-1.95996108
9	Interval Half Width	24.49951353
10	Interval Lower Limit	325.5004865
11	Interval Upper Limit	374.4995135

     (b)   No. The manufacturer cannot support a claim that the bulbs last an average 400 hours. Based on the data from the sample, a mean of 400 hours would represent a distance of 4 standard deviations above the sample mean of 350 hours.

     (c)   No. Since σ is known and $n = 64$, from the central limit theorem, we may assume that the sampling distribution of $\overline{X}$ is approximately normal.

     (d)   An individual value of 320 is only 0.30 standard deviations below the sample mean of 350. The confidence interval represents bounds on the estimate of a sample of 64, not an individual value.

     (e)   The confidence interval is narrower based on a process standard deviation of 80 hours rather than the original assumption of 100 hours.

         (a) $\overline{X} \pm Z \cdot \dfrac{\sigma}{\sqrt{n}} = 350 \pm 1.96 \cdot \dfrac{80}{\sqrt{64}}$ $330.4 \le \mu \le 369.6$

         (b)   Based on the smaller standard deviation, a mean of 400 hours would represent a distance of 5 standard deviations above the sample mean of 350 hours. No, the manufacturer cannot support a claim that the bulbs last an average of 400 hours.

7.10   (a) $t_9 = 2.2622$

       (b) $t_9 = 3.2498$

       (c) $t_{31} = 2.0395$

       (d) $t_{64} = 1.9977$

       (e) $t_{15} = 1.7531$

7.12 $\bar{X} \pm t \cdot \dfrac{s}{\sqrt{n}} = 50 \pm 2.9467 \cdot \dfrac{15}{\sqrt{16}}$ $38.9499 \le \mu \le 61.0501$

7.14   Original data: $5.8571 \pm 2.4469 \cdot \dfrac{6.4660}{\sqrt{7}}$ $-0.1229 \le \mu \le 11.8371$

      Altered data: $4.00 \pm 2.4469 \cdot \dfrac{2.1602}{\sqrt{7}}$ $2.0022 \le \mu \le 5.9978$

      The presence of an outlier in the original data increases the value of the sample mean and greatly inflates the sample standard deviation.

7.16   (a) $\bar{X} \pm t \cdot \dfrac{s}{\sqrt{n}} = 4750 \pm 2.0452 \cdot \dfrac{1200}{\sqrt{30}}$ $\$4{,}301.96 \le \mu \le \$5{,}198.04$

       (b)   It is not unusual. An individual account of \$4,000 is only 0.625 standard deviation below the sample mean of \$4,750.

7.18   (a)

	A	B
1	Dental Expenses	
2		
3	Sample Standard Deviation	138.8045789
4	Sample Mean	261.4
5	Sample Size	10
6	Confidence Level	90%
7	Standard Error of the Mean	43.89386188
8	Degrees of Freedom	9
9	t Value	1.833113856
10	Interval Half Width	80.46244642
11	Interval Lower Limit	180.94
12	Interval Upper Limit	341.86

       (b)   The population of dental expenses must be approximately normally distributed.

       (d) $\bar{X} \pm t \cdot \dfrac{s}{\sqrt{n}} = 261.40 \pm 2.2622 \cdot \dfrac{138.80}{\sqrt{10}}$ $\$162.11 \le \mu \le \$360.69$

       (e)   The additional \$500 in dental expenses, divided across the sample of 10, raises the mean by \$50 and increases the standard deviation by nearly \$20. The interval half-width increases over \$11 in the process. The new interval is:

$$\bar{X} \pm t \cdot \dfrac{s}{\sqrt{n}} = 311.40 \pm 1.8331 \cdot \dfrac{157.056}{\sqrt{10}} \qquad \$220.36 \le \mu \le \$402.22$$

7.20 (a) $\bar{X} \pm t \cdot \dfrac{s}{\sqrt{n}} = 27.892 \pm 2.0639 \cdot \dfrac{13.9697}{\sqrt{25}}$ $\qquad$ $22.167 \le \mu \le 33.617$

(b) The director should not make the statement that average waiting time at the HMO is 15 minutes. Based on these sample data, 15 minutes is 4.65 standard deviations below the sample mean of 27.892 minutes, rendering the statement extremely unlikely.

(c) Waiting times are normally distributed.

(d) Inflating one data value by 100 minutes raises the average sample waiting time by 4 minutes and increases the standard deviation from 13.9 to 19.4 minutes. The interval half-width increases from 5.725 minutes to just over 8 minutes. The new interval is:

$$\bar{X} \pm t \cdot \dfrac{s}{\sqrt{n}} = 31.892 \pm 2.0639 \cdot \dfrac{19.3847}{\sqrt{25}} \qquad 23.890 \le \mu \le 39.894$$

7.22 $\quad p_s = \dfrac{X}{n} = \dfrac{25}{400} = 0.0625 \qquad p_s \pm Z \cdot \sqrt{\dfrac{p_s(1-p_s)}{n}} = 0.25 \pm 2.58\sqrt{\dfrac{0.0625(0.9375)}{400}}$

$\qquad\qquad\qquad\qquad\qquad\qquad\qquad\qquad\qquad\qquad\qquad 0.0313 \le p \le 0.0937$

7.24 (a) $p_s = 0.4 \qquad p_s \pm Z \cdot \sqrt{\dfrac{p_s(1-p_s)}{n}} = 0.4 \pm 2.58 \cdot \sqrt{\dfrac{0.4(0.6)}{200}}$

$\qquad\qquad\qquad\qquad\qquad\qquad\qquad\qquad\qquad\qquad\qquad 0.3106 \le p \le 0.4894$

(b) The auditor should report that actual payment performance is well below the goal of 90% or more of claims that should be paid within two months. In fact, the target of 90% is 14.43 standard deviations above the sample proportion of 40%.

7.26 (a) $p_s = 0.10 \qquad p_s \pm Z \cdot \sqrt{\dfrac{p_s(1-p_s)}{n}} = 0.10 \pm 1.645 \cdot \sqrt{\dfrac{0.10(0.90)}{300}}$

$\qquad\qquad\qquad\qquad\qquad\qquad\qquad\qquad\qquad\qquad\qquad 0.0715 \le p \le 0.1285$

(b) Based on the results of this sample, the owner can return this shipment because it is likely that the shipment contains more than 5% defective pens. It is possible but highly unlikely that the owner got a 10% defective rate from a sample of 300 pens that really had only a 5% defective rate.

(c) The center of the confidence interval remains anchored at $p_s = 0.10$, but the increased confidence level increases the width of the half-interval from 0.0285 to 0.0447. The new interval is:

$p_s = 0.10 \qquad p_s \pm Z \cdot \sqrt{\dfrac{p_s(1-p_s)}{n}} = 0.10 \pm 2.58 \cdot \sqrt{\dfrac{0.10(0.90)}{300}}$

$\qquad\qquad\qquad\qquad\qquad\qquad\qquad\qquad\qquad\qquad\qquad 0.0553 \le p \le 0.1447$

7.28   (a)

	A	B
1	Purchase Additional Telephone Line	
2		
3	Sample Size	500
4	Number of Successes	135
5	Confidence Level	99%
6	Sample Proportion	0.27
7	Z Value	-2.57583451
8	Standard Error of the Proportion	0.019854471
9	Interval Half Width	0.05114183
10	Interval Lower Limit	0.21885817
11	Interval Upper Limit	0.32114183

•7.30 $n = \dfrac{Z^2\sigma^2}{e^2} = \dfrac{1.96^2 \cdot 15^2}{5^2} = 34.57$ Use $n = 35$

7.32 $n = \dfrac{Z^2 p(1-p)}{e^2} = \dfrac{2.58^2 (0.5)(0.5)}{(0.04)^2} = 1{,}040.06$ Use $n = 1{,}041$

7.34 $n = \dfrac{Z^2\sigma^2}{e^2} = \dfrac{1.96^2 \cdot 400^2}{50^2} = 245.86$ Use $n = 246$

•7.36 $n = \dfrac{Z^2\sigma^2}{e^2} = \dfrac{1.96^2 \cdot (100)^2}{(20)^2} = 96.04$ Use $n = 97$

•7.38   (a) $n = \dfrac{Z^2\sigma^2}{e^2} = \dfrac{2.58^2 \cdot 25^2}{5^2} = 166.41$ Use $n = 167$

        (b) $n = \dfrac{Z^2\sigma^2}{e^2} = \dfrac{1.96^2 \cdot 25^2}{5^2} = 96.04$ Use $n = 97$

7.40   (a) $n = \dfrac{Z^2\sigma^2}{e^2} = \dfrac{1.645^2 \cdot 45^2}{5^2} = 219.19$ Use $n = 220$

        (b) $n = \dfrac{Z^2\sigma^2}{e^2} = \dfrac{2.58^2 \cdot 45^2}{5^2} = 539.17$ Use $n = 540$

7.42   (a) $n = \dfrac{Z^2 p(1-p)}{e^2} = \dfrac{1.645^2 (0.5)(0.5)}{(0.04)^2} = 422.82$ Use $n = 423$

        (b) $n = \dfrac{Z^2 p(1-p)}{e^2} = \dfrac{1.96^2 (0.5)(0.5)}{(0.04)^2} = 600.25$ Use $n = 601$

•7.44 $n = \dfrac{Z^2 p(1-p)}{e^2} = \dfrac{1.645^2 (0.5)(0.5)}{(0.05)^2} = 270.60$ Use $n = 271$

7.46   (a) $n = \dfrac{Z^2 p(1-p)}{e^2} = \dfrac{2.58^2 (0.10)(0.90)}{(0.07)^2} = 122.26$ Use $n = 123$

(b) $n = \dfrac{Z^2 p(1-p)}{e^2} = \dfrac{1.96^2 (0.10)(0.90)}{(0.06)^2} = 96.04$ Use $n = 97$

•7.48 $\bar{X} \pm t \cdot \dfrac{s}{\sqrt{n}} \sqrt{\dfrac{N-n}{N-1}} = 75 \pm 2.0301 \cdot \dfrac{24}{\sqrt{36}} \sqrt{\dfrac{200-36}{200-1}}$ $67.6282 \le \mu \le 82.3718$

•7.50   (a) $\bar{X} \pm Z \cdot \dfrac{\sigma}{\sqrt{n}} \sqrt{\dfrac{N-n}{N-1}} = 350 \pm 1.96 \cdot \dfrac{100}{\sqrt{50}} \sqrt{\dfrac{2000-50}{2000-1}}$

$322.62 \le \mu \le 377.38$

Note: Because the process standard deviation is known, use a Z rather than a t to build the confidence interval.

(b) $n_0 = \dfrac{Z^2 \sigma^2}{e^2} = \dfrac{1.96^2 \cdot 100^2}{20^2} = 96.04$

$n = \dfrac{n_0 N}{n_0 + (N-1)} = \dfrac{96.04 \cdot 2000}{96.04 + (2000-1)} = 91.68$ Use $n = 92$

(c)(a) $\bar{X} \pm Z \cdot \dfrac{\sigma}{\sqrt{n}} \sqrt{\dfrac{N-n}{N-1}} = 350 \pm 1.96 \cdot \dfrac{100}{\sqrt{50}} \sqrt{\dfrac{1000-50}{1000-1}}$

$322.97 \le \mu \le 377.03$

(b) $n = \dfrac{n_0 N}{n_0 + (N-1)} = \dfrac{96.04 \cdot 1000}{96.04 + (1000-1)} = 87.70$ Use $n = 88$

•7.52   (a) $p_s \pm Z \sqrt{\dfrac{p_s(1-p_s)}{n}} \sqrt{\dfrac{N-n}{N-1}} = 0.3 \pm 1.645 \cdot \sqrt{\dfrac{0.3(0.7)}{100}} \sqrt{\dfrac{1000-100}{1000-1}}$

$0.2284 \le p \le 0.3716$

(b)
$n_0 = \dfrac{Z^2 p(1-p)}{e^2} = \dfrac{1.645^2 (0.5)(0.5)}{(0.05)^2} = 270.6025$

$n = \dfrac{n_0 N}{n_0 + (N-1)} = \dfrac{270.6025 \cdot 1000}{270.6025 + (1000-1)} = 213.14$

Use $n = 214$

•7.52 (b) *Note:* To be the most conservative, assume in part (b) that the population proportion is
cont. not known, using an estimate of 0.5 for p. An estimate of 0.5 maximizes the
sample size by maximizing $p(1-p)$ to produce the largest n_0 necessary.

(c) (a)

$$0.3 \pm 1.645 \cdot \sqrt{\frac{0.3(0.7)}{100}} \sqrt{\frac{2000-100}{2000-1}} \qquad 0.2265 \le p \le 0.3735$$

(b) $$n = \frac{n_0 N}{n_0 + (N-1)} = \frac{270.6025 \cdot 2000}{270.6025 + (2000-1)} = 238.46 \qquad \text{Use } n = 239$$

7.54 (a) $$\overline{X} \pm Z \cdot \frac{\sigma}{\sqrt{n}} \sqrt{\frac{N-n}{N-1}} = 1.99 \pm 1.96 \cdot \frac{0.05}{\sqrt{100}} \cdot \sqrt{\frac{2000-100}{2000-1}}$$

$$1.9804 \le \mu \le 1.9996$$

(b) $$n_0 = \frac{Z^2 \sigma^2}{e^2} = \frac{1.96^2 \cdot (0.05)^2}{(0.01)^2} = 96.04$$

$$n = \frac{n_0 N}{n_0 + (N-1)} = \frac{96.04 \cdot 2000}{96.04 + 1999} = 91.68 \qquad \text{Use } n = 92$$

(c) (a) $$\overline{X} \pm t \cdot \frac{s}{\sqrt{n}} \sqrt{\frac{N-n}{N-1}} = 1.99 \pm 1.96 \cdot \frac{0.05}{\sqrt{100}} \cdot \sqrt{\frac{1000-100}{1000-1}}$$

$$1.9807 \le \mu \le 1.9993$$

(b) $$n_0 = \frac{Z^2 \sigma^2}{e^2} = \frac{1.96^2 \cdot (0.05)^2}{(0.01)^2} = 96.04$$

$$n = \frac{n_0 N}{n_0 + (N-1)} = \frac{96.04 \cdot 1000}{96.04 + 999} = 87.70 \qquad \text{Use } n = 88$$

•7.56 (b) $$N \cdot \overline{X} \pm N \cdot t \cdot \frac{s}{\sqrt{n}} \sqrt{\frac{N-n}{N-1}} = 500 \cdot 25.7 \pm 500 \cdot 2.7969 \cdot \frac{7.8}{\sqrt{25}} \cdot \sqrt{\frac{500-25}{500-1}}$$

$$\$10,721.53 \le \text{Population Total} \le \$14,978.47$$

7.58

$$N \cdot \overline{X} \pm N \cdot t \cdot \frac{s}{\sqrt{n}} \sqrt{\frac{N-n}{N-1}}$$

$$= 2000 \cdot \$4,750 \pm 2000 \cdot 2.0452 \cdot \frac{\$1,200}{\sqrt{30}} \cdot \sqrt{\frac{2000-30}{2000-1}}$$

$$\$8,610,362.43 \le \text{Population Total} \le \$10,389,637.57$$

7.60

$$N\cdot\overline{X}\pm N\cdot t\cdot\frac{s}{\sqrt{n}}\sqrt{\frac{N-n}{N-1}}$$

$$= 3000\cdot\$261.40\pm 3000\cdot 1.8331\cdot\frac{\$138.8046}{\sqrt{10}}\cdot\sqrt{\frac{3000-10}{3000-1}}$$

$$\$543,176.96\le \text{Population Total}\le \$1,025,223.04$$

•7.62

$$N\cdot\overline{D}\pm N\cdot t\cdot\frac{s_D}{\sqrt{n}}\sqrt{\frac{N-n}{N-1}}$$

$$= 4000\cdot\$7.45907\pm 4000\cdot 2.60923\cdot\frac{\$29.55234}{\sqrt{150}}\cdot\sqrt{\frac{4000-150}{4000-1}}$$

$$\$5,125.99\le \text{Total Difference in the Population}\le \$54,546.57$$

Note: The *t*-value of 2.60923 for 95% confidence and *df* = 149 was derived on Excel.

•7.70 (a) $\overline{X}\pm t\cdot\frac{s}{\sqrt{n}}=15.3\pm 2.0227\cdot\frac{3.8}{\sqrt{40}}$ $\qquad$ $14.085\le\mu\le 16.515$

(b) $p_s\pm Z\cdot\sqrt{\frac{p_s(1-p_s)}{n}}=0.675\pm 1.96\cdot\sqrt{\frac{0.675(0.325)}{40}}$ $\qquad$ $0.530\le p\le 0.820$

(c) $n=\frac{Z^2\cdot\sigma^2}{e^2}=\frac{1.96^2\cdot 5^2}{2^2}=24.01$ $\qquad$ Use *n* = 25

(d) $n=\frac{Z^2\cdot p\cdot(1-p)}{e^2}=\frac{1.96^2\cdot(0.5)\cdot(0.5)}{(0.035)^2}=784$ $\qquad$ Use *n* = 784

(e) If a single sample were to be selected for both purposes, the larger of the two sample sizes (*n* = 784) should be used.

7.72 (a) $\overline{X}\pm t\cdot\frac{s}{\sqrt{n}}=9.7\pm 2.0639\cdot\frac{4}{\sqrt{25}}$ $\qquad$ $8.049\le\mu\le 11.351$

(b) $p_s\pm Z\cdot\sqrt{\frac{p_s(1-p_s)}{n}}=0.48\pm 1.96\cdot\sqrt{\frac{0.48(0.52)}{25}}$ $\qquad$ $0.284\le p\le 0.676$

(c) $n=\frac{Z^2\cdot\sigma^2}{e^2}=\frac{1.96^2\cdot 4.5^2}{1.5^2}=34.57$ $\qquad$ Use *n* = 35

(d) $n=\frac{Z^2\cdot p\cdot(1-p)}{e^2}=\frac{1.645^2\cdot(0.5)\cdot(0.5)}{(0.075)^2}=120.268$ $\qquad$ Use *n* = 121

(e) If a single sample were to be selected for both purposes, the larger of the two sample sizes (*n* = 121) should be used.

•7.74 (a) $\bar{X} \pm t \cdot \dfrac{s}{\sqrt{n}} = \$28.52 \pm 1.9949 \cdot \dfrac{\$11.39}{\sqrt{70}}$ $\qquad\qquad$ $\$25.80 \le \mu \le \$31.24$

(b) $p_s \pm Z \cdot \sqrt{\dfrac{p_s(1-p_s)}{n}} = 0.40 \pm 1.645 \cdot \sqrt{\dfrac{0.40(0.60)}{70}}$ $\qquad$ $0.3037 \le p \le 0.4963$

(c) $n = \dfrac{Z^2 \cdot \sigma^2}{e^2} = \dfrac{1.96^2 \cdot 10^2}{2^2} = 96.04$ $\qquad\qquad\qquad\qquad$ Use $n = 97$

(d) $n = \dfrac{Z^2 \cdot p \cdot (1-p)}{e^2} = \dfrac{1.645^2 \cdot (0.5) \cdot (0.5)}{(0.04)^2} = 422.82$ $\qquad$ Use $n = 423$

(e) $\qquad$ If a single sample were to be selected for both purposes, the larger of the two sample sizes ($n = 423$) should be used.

7.76 (a) $\bar{X} \pm t \cdot \dfrac{s}{\sqrt{n}} = \$38.54 \pm 2.0010 \cdot \dfrac{\$7.26}{\sqrt{60}}$ $\qquad\qquad$ $\$36.66 \le \mu \le \$40.42$

(b) $p_s \pm Z \cdot \sqrt{\dfrac{p_s(1-p_s)}{n}} = 0.30 \pm 1.645 \cdot \sqrt{\dfrac{0.30(0.70)}{60}}$ $\qquad$ $0.2027 \le p \le 0.3973$

(c) $n = \dfrac{Z^2 \cdot \sigma^2}{e^2} = \dfrac{1.96^2 \cdot 8^2}{1.5^2} = 109.27$ $\qquad\qquad\qquad\qquad$ Use $n = 110$

(d) $n = \dfrac{Z^2 \cdot p \cdot (1-p)}{e^2} = \dfrac{1.645^2 \cdot (0.5) \cdot (0.5)}{(0.04)^2} = 422.82$ $\qquad$ Use $n = 423$

(e) $\qquad$ If a single sample were to be selected for both purposes, the larger of the two sample sizes ($n = 423$) should be used.

7.78 (a) $p \pm Z \cdot \sqrt{\dfrac{p(1-p)}{n}} \cdot \sqrt{\dfrac{N-n}{N-1}} = 0.14 \pm 1.96 \cdot \sqrt{\dfrac{0.14(0.86)}{50}} \cdot \sqrt{\dfrac{1000-50}{1000-1}}$

$\qquad\qquad\qquad\qquad\qquad\qquad\qquad\qquad\qquad\qquad$ $0.0613 \le p \le 0.2187$

(b) $n = \dfrac{Z^2 \cdot p \cdot (1-p)}{e^2} = \dfrac{1.96^2 \cdot (0.10) \cdot (0.90)}{(0.04)^2} = 216.09$ $\qquad$ Use $n = 217$

7.80 (a) $n_0 = \dfrac{Z^2 \cdot \sigma^2}{e^2} = \dfrac{1.96^2 \cdot 30^2}{5^2} = 138.2976$

$\qquad n = \dfrac{n_0 N}{n_0 + (N-1)} = \dfrac{138.2976 \cdot 25{,}056}{138.2976 + (25{,}056 - 1)} = 137.54$ $\qquad$ Use $n = 138$

7.80

cont. (b) $p_s = \dfrac{7}{138} = 0.0507$

$$p \pm Z \cdot \sqrt{\dfrac{p(1-p)}{n}} \cdot \sqrt{\dfrac{N-n}{N-1}}$$

$$= 0.0507 \pm 1.645 \cdot \sqrt{\dfrac{0.0507(0.9493)}{138}} \cdot \sqrt{\dfrac{25,056-138}{25,056-1}}$$

$$0.0201 \le p \le 0.0813$$

(c) (1) Using Excel, we find the t-value for 95% confidence and 137 degrees of freedom is $t = 1.9774$.

$$\overline{X} \pm t \cdot \dfrac{s}{\sqrt{n}} \cdot \sqrt{\dfrac{N-n}{N-1}} = \$93.70 \pm 1.9774 \cdot \dfrac{\$34.55}{\sqrt{138}} \cdot \sqrt{\dfrac{25,056-138}{25,056-1}}$$

$$\$87.90 \le \mu_X \le \$99.50$$

(2)

$$N \cdot \overline{X} \pm N \cdot t \cdot \dfrac{s}{\sqrt{n}} \cdot \sqrt{\dfrac{N-n}{N-1}}$$

$$= 25,056 \cdot \$93.70 \pm 25,056 \cdot 1.9774 \cdot \dfrac{\$34.55}{\sqrt{138}} \cdot \sqrt{\dfrac{25,056-138}{25,056-1}}$$

$$\$2,202,427.61 \le \text{Population Total} \le \$2,493,066.79$$

(d) $\overline{D} = \dfrac{\sum D}{n} = \dfrac{241}{138} = 1.7463768 \qquad s_D = \sqrt{\dfrac{\sum(D-\overline{D})^2}{n-1}} = \sqrt{\dfrac{6432.12}{137}} = 6.85199$

$$N \cdot \overline{D} \pm N \cdot t \cdot \dfrac{s_D}{\sqrt{n}} \cdot \sqrt{\dfrac{N-n}{N-1}}$$

$$= 25,056 \cdot \$1.7463768 \pm 25,056 \cdot 1.9774 \cdot \dfrac{\$6.85199}{\sqrt{138}} \cdot \sqrt{\dfrac{25,056-138}{25,056-1}}$$

$$\$14,937.30 \le \text{Total Difference in the Population} \le \$72,577.14$$

•8.2 H_1 is used to denote the alternative hypothesis.

•8.4 β is used to denote the consumer's risk, or the chance of committing a Type II error.

8.6 α is the probability of making a Type I error – that is, the probability of incorrectly rejecting the null hypothesis when in reality the null hypothesis is true and should not be rejected.

8.8   The power of a test is the complement of the probability β of making a Type II error.

8.10   It is possible to incorrectly fail to reject a false null hypothesis because it is possible for the mean of a single sample to fall in the nonrejection region even though the hypothesized population mean is false.

8.12   Other things being equal, the closer the *hypothesized* mean is to the *actual* mean, the larger is the risk of committing a Type II error.

8.14   Under the French judicial system, unlike ours in the United States, the null hypothesis is that the defendant is assumed to be guilty, the alternative hypothesis is that the defendant is innocent. The meaning of α and β risks would also be switched.

•8.16 H_0: $\mu = 20$ minutes. 20 minutes is adequate travel time between classes.
           H_1: $\mu \neq 20$ minutes. 20 minutes is not adequate travel time between classes.

8.18   Decision rule: Reject H_0 if $Z < -1.96$ or $Z > +1.96$.
       Decision: Since $Z_{calc} = +2.21$ is greater than $Z_{crit} = +1.96$, reject H_0.

•8.20   Decision rule: Reject H_0 if $Z < -2.58$ or $Z > +2.58$.

8.22   (a)H_0: $\mu = 70$ pounds. The cloth has an average breaking strength of 70 pounds.
           H_1: $\mu \neq 70$ pounds. The cloth has an average breaking strength that differs from 70 pounds.

      (b)   Decision rule: Reject H_0 if $Z < -1.96$ or $Z > +1.96$.

$$\text{Test statistic: } Z = \frac{\overline{X} - \mu}{\sigma / \sqrt{n}} = \frac{69.1 - 70}{3.5 / \sqrt{49}} = -1.80$$

          Decision: Since $Z_{calc} = -1.80$ is between the critical bounds of ± 1.96, do not reject H_0. There is not enough evidence to conclude that the cloth has an average breaking strength that differs from 70 pounds.

8.22
cont. (c) Decision rule: Reject H_0 if $Z < -1.96$ or $Z > +1.96$.

Test statistic: $Z = \dfrac{\overline{X} - \mu}{\sigma/\sqrt{n}} = \dfrac{69.1 - 70}{1.75/\sqrt{49}} = -3.60$

Decision: Since $Z_{calc} = -3.60$ is less than the lower critical bound of -1.96, reject H_0. There is enough evidence to conclude that the cloth has an average breaking strength that differs from 70 pounds.

(d) Decision rule: Reject H_0 if $Z < -1.96$ or $Z > +1.96$.

Test statistic: $Z = \dfrac{\overline{X} - \mu}{\sigma/\sqrt{n}} = \dfrac{69 - 70}{3.5/\sqrt{49}} = -2.00$

Decision: Since $Z_{calc} = -2.00$ is less than the lower critical bound of -1.96, reject H_0. There is enough evidence to conclude that the cloth has an average breaking strength that differs from 70 pounds.

•8.24 (a), (b)

	A	B
1	Salad Dressings	
2		
3	Null Hypothesis $\mu=$	8
4	Level of Significance	0.05
5	Population Standard Deviation	0.15
6	Sample Size	50
7	Sample Mean	7.983
8	Standard Error of the Mean	0.021213203
9	Z Test Statistic	-0.80138769
10		
11	Two-Tailed Test	
12	Lower Critical Value	-1.95996108
13	Upper Critical Value	1.959961082
14	p-Value	0.422907113
15	Do not reject the null hypothesis	

(c) Decision rule: Reject H_0 if $Z < -1.96$ or $Z > +1.96$.

Test statistic: $Z = \dfrac{\overline{X} - \mu}{\sigma/\sqrt{n}} = \dfrac{7.983 - 8}{0.05/\sqrt{50}} = -2.40$

Decision: Since $Z_{calc} = -2.40$ is less than the lower critical bound of -1.96, reject H_0. There is enough evidence to conclude that the machine is filling bottles improperly.

(d) Decision rule: Reject H_0 if $Z < -1.96$ or $Z > +1.96$.

Test statistic: $Z = \dfrac{\overline{X} - \mu}{\sigma/\sqrt{n}} = \dfrac{7.952 - 8}{0.15/\sqrt{50}} = -2.26$

Decision: Since $Z_{calc} = -2.26$ is less than the lower critical bound of -1.96, reject H_0. There is enough evidence to conclude that the machine is filling bottles improperly.

•8.26 p value $= 2(0.5 - 0.4772) = 0.0456$

8.28 p value $= 2(0.5 - 0.4147) = 0.1706$

8.30   (a)   Test statistic: $Z = \dfrac{\overline{X} - \mu}{\sigma/\sqrt{n}} = \dfrac{69.1 - 70}{3.5/\sqrt{49}} = -1.80$

   p value $= 2(0.5 - 0.4641) = 0.0718$
   Interpretation: The probability of getting a sample of 49 pieces that yield a mean strength that is farther away from the hypothesized population mean than this sample is 0.0718 or 7.18%.

   (b)   Decision: Since p value $= 0.0718$ is greater than $\alpha = 0.05$, do not reject H_0.
   (c)   At the 0.05 level of significance, a p value of 0.0718 does not provide sufficient evidence to conclude that the machine is not meeting the manufacturer's specifications in terms of the average breaking strength of the cloth produced.
   (d)   Our conclusion has not changed. It is not affected by whether we base our decision on the comparison of Z-values or p values.

•8.32   (a)   Test statistic: $Z = \dfrac{\overline{X} - \mu}{\sigma/\sqrt{n}} = \dfrac{7.983 - 8}{0.15/\sqrt{50}} = -0.80$

   p value $= 2(0.5 - 0.2882) = 0.4238$
   Interpretation: The probability of getting a sample of 50 bottles of salad dressing that are more different from the hypothesized population mean of 8 ounces than this sample is 0.4238 or 42.38%.

   (b)   Decision: Since p value $= 0.4238$ is greater than $\alpha = 0.05$, do not reject H_0.
   (c)   At the 0.05 level of significance, a p value of 0.4238 does not provide enough evidence to support a conclusion that the machine is dispensing an average amount of dressing different from 8 ounces.
   (d)   Our conclusion has not changed. It is not affected by whether we base our decision on the comparison of Z-values or p values.

•8.34   (a) H_0: $\mu = 1.00$. The average amount of paint per one-gallon can is one gallon.
   H_1: $\mu \neq 1.00$. The average amount of paint per one-gallon can differs from one gallon.
   (b)   Decision rule: Reject H_0 if $Z < -2.58$ or $Z > +2.58$.

   Test statistic: $Z = \dfrac{\overline{X} - \mu}{\sigma/\sqrt{n}} = \dfrac{0.995 - 1.00}{0.02/\sqrt{50}} = -1.77$

   Decision: Since $Z_{calc} = -1.77$ is between the critical bounds of ± 2.58, do not reject H_0. There is not enough evidence to conclude that the average amount of paint per one-gallon can differs from one gallon.
   (c)   Same decision. The confidence interval includes the hypothesized value of 1.00.

8.36   (a) H_0: $\mu = 2.00$ liters. The average amount of soft drink placed in 2-liter bottles at the local bottling plant is equal to 2 liters.
H_1: $\mu \neq 2.00$ liters. The average amount of soft drink placed in 2-liter bottles at the local bottling plant differs from 2 liters.

(b)   Decision rule: Reject H_0 if $Z < -1.96$ or $Z > +1.96$.

Test statistic: $Z = \dfrac{\overline{X} - \mu}{\sigma / \sqrt{n}} = \dfrac{1.99 - 2.00}{0.05 / \sqrt{100}} = -2.00$

Decision: Since $Z_{calc} = -2.00$ is below the lower critical bounds of -1.96, reject H_0. There is enough evidence to conclude that the amount of soft drink placed in 2-liter bottles at the local bottling plant differs from 2 liters.

(c)   The results here are the same as those found in Problem 7.9. The confidence interval formed in Problem 7.9 does not include 2.00.

8.38   Since $Z_{calc} = 2.39$ is greater than $Z_{crit} = 2.33$, reject H_0.

•8.40   Since $Z_{calc} = -1.15$ is greater than $Z_{crit} = -1.28$, do not reject H_0.

•8.42   Since the p value $= 0.0228$ is less than $\alpha = 0.10$, reject H_0.

8.44   Since the p value $= 0.0838$ is greater than $\alpha = 0.01$, reject H_0.

•8.46   (a) H_0: $\mu \geq 2.8$ feet.
The average length of steel bars produced is at least 2.8 feet and the production equipment does not need immediate adjustment.
H_1: $\mu < 2.8$ feet.
The average length of steel bars produced is less than 2.8 feet and the production equipment does need immediate adjustment.

(b)   Decision rule: If $Z < -1.645$, reject H_0.

Test statistic: $Z = \dfrac{\overline{X} - \mu}{\sigma / \sqrt{n}} = \dfrac{2.73 - 2.8}{0.2 / \sqrt{25}} = -1.75$

Decision: Since $Z_{calc} = -1.75$ is less than $Z_{crit} = -1.645$, reject H_0. There is enough evidence to conclude the production equipment needs adjustment.

(c)   Decision rule: If p value < 0.05, reject H_0.

Test statistic: $Z = \dfrac{\overline{X} - \mu}{\sigma / \sqrt{n}} = \dfrac{2.73 - 2.8}{0.2 / \sqrt{25}} = -1.75$

p value $= 0.5 - 0.4599 = 0.0401$

Decision: Since p value $= 0.0401$ is less than $\alpha = 0.05$, reject H_0. There is enough evidence to conclude the production equipment needs adjustment.

(d)   The probability of obtaining a sample whose mean is 2.73 feet or less when the null hypothesis is true is 0.0401.

(e)   The conclusions are the same.

•8.48　(a)　H_0: $\mu \geq 8$ ounces.

The mean amount of salad dressing dispensed is at least 8 ounces. The machine is working properly. No work stoppage should occur.

H_1: $\mu < 8$ ounces.

The mean amount of salad dressing dispensed is less than 8 ounces. The machine is not working properly. The filling line should be stopped.

(b)　Decision rule: If $Z < -1.645$, reject H_0.

Test statistic: $Z = \dfrac{\bar{X} - \mu}{\sigma / \sqrt{n}} = \dfrac{7.983 - 8}{0.15 / \sqrt{50}} = -0.80$

Decision: Since $Z_{calc} = -0.80$ is greater than $Z_{crit} = -1.645$, do not reject H_0. There is not enough evidence to conclude that the mean amount of salad dressing dispensed is less than 8 ounces. There is insufficient evidence to conclude the machine is not working properly. The filling line should not be stopped.

(c)　Decision rule: If p value < 0.05, reject H_0.

Test statistic: $Z = \dfrac{\bar{X} - \mu}{\sigma / \sqrt{n}} = \dfrac{7.983 - 8}{0.15 / \sqrt{50}} = -0.80$

p value $= 0.5 - 0.2881 = 0.2119$

Decision: Since p value $= 0.2119$ is greater than $\alpha = 0.05$, do not reject H_0. There is not enough evidence to conclude that the mean amount of salad dressing dispensed is less than 8 ounces. There is insufficient evidence to conclude the machine is not working properly. The filling line should not be stopped.

(d)　The probability of obtaining a sample whose mean is 7.983 ounces or less when the null hypothesis is true is 0.2119.

(e)　The conclusions are the same.

8.50　H_0: $\mu \leq 25$ mgs/mm.

The average margin by which a new pill reduces the systolic blood pressure of hypertensive patients is less than or equal to 25 mgs/mm.

H_1: $\mu > 25$ mgs/mm.

The average margin by which a new pill reduces the systolic blood pressure of hypertensive patients is greater than 25 mgs/mm.

•8.52　$df = n - 1 = 16 - 1 = 15$

8.54　(a)　Since $t_{calc} = 2.00$ is between the critical bounds of $t_{crit} = \pm 2.1315$, do not reject H_0.

(b)　Since $t_{calc} = 2.00$ is above the critical bound of $t_{crit} = +1.7531$, reject H_0.

8.56　Yes, you may use the t test to test the null hypothesis that $\mu = 60$ on a population is left-skewed if the sample size is sufficiently large($n = 160$). The t test assumes that, if the underlying population is not normally distributed, the sample size is sufficiently large to enable the test statistic t to be influenced by the central limit theorem. With large sample sizes ($n > 30$), the t test may be used because the sampling distribution of the mean does meet the requirements of the central limit theorem.

8.58 (a)

	A	B
1	Detergent Weights	
2		
3	Null Hypothesis μ=	3.25
4	Level of Significance	0.01
5	Sample Size	64
6	Sample Mean	3.238
7	Sample Standard Deviation	0.117
8	Standard Error of the Mean	0.014625
9	Degrees of Freedom	63
10	*t* Test Statistic	-0.82051282
11		
12	Two-Tailed Test	
13	Lower Critical Value	-2.6561429
14	Upper Critical Value	2.656142897
15	*p*-Value	0.415017678
16	Do not reject the null hypothesis	

(b) H_0: $\mu = 3.25$ pounds. The average weight of the boxes is 3.25 pounds.

H_1: $\mu \neq 3.25$ pounds. The average weight of the boxes of detergent is not equal to 3.25 pounds.

Decision rule: $df = 63$. If $t > 2.6561$ or $t < -2.6561$, reject H_0.

Test statistic: $t = \dfrac{\overline{X} - \mu}{S/\sqrt{n}} = \dfrac{3.238 - 3.25}{0.05/\sqrt{64}} = -1.9200$

Decision: Since $t_{calc} = -1.9200$ is between the critical bounds of $t = \pm 2.6561$, do not reject H_0. There is not enough evidence to conclude that the average weight of the boxes of detergent is not equal to 3.25 pounds.

(c) H_0: $\mu = 3.25$ pounds. The average weight of the boxes is 3.25 pounds.

H_1: $\mu \neq 3.25$ pounds. The average weight of the boxes of detergent is not equal to 3.25 pounds.

Decision rule: $df = 63$. If $t > 2.6561$ or $t < -2.6561$, reject H_0.

Test statistic: $t = \dfrac{\overline{X} - \mu}{S/\sqrt{n}} = \dfrac{3.211 - 3.25}{0.117/\sqrt{64}} = -2.6667$

Decision: Since $t_{calc} = -2.6667$ is below the critical bound of $t = -2.6561$, reject H_0. There is enough evidence to conclude that the average weight of the boxes of detergent is not equal to 3.25 pounds.

•8.60 (a) H_0: $\mu = 9.0$ The average energy efficiency rating of window-mounted large capacity air conditioning units is equal to 9.0.

H_1: $\mu \neq 9.0$ The average energy efficiency rating of window-mounted large-capacity air-conditioning units is not equal to 9.0.

Decision rule: $df = 35$. If $t > 2.0301$ or $t < -2.0301$, reject H_0.

Test statistic: $t = \dfrac{\overline{X} - \mu}{S/\sqrt{n}} = \dfrac{9.2111 - 9.0}{0.3838/\sqrt{36}} = 3.3002$

Decision: Since $t_{calc} = 3.3002$ is above the upper critical bound of $t = 2.0301$, reject H_0. There is enough evidence to conclude that the average energy efficiency rating of window-mounted large-capacity air-conditioning units is not equal to 9.0.

(b) To perform this test, you must assume that (1) the observed sequence in which the data were collected is random, and (2) the sample size is sufficiently large for the central limit theorem to apply, meaning that the sampling distribution of the mean is approximately normally distributed.

(c) p value = 0.0022. The probability of obtaining a sample whose mean is further away from the hypothesized value of 9.0 than 9.2111 is 0.0022.

(d) H_0: $\mu = 9.0$ The average energy efficiency rating of window-mounted large capacity air-conditioning units is equal to 9.0.

H_1: $\mu \neq 9.0$ The average energy efficiency rating of window-mounted large-capacity air-conditioning units is not equal to 9.0.

Decision rule: $df = 35$. If $t > 2.0301$ or $t < -2.0301$, reject H_0.

Test statistic: $t = \dfrac{\overline{X} - \mu}{S/\sqrt{n}} = \dfrac{9.1556 - 9.0}{0.4102/\sqrt{36}} = 2.2754$

Decision: Since $t_{calc} = 2.2754$ is above the critical bound of $t = 2.0301$, reject H_0. There is enough evidence to conclude that the average energy efficiency rating of window-mounted large-capacity air-conditioning units is not equal to 9.0.

8.62 (a) H_0: $\mu = 15$ ounces. The average weight of raisins is 15 ounces per box.

H_1: $\mu \neq 15$ ounces. The average weight of raisins is not equal to 15 ounces per box.

Decision rule: $df = 29$. If $t > 2.0452$ or $t < -2.0452$, reject H_0.

Test statistic: $t = \dfrac{\overline{X} - \mu}{S/\sqrt{n}} = \dfrac{15.1133 - 15.0}{0.4058/\sqrt{30}} = 1.5298$

Decision: Since $t_{calc} = 1.5298$ is between the critical bounds of $t = \pm 2.0452$, do not reject H_0. There is not enough evidence to conclude that the average weight of raisins is not equal to 15 ounces per box.

(b) In addition to assuming that the observed sequence in which the data were collected is random, to perform this test, you must assume that the sample size is sufficiently large for the central limit theorem to apply, meaning that the sampling distribution of the mean is approximately normally distributed.

8.62 cont. (c)H_0: $\mu = 15$ ounces. The average weight of raisins is 15 ounces per box.

H_1: $\mu \neq 15$ ounces. The average weight of raisins is not equal to 15 ounces per box.

Decision rule: $df = 29$. If $t > 2.0452$ or $t < -2.0452$, reject H_0.

Test statistic: $t = \dfrac{\bar{X} - \mu}{S/\sqrt{n}} = \dfrac{15.18 - 15.0}{0.4909/\sqrt{30}} = 2.0084$

Decision: Since $t_{calc} = 2.0084$ is between the critical bounds of $t = \pm 2.0452$, do not reject H_0. There is not enough evidence to conclude that the average weight of raisins is not equal to 15 ounces per box.

8.64 (a)H_0: $\mu \leq 70$ miles. The average miles logged per taxi per day is no more than 70 miles. There is no need to alter the contract.

H_1: $\mu > 70$ miles. The average miles logged per taxi per day is more than 70 miles. There is a need to alter the contract.

Decision rule: $df = 15$. If $t > 1.7531$, reject H_0.

Test statistic: $t = \dfrac{\bar{X} - \mu}{S/\sqrt{n}} = \dfrac{81.2125 - 70}{19.9393/\sqrt{16}} = 2.2493$

Decision: Since $t_{calc} = 2.2493$ is above the critical bound of $t = 1.7531$, reject H_0. There is enough evidence to conclude that the average miles logged per taxi per day is more than 70 miles. There is a need to alter the contract.

(b) Box-and-whisker plot:

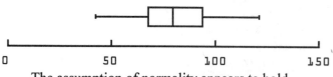

The assumption of normality appears to hold.

•8.66 (a) $Z = \dfrac{p_s - p}{\sqrt{\dfrac{p(1-p)}{n}}} = \dfrac{0.22 - 0.20}{\sqrt{\dfrac{0.20(0.80)}{400}}} = 1.00$

(b) $Z = \dfrac{X - np}{\sqrt{n \cdot p \cdot (1-p)}} = \dfrac{88 - 400 \cdot (0.20)}{\sqrt{400 \cdot (0.20) \cdot (0.80)}} = 1.00$

8.68 (a) H_0: $p \leq 0.10$. No more than 10% of the television sets manufactured required repair during their first 2 years of operation. There is no reason to doubt the manufacturer's claim.

H_1: $p > 0.10$. More than 10% of the television sets manufactured required repair during their first 2 years of operation. There is enough evidence to doubt the manufacturer's claim.

Decision rule: If $Z > 2.33$, reject H_0.

Test statistic: $Z = \dfrac{p_s - p}{\sqrt{\dfrac{p(1-p)}{n}}} = \dfrac{0.14 - 0.10}{\sqrt{\dfrac{0.10(0.90)}{100}}} = 1.33$

Decision: Since $Z_{calc} = 1.33$ is below the critical bound of $Z = 2.33$, do not reject H_0. There is not enough evidence to cast doubt on the manufacturer's claim.

8.68
cont. (b) p value = 0.0918. The probability of getting a sample with a higher rate of television sets requiring repair during their first 2 years of operation when the null hypothesis is true is 0.0918.

(c) H_0: $p \leq 0.10$. No more than 10% of the television sets manufactured required repair during their first 2 years of operation. There is no reason to doubt the manufacturer's claim.
H_1: $p > 0.10$. More than 10% of the television sets manufactured required repair during their first 2 years of operation. There is enough evidence to doubt the manufacturer's claim.
Decision rule: If $Z > 2.33$, reject H_0.

Test statistic: $Z = \dfrac{p_s - p}{\sqrt{\dfrac{p(1-p)}{n}}} = \dfrac{0.18 - 0.10}{\sqrt{\dfrac{0.10(0.90)}{100}}} = 2.67$

Decision: Since $Z_{calc} = 2.67$ is above the critical bound of $Z = 2.33$, reject H_0. There is enough evidence to doubt the manufacturer's claim.

•8.70 (a) (b)

	A	B
1	Training of Clerks	
2		
3	Null Hypothesis p=	0.25
4	Level of Significance	0.01
5	Number of Successes	29
6	Sample Size	150
7	Sample Proportion	0.193333333
8	Standard Error	0.035355339
9	Z Test Statistic	-1.60277537
10		
11	Lower-Tail Test	
12	Lower Critical Value	-2.32634193
13	p-Value	0.054492125
14	Do not reject the null hypothesis	

(c) H_0: $p \geq 0.25$. At least 25% of the data processing clerks who have gone through the new training are no longer employed at the company after one year.
H_1: $p < 0.25$. Less than 25% of the data processing clerks who have gone through the new training are no longer employed at the company after one year.
Decision rule: If $Z < -2.33$, reject H_0.

Test statistic: $Z = \dfrac{p_s - p}{\sqrt{\dfrac{p(1-p)}{n}}} = \dfrac{0.1467 - 0.25}{\sqrt{\dfrac{0.25(0.75)}{150}}} = -2.92$

Decision: Since $Z_{calc} = -2.92$ is below the critical bound of $Z = -2.33$, reject H_0. There is enough evidence to show that the new training approaches are effective in reducing the turnover rate.

8.72   (a) H_0: $p \leq 0.40$. The proportion of tourists who purchase silver jewelry while vacationing in Mexico is no more than 40%.

H_1: $p > 0.40$. The proportion of tourists who purchase silver jewelry while vacationing in Mexico is greater than 40%.

Decision rule: If $Z > 1.645$, reject H_0.

Test statistic: $Z = \dfrac{p_s - p}{\sqrt{\dfrac{p(1-p)}{n}}} = \dfrac{0.454 - 0.40}{\sqrt{\dfrac{0.40(0.60)}{500}}} = 2.46$

Decision: Since $Z_{calc} = 2.46$ is above the critical bound of $Z = 1.645$, reject H_0. There is enough evidence to conclude that the proportion of tourists who purchase silver jewelry while vacationing in Mexico is greater than 40%.

   (b) p value = 0.0069. The probability of obtaining a sample that has a proportion further away from 0.40 when the null hypothesis is true is 0.0069.

   (c) H_0: $p \leq 0.40$. The proportion of tourists who purchase silver jewelry while vacationing in Mexico is no more than 40%.

H_1: $p > 0.40$. The proportion of tourists who purchase silver jewelry while vacationing in Mexico is greater than 40%.

Decision rule: If $Z > 1.645$, reject H_0.

Test statistic: $Z = \dfrac{p_s - p}{\sqrt{\dfrac{p(1-p)}{n}}} = \dfrac{0.426 - 0.40}{\sqrt{\dfrac{0.40(0.60)}{500}}} = 1.19$

Decision: Since $Z_{calc} = 1.19$ is below the critical bound of $Z = 1.645$, do not reject H_0. There is not enough evidence to conclude that the proportion of tourists who purchase silver jewelry while vacationing in Mexico is greater than 40%.

8.74   (a) H_0: $p = 0.378$. The proportion of market share for Kellogg ready-to-eat breakfast cereals is 37.8%.

H_1: $p \neq 0.378$. The proportion of market share for Kellogg ready-to-eat breakfast cereals differs from 37.8%.

Decision rule: If $Z < -1.96$ or $Z > 1.96$, reject H_0.

Test statistic: $Z = \dfrac{p_s - p}{\sqrt{\dfrac{p(1-p)}{n}}} = \dfrac{0.39 - 0.378}{\sqrt{\dfrac{0.378(0.622)}{200}}} = 0.35$

Decision: Since $Z_{calc} = 0.35$ is between the critical bounds of $Z = \pm 1.96$, do not reject H_0. There is not enough evidence to conclude that the proportion of market share for Kellogg ready-to-eat breakfast cereals differs from the previous 1996-1997 market share.

   (b) p value = 2(0.5 − 0.1368) = 0.7264. The probability of obtaining a sample that has a proportion further away from 0.378 than this sample proportion when the null hypothesis is true is 0.7264.

8.84   (a) $H_0: p \geq 0.90$. At least 90% of the batteries last three years and can be called "reliable."
$H_1: p < 0.90$. Less than 90% of the batteries last three years and can be called "reliable."
Decision rule: If $Z < -1.645$, reject H_0.

Test statistic: $Z = \dfrac{p_s - p}{\sqrt{\dfrac{p(1-p)}{n}}} = \dfrac{0.8214 - 0.90}{\sqrt{\dfrac{0.90(0.10)}{28}}} = -1.39$

Decision: Since $Z_{calc} = -1.39$ is above the critical bound of $Z = -1.645$, do not reject H_0. There is not enough evidence to conclude that less than 90% of the batteries last three years and can be called "reliable."

(b) $H_0: \mu \geq 48$ months. The average useful life of a certain type of battery is at least 48 months.
$H_1: \mu < 48$ months. The average useful life of a certain type of battery is less than 48 months.
Decision rule: $df = 27$. If $t < -1.7033$, reject H_0.

Test statistic: $t = \dfrac{\bar{X} - \mu}{S / \sqrt{n}} = \dfrac{43.325 - 48}{8.5439 / \sqrt{28}} = -2.8954$

Decision: Since $t_{calc} = -2.8954$ is below the critical bound of $t = -1.7033$, reject H_0. There is enough evidence to conclude that the average useful life of a certain type of battery is less than 48 months.

(c)   To perform the t-test, you must assume that the data are approximately normally distributed.

(d)   Box-and-whisker plot:

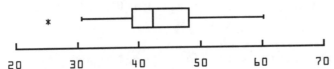

The data seem slightly right-skewed. But the sample size is nearly 30 so the accuracy of the test is not seriously affected.

(e)   (b) $H_0: \mu \geq 48$ months. The average useful life of a certain type of battery is at least 48 months.
$H_1: \mu < 48$ months. The average useful life of a certain type of battery is less than 48 months.
Decision rule: $df = 27$. If $t < -1.7033$, reject H_0.

Test statistic: $t = \dfrac{\bar{X} - \mu}{S / \sqrt{n}} = \dfrac{44.3964 - 48}{8.4969 / \sqrt{28}} = -2.2441$

Decision: Since $t_{calc} = -2.2441$ is below the critical bound of $t = -1.7033$, reject H_0. There is enough evidence to conclude that the average useful life of a certain type of battery is less than 48 months.

•8.86 (a) H_0: $\mu \geq \$100$. The average reimbursement for office visits to doctors paid by Medicare is at least $100.

H_1: $\mu < \$100$. The average reimbursement for office visits to doctors paid by Medicare is less than $100.

Decision rule: $df = 74$. If $t < -1.6657$, reject H_0.

Test statistic: $t = \dfrac{\overline{X} - \mu}{S/\sqrt{n}} = \dfrac{\$93.70 - \$100}{\$34.55/\sqrt{75}} = -1.5791$

Decision: Since the test statistic of $t_{calc} = -1.5791$ is above the critical bound of $t = -1.6657$, do not reject H_0. There is not enough evidence to conclude that the average reimbursement for office visits to doctors paid by Medicare is less than $100.

(b) H_0: $p \leq 0.10$. At most 10% of all reimbursements for office visits to doctors paid by Medicare are incorrect.

H_1: $p > 0.10$. More than 10% of all reimbursements for office visits to doctors paid by Medicare are incorrect.

Decision rule: If $Z > 1.645$, reject H_0.

Test statistic: $Z = \dfrac{p_s - p}{\sqrt{\dfrac{p(1-p)}{n}}} = \dfrac{0.16 - 0.10}{\sqrt{\dfrac{0.10(0.90)}{75}}} = 1.73$

Decision: Since the test statistic of $Z_{calc} = 1.73$ is above the critical bound of $Z = 1.645$, reject H_0. There is sufficient evidence to conclude that more than 10% of all reimbursements for office visits to doctors paid by Medicare are incorrect.

(c)   To perform the t-test on the population mean, you must assume that the observed sequence in which the data were collected is random and that the data are approximately normally distributed.

(d) H_0: $\mu \geq \$100$. The average reimbursement for office visits to doctors paid by Medicare is at least $100.

H_1: $\mu < \$100$. The average reimbursement for office visits to doctors paid by Medicare is less than $100.

Decision rule: $df = 74$. If $t < -1.6657$, reject H_0.

Test statistic: $t = \dfrac{\overline{X} - \mu}{S/\sqrt{n}} = \dfrac{\$90 - \$100}{\$34.55/\sqrt{75}} = -2.5066$

Decision: Since the test statistic of $t_{calc} = -2.5066$ is below the critical bound of $t = -1.6657$, reject H_0. There is enough evidence to conclude that the average reimbursement for office visits to doctors paid by Medicare is less than $100.

•8.86 (e) $H_0: p \le 0.10$. At most 10% of all reimbursements for office visits to
cont.   doctors paid by Medicare are incorrect.
           $H_1: p > 0.10$. More than 10% of all reimbursements for office visits to doctors paid by
           Medicare are incorrect.
           Decision rule: If $Z > 1.645$, reject H_0.

           Test statistic: $Z = \dfrac{p_s - p}{\sqrt{\dfrac{p(1-p)}{n}}} = \dfrac{0.20 - 0.10}{\sqrt{\dfrac{0.10(0.90)}{75}}} = 2.89$

           Decision: Since the test statistic of $Z_{calc} = 2.89$ is above the critical bound of $Z = 1.645$,
           reject H_0. There is sufficient evidence to conclude that more than 10% of all
           reimbursements for office visits to doctors paid by Medicare are incorrect.

8.88 (a) $H_0: \mu \le 20$ days. The average length of time to resolve a formal complaint is no more
          than 20 days.
          $H_1: \mu > 20$ days. The average length of time to resolve a formal complaint is more than 20
          days.
          Decision rule: $df = 49$. If $t > 1.6766$, reject H_0.

          Test statistic: $t = \dfrac{\overline{X} - \mu}{S/\sqrt{n}} = \dfrac{43.04 - 20}{41.926/\sqrt{50}} = 3.8858$

          Decision: Since the test statistic of $t_{calc} = 3.8858$ is above the critical value of $t = 1.6766$,
          reject H_0. There is sufficient evidence on which to conclude that the average length of
          time to resolve a formal complaint is more than 20 days.

(b) To perform the t-test on the population mean, you must assume that the observed
     sequence in which the data were collected is random and that the sample size is
     sufficiently large for the central limit theorem to apply, meaning the sampling
     distribution of the mean is approximately normal.

(c) Box-and-whisker plot:

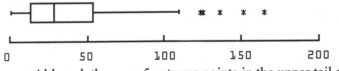

     Although there are 5 extreme points in the upper tail of the distribution, the sample size
     of $n = 50$ is sufficiently large for the central limit theorem to apply.

(d) p value = 0.00015. The probability of obtaining a sample whose mean is at most 20 days
     when the null hypothesis is true is 0.00015, a very small likelihood. The floor manager is
     not making a judicious statement.
     Note: The p value was found using Excel.

CHAPTER 9

•9.2 H_0: $\mu_1 = \mu_2$

H_1: $\mu_1 \neq \mu_2$

Decision rule: If $Z < -2.58$ or $Z > 2.58$, reject H_0.

Test statistic: $Z = \dfrac{(\bar{X}_1 - \bar{X}_2) - (\mu_1 - \mu_2)}{\sqrt{\dfrac{\sigma_1^2}{n_1} + \dfrac{\sigma_2^2}{n_2}}} = \dfrac{(72 - 66) - 0}{\sqrt{\dfrac{20^2}{40} + \dfrac{10^2}{50}}} = 1.73$

Decision: Since $Z_{calc} = 1.73$ is between the critical bounds of $Z = \pm 2.58$, do not reject H_0. There is inadequate evidence to conclude the two population means are different.

9.4   (a) $S_p^{\ 2} = \dfrac{(n_1 - 1) \cdot S_1^2 + (n_2 - 1) \cdot S_2^2}{(n_1 - 1) + (n_2 - 1)} = \dfrac{(7) \cdot 4^2 + (14) \cdot 5^2}{7 + 14} = 22$

$t = \dfrac{(\bar{X}_1 - \bar{X}_2) - (\mu_1 - \mu_2)}{\sqrt{S_p^{\ 2}\left(\dfrac{1}{n_1} + \dfrac{1}{n_2}\right)}} = \dfrac{(42 - 34) - 0}{\sqrt{22\left(\dfrac{1}{8} + \dfrac{1}{15}\right)}} = 3.8959$

(b) $df = (n_1 - 1) + (n_2 - 1) = 7 + 14 = 21$

(c)   Decision rule: $df = 21$. If $t > 2.5177$, reject H_0.

(d)   Decision: Since $t_{calc} = 3.8959$ is above the critical bound of $t = 2.5177$, reject H_0. There is enough evidence to conclude that the first population mean is larger than the second population mean.

9.6   (a) H_0: $\mu_1 \leq \mu_2$ where Populations: 1 = new machine, 2 = old machine
The average breaking strength of parts produced by the new machine is not greater than the average breaking strength of parts produced by the old machine.
H_1: $\mu_1 > \mu_2$
The average breaking strength of parts produced by the new machine is greater than the average breaking strength of parts produced by the old machine.

Decision rule: If $Z > 2.33$, reject H_0.

Test statistic: $Z = \dfrac{(\bar{X}_1 - \bar{X}_2) - (\mu_1 - \mu_2)}{\sqrt{\dfrac{\sigma_1^2}{n_1} + \dfrac{\sigma_2^2}{n_2}}} = \dfrac{(72 - 65) - 0}{\sqrt{\dfrac{9^2}{100} + \dfrac{10^2}{100}}} = 5.20$

Decision: Since $Z_{calc} = 5.20$ is above the critical bound of 2.33, reject H_0. There is enough evidence to conclude that the average breaking strength of parts produced by the new machine is greater than the average breaking strength of parts produced by the old machine.

(b) p value = virtually zero.
The probability of obtaining samples whose means differ by 7 or more units of stength when the null hypothesis is true is virtually zero.

•9.8 (a) H_0: $\mu_1 = \mu_2$ where Populations: 1 = day shift, 2 = evening shift

Average output for day shift workers is the same as the average output for evening shift workers.

H_1: $\mu_1 \neq \mu_2$

Average output for day shift workers is not the same as the average output for evening shift workers.

Decision rule: $df = 198$. If $Z < -1.645$ or $Z > 1.645$, reject H_0.

Note: Because the degrees of freedom are so large, we use a Z-value to establish the bounds of the rejection region.

Test statistic: $S_p^2 = \dfrac{(n_1-1)\cdot S_1^2 + (n_2-1)\cdot S_2^2}{(n_1-1)+(n_2-1)} = \dfrac{(99)\cdot 16^2 + (99)\cdot 18^2}{99+99} = 290$

$t = \dfrac{(\overline{X}_1 - \overline{X}_2)-(\mu_1-\mu_2)}{\sqrt{S_p^2\left(\dfrac{1}{n_1}+\dfrac{1}{n_2}\right)}} = \dfrac{(74.3-69.7)-0}{\sqrt{290\left(\dfrac{1}{100}+\dfrac{1}{100}\right)}} = 1.9100$

Decision: Since $t_{calc} = 1.9100$ is above the upper critical bound of 1.645, reject H_0. There is enough evidence to conclude that the average output for day shift workers is not the same as the average output for evening shift workers.

Note: Because our initial hypothesis was two-tailed, we are not free to comment on which shift had higher output, only that they were not equal.

(b) Using the normal distribution, the p value $= 2(0.5 - 0.4719) = 0.0562$

The probability of obtaining samples whose means differ by 4.6 parts per hour or more when the null hypothesis is true is 0.0562.

9.10 (a) H_0: $\mu_1 = \mu_2$ where Populations: 1 = store A, 2 = store B

Average delivery time for the two major outlet stores is the same.

H_1: $\mu_1 \neq \mu_2$

Average delivery time for the two major outlet stores is different.

Decision rule: $df = 70$. If $t < -2.6479$ or $t > 2.6479$, reject H_0.

Test statistic:

$S_p^2 = \dfrac{(n_1-1)\cdot S_1^2 + (n_2-1)\cdot S_2^2}{(n_1-1)+(n_2-1)} = \dfrac{(40)\cdot 2.4^2 + (30)\cdot 3.1^2}{40+30} = 7.41$

$t = \dfrac{(\overline{X}_1 - \overline{X}_2)-(\mu_1-\mu_2)}{\sqrt{S_p^2\left(\dfrac{1}{n_1}+\dfrac{1}{n_2}\right)}} = \dfrac{(34.3-43.7)-0}{\sqrt{7.41\left(\dfrac{1}{41}+\dfrac{1}{31}\right)}} = -14.5086$

Decision: Since $t_{calc} = -14.5086$ is below the lower critical bound of -2.6479, reject H_0. There is enough evidence to conclude that the average delivery time for the two major outlet stores is different.

9.10   (b)   Using the *t*-table, the *p* value < 0.005, or using Excel, the *p* value =
cont.   8.6897 x 10^{-23}, an exceedingly small probability.
                The probability of obtaining samples whose means differ by 9.4 days or more when the
                null hypothesis is true is virtually zero.

•9.12   (a) – (c)

	A	B	C
1	t-Test: Two-Sample Assuming Equal Variances		
2			
3		Cadmium	Metal Hydride
4	Mean	70.748	79.728
5	Variance	195.7884	226.0296
6	Observations	25	25
7	Pooled Variance	210.909	
8	Hypothesized Mean Difference	0	
9	df	48	
10	t Stat	-2.18617	
11	P(T<=t) one-tail	0.016856	
12	t Critical one-tail	1.677224	
13	P(T<=t) two-tail	0.033712	
14	t Critical two-tail	2.010634	

9.14   (a)

	A	B	C
1	t-Test: Two-Sample Assuming Equal Variances		
2			
3		Urban	Suburban
4	Mean	77.325	70.9
5	Variance	6.400667	28.19333
6	Observations	16	16
7	Pooled Variance	17.297	
8	Hypothesized Mean Difference	0	
9	df	30	
10	t Stat	4.36951	
11	P(T<=t) one-tail	6.86E-05	
12	t Critical one-tail	1.69726	
13	P(T<=t) two-tail	0.000137	
14	t Critical two-tail	2.04227	

Decision: Since t_{calc} = 4.3695 is above the upper critical bound of 2.0423, reject H_0. There
is enough evidence to conclude that the average occupancy rates in urban and suburban
hospitals in this state are different.

(b)   One must assume that each of the two populations is normally distributed
       and that they have equal variances.

•9.16   (a) $F_U = 2.20$, $F_L = \dfrac{1}{2.33} = 0.429$

        (b) $F_U = 2.57$, $F_L = \dfrac{1}{2.76} = 0.362$

        (c) $F_U = 3.09$, $F_L = \dfrac{1}{3.37} = 0.297$

•9.16

cont.   (d) $F_U = 3.50$, $F_L = \dfrac{1}{3.88} = 0.258$

(e) As α gets smaller, the rejection region gets narrower and the nonrejection region gets wider. F_L gets smaller and F_U gets larger.

•9.18   (a) $F_L = \dfrac{1}{2.33} = 0.429$

(b) $F_L = \dfrac{1}{2.76} = 0.362$

(c) $F_L = \dfrac{1}{3.37} = 0.297$

(d) $F_L = \dfrac{1}{3.88} = 0.258$

(e)   As α gets smaller, the rejection region gets narrower and the nonrejection region gets wider. F_L gets smaller (approaching zero).

9.20   The degrees of freedom for the numerator is 24 and for the denominator is 24.

9.22   Since $F_{calc} = 0.826$ is between the critical bounds of $F_U = 2.27$ and $F_L = 0.441$, do not reject H_0. There is not enough evidence to conclude that the two population variances are different.

•9.24   (a) H_0: $\sigma_1^2 = \sigma_2^2$ The population variances are the same.
H_1: $\sigma_1^2 \neq \sigma_2^2$ The population variances are different.
Decision rule: If $F > 3.18$ or $F < 0.338$, reject H_0.
Test statistic: $F = \dfrac{S_1^2}{S_2^2} = \dfrac{47.3}{36.4} = 1.299$

Decision: Since $F_{calc} = 1.299$ is between the critical bounds of $F_U = 3.18$ and $F_L = 0.338$, do not reject H_0. There is not enough evidence to conclude that the two population variances are different.

(b) H_0: $\sigma_1^2 \leq \sigma_2^2$ The variance for population 1 is less than or equal to the variance for population 2.
H_1: $\sigma_1^2 > \sigma_2^2$ The variance for population 1 is greater than the variance for population 2.
Decision rule: If $F > 2.62$, reject H_0.
Test statistic: $F = \dfrac{S_1^2}{S_2^2} = \dfrac{47.3}{36.4} = 1.299$

Decision: Since $F_{calc} = 1.299$ is below the critical bound of $F_U = 2.62$, do not reject H_0. There is not enough evidence to conclude that the variance for population 1 is greater than the variance for population 2.

(c) H_0: $\sigma_1^2 \geq \sigma_2^2$ The variance for population 1 is greater than or equal to the variance for population 2.
H_1: $\sigma_1^2 < \sigma_2^2$ The variance for population 1 is less than the variance for population 2.
Decision rule: If $F < 0.403$, reject H_0.

Test statistic: $F = \dfrac{S_1^2}{S_2^2} = \dfrac{47.3}{36.4} = 1.299$

Decision: Since $F_{\text{calc}} = 1.299$ is above the critical bound of $F_L = 0.403$, do not reject H_0. There is not enough evidence to conclude that the variance for population 1 is less than the variance for population 2.

9.26 (a) H_0: $\sigma_1^2 = \sigma_2^2$ where Populations: 1 = store A, 2 = store B

The population variances in the shipping times between the two major outlet stores are the same.
H_1: $\sigma_1^2 \neq \sigma_2^2$

The population variances in the shipping times between the two major outlet stores are different.

Decision rule: If $F > 2.52$ or $F < 0.417$, reject H_0.

Test statistic: $F = \dfrac{S_1^2}{S_2^2} = \dfrac{2.4^2}{3.1^2} = 0.599$

Decision: Since $F_{\text{calc}} = 0.599$ is between the critical bounds of $F_U = 2.52$ and $F_L = 0.417$, do not reject H_0. There is not enough evidence to conclude that the two population variances in the shipping times between the two major outlet stores are different.

(b) Using Excel, p value = 0.9353
(c) One must assume that the two populations are each normally distributed.
(d) Assuming the underlying normality in the two populations is met, based on the results of part (a) above, it is appropriate to use the pooled-variance t-test to compare the mean shipping times of the two outlets.

•9.28 (a)

	A	B	C
1	F-Test Two-Sample for Variances		
2			
3		Cadmium	Metal Hydride
4	Mean	70.748	79.728
5	Variance	195.7884	226.0296
6	Observations	25	25
7	df	24	24
8	F	0.866207	
9	P(F<=f) one-tail	0.363909	
10	F Critical one-tail	0.504093	

Decision: Since $F_{calc} = 0.866$ is between the critical bounds of $F_U = 2.27$ and $F_L = 0.441$, do not reject H_0. There is not enough evidence to conclude that the two population variances in talking time in minutes prior to recharging are different for the two types of batteries.

(b)   Assuming the underlying normality in the two populations is met, based on the results obtained in part (a), it is appropriate to use the pooled-variance t-test to compare the talking time in minutes prior to recharging for the two types of batteries.

9.30 (a) H_0: $\sigma_1^2 = \sigma_2^2$ where Populations: 1 = Computer-assisted individual, 2 = Team-based program

The population variances in assembly times in seconds are the same for employees trained in a computer-assisted, individual program and those trained in a team-based program.

H_1: $\sigma_1^2 \neq \sigma_2^2$

The population variances in assembly times in seconds are different for employees trained in a computer-assisted, individual program and those trained in a team-based program.

Decision rule: If $F > 2.46$ or $F < 0.407$, reject H_0.

Test statistic: $F = \dfrac{S_1^2}{S_2^2} = \dfrac{1.9333^2}{4.5767^2} = 0.178$

Decision: Since $F_{calc} = 0.178$ is below the critical bound of $F_L = 0.407$, reject H_0. There is enough evidence to conclude that the two population variances in assembly times in seconds are different for employees trained in a computer-assisted, individual program and those trained in a team-based program.

(b)   Assuming the underlying normality in the two populations is met, based on the results obtained in part (a), it is more appropriate to use the separate-variance t-test to compare assembly times in seconds for employees trained in a computer-assisted, individual program and those trained in a team-based program.

9.32 $df = n - 1 = 15 - 1 = 14$, where n = number of pairs of data

9.34 **(a)** H_0: $\mu_D = 0$

There is no difference in the average wear for the new and old material.

H_1: $\mu_D \neq 0$

There is a difference in the average wear for the new and old material.

Decision rule: $df = 9$. If $t < -2.2622$ or $t > 2.2622$, reject H_0.

Test statistic: $t = \dfrac{\overline{D} - \mu_D}{S_D/\sqrt{n}} = \dfrac{0.3 - 0}{1.7667/\sqrt{10}} = 0.5369$

Decision: Since $t_{calc} = 0.5369$ is between the critical bounds of ± 2.2622, do not reject H_0. There is not enough evidence to conclude that there is a difference in the average wear for the new and old material.

(b) One must assume that the distribution of the differences between the average wear for the new and old material is approximately normally distributed.

(c) Using the t-table, p value $> 2(0.25) = 0.50$. Using Excel, p value $= 0.6044$
The probability of obtaining a mean difference that deviates from 0 by 0.5369 or more when the null hypothesis is true is 0.6044.

9.36 **(a)**

	A	B	C
1	t-Test: Paired Two Sample for Means		
2			
3		With Campaign	Without Campaign
4	Mean	62.84615385	59.19230769
5	Variance	401.029359	379.8557692
6	Observations	13	13
7	Pearson Correlation	0.987367916	
8	Hypothesized Mean Difference	0	
9	df	12	
10	t Stat	4.13559773	
11	P(T<=t) one-tail	0.000690816	
12	t Critical one-tail	1.782286745	
13	P(T<=t) two-tail	0.001381632	
14	t Critical two-tail	2.178812792	

Decision: Since $t_{calc} = 4.1356$ is above the critical bound of 2.1788, reject H_0. There is enough evidence to conclude that there is a difference in the average sales of nonsale items with and without a sales campaign.

(b) One must assume that the distribution of the differences between the average sales of nonsale items with and without a sales campaign is approximately normally distributed.

(c) Using the t-table, p value $< 2(0.005) = 0.01$. Using Excel, p value $= 0.0014$.
The probability of obtaining a mean difference that deviates from 0 by 4.1356 or more when the null hypothesis is true is 0.0014.

9.38   (a) H_0: $\mu_{\overline{D}} = 0$

There is no difference in the average of median prices over the period from the third quarter of 1996 to the third quarter of 1997.

H_1: $\mu_{\overline{D}} \neq 0$

There is a difference in the average of median prices over the period from the third quarter of 1996 to the third quarter of 1997.

Decision rule: $df = 14$. If $t < -2.1448$ or $t > 2.1448$, reject H_0.

Test statistic: $t = \dfrac{\overline{D} - \mu_{\overline{D}}}{S_{\overline{D}}/\sqrt{n}} = \dfrac{3.7333 - 0}{7.3736/\sqrt{15}} = 1.9609$

Decision: Since $t_{calc} = 1.9609$ is between the critical bounds of ± 2.1448, do not reject H_0. There is not enough evidence to conclude that there is a difference in the average of median prices over the period from the third quarter of 1996 to the third quarter of 1997.

        (b)   One must assume that the distribution of the differences between the average of median prices over the third quarter of 1996 to the third quarter of 1997 is approximately normally distributed.

        (c)   Using the t-table, $2(0.025) < p$ value $< 2(0.05)$, or $0.05 < p$ value < 0.10. Using Excel, p value $= 0.0701$.
The probability of obtaining a mean difference that deviates from 0 by 1.9609 or more when the null hypothesis is true is 0.0701.

    (d)-(e) H_0: $\mu_{\overline{D}} = 6.0$ thousand dollars

The average rise in the median price over the period from the third quarter of 1996 to the third quarter of 1997 is 6.0 thousand dollars.

H_1: $\mu_{\overline{D}} \neq 6.0$ thousand dollars

The average rise in the median price over the period from the third quarter of 1996 to the third quarter of 1997 is not 6.0 thousand dollars.

Decision rule: $df = 14$. If $t < -2.1448$ or $t > 2.1448$, reject H_0.

Test statistic: $t = \dfrac{\overline{D} - \mu_{\overline{D}}}{S_{\overline{D}}/\sqrt{n}} = \dfrac{3.7333 - 6.0}{7.3736/\sqrt{15}} = -1.1906$

Decision: Since $t_{calc} = -1.1906$ is between the critical bounds of ± 2.1448, do not reject H_0. There is not enough evidence to conclude that there is a difference in the average rise in the median price over the period from the third quarter of 1996 to the third quarter of 1997 is not 6.0 thousand dollars.

•9.40   (a)   The lower and upper critical values are 31 and 59, respectively.
        (b)   The lower and upper critical values are 29 and 61, respectively.
        (c)   The lower and upper critical values are 25 and 65, respectively.
        (d)   As the level of significance α gets smaller, the width of the nonrejection region gets wider.

•9.42   (a)   The lower critical value is 31.
        (b)   The lower critical value is 29.
        (c)   The lower critical value is 27.
        (d)   The lower critical value is 25.
        (e)   As the level of significance α gets smaller, the width of the nonrejection region gets wider.

9.44 The lower and upper critical values are 40 and 79, respectively.

•9.46 (a) The ranks for Sample 1 are 1, 2, 4, 5, and 10, respectively.
The ranks for Sample 2 are 3, 6.5, 6.5, 8, 9, and 11, respectively.

(b) $T_1 = 1 + 2 + 4 + 5 + 10 = 22$

(c) $T_2 = 3 + 6.5 + 6.5 + 8 + 9 + 11 = 44$

(d) $$T_1 + T_2 = \frac{n(n+1)}{2} = \frac{11(12)}{2} = 66 \qquad T_1 + T_2 = 22 + 44 = 66$$

•9.48 Decision: Since $T_1 = 22$ is above the lower critical bound of 20, do not reject H_0.

9.50 $H_0: M_1 \geq M_2$ where Populations: 1 = MBA, 2 = MPH
MBA applicants were not more preferred than MPH candidates.
$H_1: M_1 < M_2$ MBA applicants were more preferred than MPH candidates.
Decision rule: If $Z < -1.645$, reject H_0.
Test statistic: $T_1 = 84$,

$$\mu_{T_1} = \frac{n_1 \cdot (n+1)}{2} = \frac{10 \cdot (23)}{2} = 115, \quad \sigma_{T_1} = \sqrt{\frac{n_1 \cdot n_2 \cdot (n+1)}{12}} = \sqrt{\frac{10 \cdot 12 \cdot 23}{12}} = 15.1658$$

$$Z = \frac{T_1 - \mu_{T_1}}{\sigma_{T_1}} = \frac{84 - 115}{15.1658} = -2.04$$

Decision: Since $Z_{calc} = -2.04$ is below the lower critical bound of $Z = -1.645$, reject H_0. There is enough evidence to conclude that MBA applicants were more preferred than MPH candidates.

9.52 (a) $H_0: M_1 \geq M_2$ where Populations: 1 = hourly rate, 2 = commission
The use of commission wage incentives do not yield greater median sales volume than salary based on hourly rates.
$H_1: M_1 < M_2$ The use of commission wage incentives does yield greater median sales volume than salary based on hourly rates.
Decision rule: If $Z < -2.33$, reject H_0.
Test statistic: $T_1 = 110$

$$\mu_{T_1} = \frac{n_1 \cdot (n+1)}{2} = \frac{12 \cdot (25)}{2} = 150, \quad \sigma_{T_1} = \sqrt{\frac{n_1 \cdot n_2 \cdot (n+1)}{12}} = \sqrt{\frac{12 \cdot 12 \cdot 25}{12}} = 17.3205$$

$$Z = \frac{T_1 - \mu_{T_1}}{\sigma_{T_1}} = \frac{110 - 150}{17.3205} = -2.31$$

Decision: Since $Z_{calc} = -2.31$ is just above the critical bound of -2.33, do not reject H_0. There is not enough evidence to conclude that use of commission wage incentives yields greater median sales volume than salary based on hourly rates.

(b) One must assume approximately equal variability in the two populations.

(c) Using the pooled-variance t-test allowed us to reject the null hypothesis and conclude that wage incentives did yield greater sales volume than hourly rates in Problem 9.11. In contrast, the test statistic using the Wilcoxon rank sum test with large-sample Z-approximation fell just short of the critical bound and we failed to reject the null hypothesis here.

9.54   (a) H_0: $M_1 = M_2$ where Populations: 1 = urban, 2 = suburban

Median occupancy rates for urban and suburban hospitals are the same.

H_1: $M_1 \neq M_2$ Median occupancy rates for the hospitals are different.

Decision rule: If $Z < -1.96$ or $Z > 1.96$, reject H_0.

Test statistic: $T_1 = 366.5$

$$\mu_{T_1} = \frac{n_1 \cdot (n+1)}{2} = \frac{16 \cdot (33)}{2} = 264,$$

$$\sigma_{T_1} = \sqrt{\frac{n_1 \cdot n_2 \cdot (n+1)}{12}} = \sqrt{\frac{16 \cdot 16 \cdot 33}{12}} = 26.5330$$

$$Z = \frac{T_1 - \mu_{T_1}}{\sigma_{T_1}} = \frac{366.5 - 264}{26.5330} = 3.86$$

Decision: Since $Z_{calc} = 3.86$ is above the upper critical bound of 1.96, reject H_0. There is enough evidence to conclude that median occupancy rates for urban and suburban hospitals are different.

   (b)   One must assume approximately equal variability in the two populations.

   (c)   Using both the pooled-variance t-test and the separate-variance t-test allowed us to reject the null hypothesis and conclude in Problem 9.14 that the average occupancy rates for urban and suburban hospitals are different. In this test, using the Wilcoxon rank sum test with large-sample Z-approximation also allowed us to reject the null hypothesis and conclude that the median occupancy rates for urban and suburban hospitals are different.

9.64   (a) $\bar{X}_I \pm t \cdot \dfrac{S_I}{\sqrt{n_I}} = \$115 \pm 2.0639 \cdot \dfrac{\$30}{\sqrt{25}}$ $\$102.62 < \mu_{X_I} < \$127.38$

   (b) H_0: $\mu_{II} \leq \$80$ The average monthly electric bill is no more than $80 for single-family homes in County II during the summer season.

H_1: $\mu_{II} > \$80$ The average monthly electric bill is more than $80 for single-family homes in County II during the summer season.

Decision rule: $df = 20$. If $t > 1.7247$, reject H_0.

Test statistic: $t = \dfrac{\bar{X} - \mu}{S/\sqrt{n}} = \dfrac{\$98 - \$80}{\$18/\sqrt{21}} = 4.5826$

Decision: Since $t_{calc} = 4.5826$ is above the critical bound of 1.7247, reject H_0. There is sufficient evidence to conclude that the average monthly electric bill is more than $80 for single-family homes in County II during the summer season.

92

9.64
cont. **(c)** H_0: $\sigma_I^2 = \sigma_{II}^2$ The population variances for monthly electric bills in County I and II are the same.
H_1: $\sigma_I^2 \neq \sigma_{II}^2$ County I and II have different population variances for monthly electric bills.
Decision rule: If $F < 0.429$ or $F > 2.41$, reject H_0.
Test statistic: $F = \dfrac{S_I^2}{S_{II}^2} = \dfrac{30^2}{18^2} = 2.78$

Decision: Since $F_{calc} = 2.78$ is above the upper critical bound of 2.41, reject H_0. There is enough evidence to conclude that County I and II have different population variances for monthly electric bills.

(d) H_0: $\mu_I \leq \mu_{II}$ The average monthly electric bill is not higher in County I than in County II.
H_1: $\mu_I > \mu_{II}$ The average monthly electric bill is higher in County I than in County II.
Based on the results in (c) the separate-variance t-test should be used here.

(e) **(b)** Given $t_{calc} = 4.5826$, $df = 20$ for a one-tailed hypothesis test, using Excel, we find the p value $= 9.0251 \times 10^{-5}$, an exceedingly small probability.

(c) Given $F_{calc} = 2.78$, numerator $df = 24$ and denominator $df = 20$, using Excel for a two-tailed hypothesis test:
$$P(F_{24,20} > 2.78) = 0.0117$$
$$P\left(\frac{1}{F_{20,24}} < \frac{1}{2.78}\right) = 0.0117$$
$$p - \text{value} = P(F_{24,20} > 2.78) + P\left(\frac{1}{F_{20,24}} < \frac{1}{2.78}\right)$$
$$= 0.0117 + 0.0117 = 0.0234$$

9.66 **(a)** H_0: $\mu \leq 10$ minutes. Introductory computer students required no more than an average of 10 minutes to write and run a program in Visual Basic.
H_1: $\mu > 10$ minutes. Introductory computer students required more than 10 minutes on the average to write and run a program in Visual Basic.
Decision rule: $df = 8$. If $t > 1.8595$, reject H_0.
Test statistic: $t = \dfrac{\bar{X} - \mu}{S/\sqrt{n}} = \dfrac{12 - 10}{1.8028/\sqrt{9}} = 1.5504$

Decision: Since $t_{calc} = 1.5504$ is below the critical bound of 1.8595, do not reject H_0. There is not enough evidence to conclude that the introductory computer students required more than 10 minutes on the average to write and run a program in Visual Basic.

9.66
cont. **(b)** H_0: $\mu \le 10$ minutes. Introductory computer students required no more than an average of 10 minutes to write and run a program in Visual Basic.
H_1: $\mu > 10$ minutes. Introductory computer students required more than 10 minutes on the average to write and run a program in Visual Basic.
Decision rule: $df = 8$. If $t > 1.8595$, reject H_0.
Test statistic: $t = \dfrac{\overline{X} - \mu}{S / \sqrt{n}} = \dfrac{16 - 10}{13.2004 / \sqrt{9}} = 1.3636$

Decision: Since $t_{calc} = 1.3636$ is below the critical bound of 1.8595, do not reject H_0. There is not enough evidence to conclude that the introductory computer students required more than 10 minutes on the average to write and run a program in Visual Basic.

(c) Although the average time necessary to complete the assignment increased from 12 to 16 minutes as a result of the increase in one data value, the standard deviation went from 1.8 to 13.2, which in turn brought the t-value down because of the increased denominator.

(d) H_0: $\sigma_1^2 = \sigma_2^2$ where Population: 1 = introductory students, 2 = majors
The population variances for average time to complete the assignment are the same.
H_1: $\sigma_1^2 \ne \sigma_2^2$ The population variances for average time to complete the assignment are different.
Decision rule: If $F < 0.233$ or $F > 3.85$, reject H_0.
Test statistic: $F = \dfrac{S_1^2}{S_2^2} = \dfrac{1.8028^2}{2.0^2} = 0.8125$

Decision: Since $F_{calc} = 0.8125$ is between the critical bounds of 0.233 and 3.85, do not reject H_0. There is not enough evidence to conclude that the population variances for average time to complete the assignment are different. If the populations are normally distributed, a pooled-variance t-test can be performed.

H_0: $\mu_1 \le \mu_2$ where Population: 1 = introductory students, 2 = majors
Introductory students on the average require no more time to complete the assignment than students majoring in the area.
H_1: $\mu_1 > \mu_2$ Introductory students on the average do require more time to complete the assignment than students majoring in the area.
Decision rule: $df = 18$. If $t > 1.7341$, reject H_0.
Test statistic:
$$S_p^2 = \frac{(n_1 - 1) \cdot S_1^2 + (n_2 - 1) \cdot S_2^2}{(n_1 - 1) + (n_2 - 1)} = \frac{8 \cdot 1.8028^2 + 10 \cdot 2.0^2}{8 + 10} = 3.6667$$
$$t = \frac{(\overline{X}_1 - \overline{X}_2) - (\mu_1 - \mu_2)}{\sqrt{S_p^2 \left(\dfrac{1}{n_1} + \dfrac{1}{n_2} \right)}} = \frac{12 - 8.5}{\sqrt{3.6667 \left(\dfrac{1}{9} + \dfrac{1}{11} \right)}} = 4.0666$$

Decision: Since $t_{calc} = 4.0666$ is above the critical bound of $t = 1.7341$, reject H_0. There is enough evidence to support a conclusion that the introductory students on the average do require more time to complete the assignment than students majoring in the area.

•9.68   From an examination of the box-and-whisker plots, one cannot assume the two populations are normally distributed.

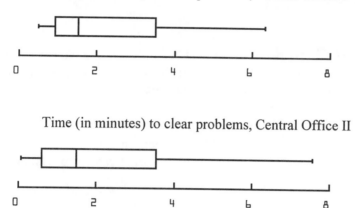

Time (in minutes) to clear problems, Central Office I

Time (in minutes) to clear problems, Central Office II

But, from the F-test of two variances, there is not enough evidence at the 0.05 level of significance to doubt that the variability in the two populations is approximately equal, since F_{calc} = 0.82 is between the critical bounds of $F = 0.40$ and $F = 2.53$. To test evidence at the 0.05 level of significance for a difference in the median amount of time required to clear problems, the large-sample approximation formula for the Wilcoxon rank sum test statistic is $Z = 0.66$. Since the p value = 0.5070 is greater than the desired 0.05 level of significance, we are unable to conclude that there is any real difference in the median amount of time required to clear problems at the two offices.

9.70   (a) H_0: $\sigma_1^2 = \sigma_2^2$ where Populations: 1 = American League pitchers
                        2 = National League pitchers
There is no difference in salary variability between American versus National League pitcher salaries.

H_1: $\sigma_1^2 \neq \sigma_2^2$
There is a difference in salary variability between American versus National League pitcher salaries.

Decision rule: If $F < 0.3210$ or $F > 3.1150$, reject H_0.

Test statistic: $F = \dfrac{S_1^2}{S_2^2} = \dfrac{0.9440}{0.9764} = 0.967$

Decision: Since $F_{calc} = 0.967$ is between the critical bounds of 0.321 and 3.115, do not reject H_0. There is insufficient evidence to conclude that the variances in salaries for American League pitchers is different from the variances in salaries for National League pitchers. If the populations are normally distributed, a Wilcoxon rank sum test with large-sample Z-approximation can be performed.

H_0: $M_1 = M_2$ There is no difference in the median salaries for American League pitchers and National League pitchers.

H_1: $M_1 \neq M_2$ There is a difference in the median salaries for American League pitchers and National League pitchers.

Decision rule: If $Z < -1.96$ or $Z > 1.96$, reject H_0.

Test statistic: $T_1 = 214.5$

$$\mu_{T_1} = \frac{n_1 \cdot (n+1)}{2} = \frac{14 \cdot 29}{2} = 203, \quad \sigma_{T_1} = \sqrt{\frac{n_1 \cdot n_2 \cdot (n+1)}{12}} = \sqrt{\frac{14 \cdot 14 \cdot 29}{12}} = 21.7639$$

9.70
cont.

$$Z = \frac{T_1 - \mu_{T_1}}{\sigma_{T_1}} = \frac{214.5 - 203}{21.7639} = 0.53$$

Decision: Since $Z_{calc} = 0.53$ is between the critical bounds of ± 1.96, do not reject H_0. There is not enough evidence to conclude that there is a difference in the median salaries for American League pitchers and National League pitchers.

(b) H_0: $\sigma_1^2 = \sigma_2^2$ where Populations: 1 = American League outfielders

2 = National League outfielders

There is no difference in salary variability between American versus National League outfielder salaries.

H_1: $\sigma_1^2 \neq \sigma_2^2$

There is a difference in salary variability between American versus National League outfielder salaries.

Decision rule: If $F < 0.3210$ or $F > 3.1150$, reject H_0.

Test statistic: $F = \dfrac{S_1^2}{S_2^2} = \dfrac{0.7604}{2.3253} = 0.327$

Decision: Since $F_{calc} = 0.327$ is between the critical bounds of 0.321 and 3.115, do not reject H_0. There is insufficient evidence to conclude that the variances in salaries for American League outfielders is different from the variances in salaries for National League outfielders. If the populations are normally distributed, a Wilcoxon rank sum test with large-sample Z-approximation can be performed.

H_0: $M_1 = M_2$ There is no difference in the median salaries for American League outfielders and National League outfielders.

H_1: $M_1 \neq M_2$ There is a difference in the median salaries for American League outfielders and National League outfielders.

Decision rule: If $Z < -1.96$ or $Z > 1.96$, reject H_0.

Test statistic: $T_1 = 194.5$

$$\mu_{T_1} = \frac{n_1 \cdot (n+1)}{2} = \frac{14 \cdot 29}{2} = 203, \ \sigma_{T_1} = \sqrt{\frac{n_1 \cdot n_2 \cdot (n+1)}{12}} = \sqrt{\frac{14 \cdot 14 \cdot 29}{12}} = 21.7639$$

$$Z = \frac{T_1 - \mu_{T_1}}{\sigma_{T_1}} = \frac{194.5 - 203}{21.7639} = -0.39$$

Decision: Since $Z_{calc} = -0.39$ is between the critical bounds of ± 1.96, do not reject H_0. There is not enough evidence to conclude that there is a difference in the median salaries for American League outfielders and National League outfielders.

9.70
cont. (c) H_0: $\sigma_1^2 = \sigma_2^2$ where Populations: 1 = American League pitchers

2 = American League outfielders

There is no difference in salary variability between American League pitcher versus outfielder salaries.

H_1: $\sigma_1^2 \neq \sigma_2^2$ There is a difference in salary variability between American League pitcher versus outfielder salaries.

Decision rule: If $F < 0.3210$ or $F > 3.1150$, reject H_0.

Test statistic: $F = \dfrac{S_1^2}{S_2^2} = \dfrac{0.9440}{0.7604} = 1.2413$

Decision: Since $F_{calc} = 1.2413$ is between the critical bounds of 0.321 and 3.115, do not reject H_0. There is insufficient evidence to conclude that the variances in salaries for American League pitchers is different from the variances in salaries for American League outfielders. If the populations are normally distributed, a Wilcoxon rank sum test with large-sample Z-approximation can be performed.

H_0: $M_1 = M_2$ There is no difference in the median salaries for American League pitchers and American League outfielders.

H_1: $M_1 \neq M_2$ There is a difference in the median salaries for American League pitchers and American League outfielders.

Decision rule: If $Z < -1.96$ or $Z > 1.96$, reject H_0.

Test statistic: $T_1 = 239$

$$\mu_{T_1} = \frac{n_1 \cdot (n+1)}{2} = \frac{14 \cdot 29}{2} = 203, \quad \sigma_{T_1} = \sqrt{\frac{n_1 \cdot n_2 \cdot (n+1)}{12}} = \sqrt{\frac{14 \cdot 14 \cdot 29}{12}} = 21.7639$$

$$Z = \frac{T_1 - \mu_{T_1}}{\sigma_{T_1}} = \frac{239 - 203}{21.7639} = 1.65$$

Decision: Since $Z_{calc} = 1.65$ is between the critical bounds of ± 1.96, do not reject H_0. There is not enough evidence to conclude that there is a difference in the median salaries for American League pitchers and American League outfielders.

(d) H_0: $\sigma_1^2 = \sigma_2^2$ where Populations: 1 = National League pitchers

2 = National League outfielders

There is no difference in salary variability between National League pitcher versus outfielder salaries.

H_1: $\sigma_1^2 \neq \sigma_2^2$

There is a difference in salary variability between National League pitcher versus outfielder salaries.

Decision rule: If $F < 0.3210$ or $F > 3.1150$, reject H_0.

Test statistic: $F = \dfrac{S_1^2}{S_2^2} = \dfrac{0.9764}{2.3253} = 0.4199$

Decision: Since $F_{calc} = 0.4199$ is between the critical bounds of 0.321 and 3.115, do not reject H_0. There is insufficient evidence to conclude that the variances in salaries for National League pitchers is different from the variances in salaries for National League outfielders.

9.70
cont.
(d) $H_0: M_1 = M_2$ There is no difference in the median salaries for National League pitchers and National League outfielders.
$H_1: M_1 \neq M_2$ There is a difference in the median salaries for National League pitchers and National League outfielders.
Decision rule: If $Z < -1.96$ or $Z > 1.96$, reject H_0.
Test statistic: $T_1 = 210$

$$\mu_{T_1} = \frac{n_1 \cdot (n+1)}{2} = \frac{14 \cdot 29}{2} = 203, \ \sigma_{T_1} = \sqrt{\frac{n_1 \cdot n_2 \cdot (n+1)}{12}} = \sqrt{\frac{14 \cdot 14 \cdot 29}{12}} = 21.7639$$

$$Z = \frac{T_1 - \mu_{T_1}}{\sigma_{T_1}} = \frac{210 - 203}{21.7639} = 0.32$$

Decision: Since $Z_{calc} = 0.32$ is between the critical bounds of ± 1.96, do not reject H_0. There is not enough evidence to conclude that there is a difference in the median salaries for National League pitchers and National League outfielders.

(e) $H_0: \sigma_1^2 = \sigma_2^2$ where Populations: 1 = pitchers, 2 = outfielders
There is no difference in salary variability between pitcher versus outfielder salaries.
$H_1: \sigma_1^2 \neq \sigma_2^2$
There is a difference in salary variability between pitcher versus outfielder salaries.
Decision rule: If $F < 0.3210$ or $F > 3.1150$, reject H_0.
Test statistic: $F = \frac{S_1^2}{S_2^2} = \frac{0.9322}{1.5610} = 0.5972$

Decision: Since $F_{calc} = 0.5972$ is between the critical bounds of 0.321 and 3.115, do not reject H_0. There is insufficient evidence to conclude that the variances in salaries for pitchers is different from the variances in salaries for outfielders. If the populations are normally distributed, a Wilcoxon rank sum test with large-sample Z-approximation can be performed.

$H_0: M_1 = M_2$ There is no difference in the median salaries for pitchers and outfielders.
$H_1: M_1 \neq M_2$ There is a difference in the median salaries for pitchers and outfielders.
Decision rule: If $Z < -1.96$ or $Z > 1.96$, reject H_0.
Test statistic: $T_1 = 874$

$$\mu_{T_1} = \frac{n_1 \cdot (n+1)}{2} = \frac{28 \cdot 57}{2} = 798, \ \sigma_{T_1} = \sqrt{\frac{n_1 \cdot n_2 \cdot (n+1)}{12}} = \sqrt{\frac{28 \cdot 28 \cdot 57}{12}} = 61.0246$$

$$Z = \frac{T_1 - \mu_{T_1}}{\sigma_{T_1}} = \frac{874 - 798}{61.0246} = 1.25$$

Decision: Since $Z_{calc} = 1.25$ is between the critical bounds of ± 1.96, do not reject H_0. There is not enough evidence to conclude that there is a difference in the median salaries for pitchers and outfielders.

CHAPTER 10

•10.2 (a) $SSW = SST - SSA = 210 - 60 = 150$

(b) $MSA = \dfrac{SSA}{c-1} = \dfrac{60}{5-1} = 15$

(c) $MSW = \dfrac{SSW}{n-c} = \dfrac{150}{35-5} = 5$

(d) $F = \dfrac{MSA}{MSW} = \dfrac{15}{5} = 3$

10.4 (a) $df\,A = c - 1 = 3 - 1 = 2$
(b) $df\,W = n - c = 21 - 3 = 18$
(c) $df\,T = n - 1 = 21 - 1 = 20$

10.6

Source	df	SS	MS	F
Among groups	4 – 1 = 3	80 x (3) = 240	80	80 ÷ 20 = 4
Within groups	32 – 4 = 28	560	560 ÷ 28 = 20	
Total	32 – 1 = 31	240 + 560 = 800		

•10.8 (a) Box-and-Whisker Plots, Programs A - D:

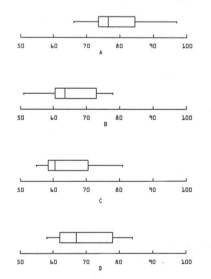

(b) Scores for Program A appear to be higher than those for other programs.

(c) To perform the ANOVA, the assumption must be made that the underlying populations have equal variances (H_0: $\sigma_A^2 = \sigma_B^2 = \sigma_C^2 = \sigma_D^2$). From the box-and-whisker plots there is not enough evidence to conclude that the variances are not equal.

•10.8 (d)
cont.

	A	B	C	D	E	F	G
1	Anova: Single Factor						
2							
3	SUMMARY						
4	Groups	Count	Sum	Average	Variance		
5	1	8	632	79	92		
6	2	8	523	65.375	77.69643		
7	3	8	515	64.375	77.69643		
8	4	8	556	69.5	90		
9							
10							
11	ANOVA						
12	Source of Variation	SS	df	MS	F	P-value	F crit
13	Between Groups	1068.125	3	356.0417	4.221093	0.013934	2.946685
14	Within Groups	2361.75	28	84.34821			
15							
16	Total	3429.875	31				

Test statistic: $F = 4.22$

Decision: Since $F_{calc} = 4.22$ is above the critical bound of $F = 2.95$, reject H_0. There is e nough evidence to conclude that employees from at least two of the sales programs have different exam scores.

(e) At the 95% level, Program A produces higher average exam scores than Programs B and C.

10.10 (a) Box-and-whisker plots, four formulation methods:

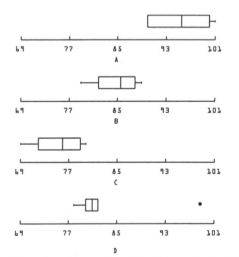

Based on the box-and-whisker plots, formulation A stands out from the other formulations in length of shelf life.

To perform the ANOVA, we must assume that the variances from the underlying populations are equal (H_0: $\sigma_A^2 = \sigma_B^2 = \sigma_C^2 = \sigma_D^2$).

From the box-and-whisker plots there is not enough evidence to conclude that the variances are not equal.

10.10
cont.

To test at the 0.05 level of significance whether the average profits/losses are different across the four strategies, we conduct an F test:

H_0: $\mu_A = \mu_B = \mu_C = \mu_D$ H_1: At least one mean is different.

	A	B	C	D	E	F	G
1	Anova: Single Factor						
2							
3	SUMMARY						
4	Groups	Count	Sum	Average	Variance		
5	1	6	572	95.33333	23.06667		
6	2	6	509	84.83333	16.56667		
7	3	6	452	75.33333	17.46667		
8	4	6	491	81.83333	14.56667		
9							
10							
11	ANOVA						
12	Source of Variation	SS	df	MS	F	P-value	F crit
13	Between Groups	1251	3	417	23.27442	9.9E-07	3.098393
14	Within Groups	358.3333	20	17.91667			
15							
16	Total	1609.333	23				

Test statistic: $F = 23.27$
Decision: Since $F_{calc} = 23.27$ is above the critical bound of $F = 3.10$, reject H_0. There is enough evidence to conclude that the average shelf life in days until the product was deemed to be lacking in freshness differed across the four product formulations.

(b)   To determine which of the means are significantly different from one another, we use the Tukey-Kramer procedure to establish the critical range:
$Q_{U(c,\ n-c)} = Q_{U(4,\ 20)} = 3.96$

$$\text{critical range} = Q_{U(c,n-c)} \cdot \sqrt{\frac{MSW}{2} \cdot \left(\frac{1}{n_j} + \frac{1}{n_{j'}}\right)} = 3.96 \cdot \sqrt{\frac{17.9}{2} \cdot \left(\frac{1}{6} + \frac{1}{6}\right)} = 6.782$$

Pairs of means that differ at the 0.05 level are marked with * below.
$\left|\bar{X}_1 - \bar{X}_2\right| = 10.500*$ $\left|\bar{X}_1 - \bar{X}_3\right| = 20.000*$ $\left|\bar{X}_1 - \bar{X}_4\right| = 13.500*$
$\left|\bar{X}_2 - \bar{X}_3\right| = 9.500*$ $\left|\bar{X}_2 - \bar{X}_4\right| = 3.000$ $\left|\bar{X}_3 - \bar{X}_4\right| = 6.500$

(c)   The manager can conclude with at least 95% confidence that formulation A gives superior product longevity over all three other formulations, and that formulation B creates a longer shelf life than formulation C.

10.12　(a)　To perform the ANOVA, we must assume that the underlying variation within the groups is the same for all groups (H_0: $\sigma^2_{Green} = \sigma^2_{Blue} = \sigma^2_{Red}$).

To test at the 0.05 level of significance whether the attitudes toward work are different across the three room colors, we conduct an F test:
H_0: $\mu_{Green} = \mu_{Blue} = \mu_{Red}$　　H_1: At least one mean is different.
Decision rule: df: 2, 15. If $F > 3.68$, reject H_0.
Test statistic: $F = 10.13$
Decision: Since $F_{calc} = 10.13$ is above the critical bound of $F = 3.68$, reject H_0. There is enough evidence to conclude that the average employee attitudes toward work are different for different room colors.

To determine which of the means are significantly different from one another, we use the Tukey-Kramer procedure to establish the critical range:
$Q_{U(c,\,n-c)} = Q_{U(3,\,15)} = 3.96$

$$\text{critical range} \quad = Q_{U(c,n-c)} \cdot \sqrt{\frac{MSW}{2} \cdot \left(\frac{1}{n_j} + \frac{1}{n_{j'}}\right)} = 3.67 \cdot \sqrt{\frac{32.8}{2} \cdot \left(\frac{1}{6} + \frac{1}{6}\right)} = 8.581$$

Pairs of means that differ at the 0.05 level are marked with * below.
$\left|\overline{X}_1 - \overline{X}_2\right| = 2.167$　　$\left|\overline{X}_1 - \overline{X}_3\right| = 11.667*$　　$\left|\overline{X}_2 - \overline{X}_3\right| = 13.833*$

10.14　(a)　To perform the ANOVA, we must assume that the underlying variation within the groups is the same for all groups (H_0: $\sigma^2_A = \sigma^2_B = \sigma^2_C$).

To test at the 0.05 level of significance whether the average assembly times are different across the team-based methods, we conduct an F test:
H_0: $\mu_A = \mu_B = \mu_C$　　H_1: At least one mean is different.

	A	B	C	D	E	F	G
1	Anova: Single Factor						
2							
3	SUMMARY						
4	Groups	Count	Sum	Average	Variance		
5	1	9	80.8	8.977778	0.157694		
6	2	9	71.42	7.935556	0.389228		
7	3	8	69.91	8.73875	0.46467		
8							
9							
10	ANOVA						
11	Source of Variation	SS	df	MS	F	P-value	F crit
12	Between Groups	5.328723	2	2.664362	8.033533	0.00226	3.42213
13	Within Groups	7.628065	23	0.331655			
14							
15	Total	12.95679	25				

10.14
cont.

Test statistic: $F = 8.03$

Decision: Since $F_{calc} = 8.03$ is above the critical bound of $F = 3.42$, reject H_0. There is enough evidence to conclude that the average assembly times are different across the various team-based methods.

(b)   To determine which of the means are significantly different from one another, we use the Tukey-Kramer procedure to establish the critical range

~ for comparing the first two samples of equal size:

$$\text{critical range} = Q_{U(c,n-c)} \cdot \sqrt{\frac{MSW}{2} \cdot \left(\frac{1}{n_j} + \frac{1}{n_{j'}}\right)} = 3.58 \cdot \sqrt{\frac{0.332}{2} \cdot \left(\frac{1}{9} + \frac{1}{9}\right)}$$

$$= 0.6876$$

$$\left|\overline{X}_1 - \overline{X}_2\right| = 1.0422*$$

~ for comparing the first and third and the second and third samples:

$$\text{critical range} = Q_{U(c,n-c)} \cdot \sqrt{\frac{MSW}{2} \cdot \left(\frac{1}{n_j} + \frac{1}{n_{j'}}\right)} = 3.58 \cdot \sqrt{\frac{0.332}{2} \cdot \left(\frac{1}{9} + \frac{1}{8}\right)}$$

$$= 0.7088$$

$$\left|\overline{X}_1 - \overline{X}_3\right| = 0.2391 \quad \left|\overline{X}_2 - \overline{X}_3\right| = 0.8031*$$

Pairs of means that differ at the 0.05 level are marked with * above.

Note: Table E.10 does not show a value for 23 degrees of freedom. We have used the studentized range Q for 20 degrees of freedom, $Q = 3.58$, understanding that the actual Q for 23 degrees of freedom will be slightly smaller and will fit inside the range we calculated.

•10.16 (a) $df\,A = r - 1 = 3 - 1 = 2$
        (b) $df\,B = c - 1 = 3 - 1 = 2$
        (c) $df\,AB = (r - 1)(c - 1) = (3 - 1)(3 - 1) = 4$
        (d) $df\,E = rc(n' - 1) = 3 \times 3 \times (4 - 1) = 27$
        (e) $df\,T = n - 1 = 35$

10.18   (a) $F_{(2, 27)} = 3.35$ (b) $F_{(2, 27)} = 3.35$ (c) $F_{(4, 27)} = 2.73$
        (d)   Decision: Since $F_{calc} = 1.00$ is below the critical bound of $F = 2.73$, do not reject H_0. There is insufficient evidence to conclude there is an interaction effect.
        (e)   Decision: Since $F_{calc} = 6.00$ is above the critical bound of $F = 3.35$, reject H_0. There is evidence of a difference among treatment means.
        (f)   Decision: Since $F_{calc} = 5.50$ is above the critical bound of $F = 3.35$, reject H_0. There is evidence of a difference among block means.

10.20

Source	df	SS	MS	F
Factor A	2	2 x 80 = 160	80	80 ÷ 5 = 16.00
Factor B	5-1 = 4	220	220 ÷ 4 = 55	11.00
Interaction, AB	8	8 x 10 = 80	10	10 ÷ 5 = 2.00
Error, E	30	30 x 5 = 150	150 ÷ 30 = 5	
Total, T	45-1 44	160+220+80+150 = 610		

•10.22 (a) (1) H_0: There is no interaction between service centers and VCR brands.
H_1: There is an interaction between service centers and VCR brands.
Decision rule: If $F > 3.63$, reject H_0.
Test statistic: $F = 3.36$
Decision: Since $F_{calc} = 3.36$ is below the critical bound of $F = 3.63$, do not reject H_0. There is insufficient evidence to conclude that there is any interaction between service centers and VCR brands that affects the average repair time.

(2) H_0: $\mu_1 = \mu_2 = \mu_3$ H_1: At least one mean differs.

	ANOVA						
29	ANOVA						
30	Source of Variation	SS	df	MS	F	P-value	F crit
31	Sample (Centers)	27.44444	2	13.72222	0.510331	0.616677	4.256492
32	Columns (Brands)	945.7778	2	472.8889	17.58678	0.000778	4.256492
33	Interaction	361.2222	4	90.30556	3.358471	0.060618	3.63309
34	Within	242	9	26.88889			
35							
36	Total	1576.444	17				

Decision: Since $F_{calc} = 0.51$ is below the critical bound of $F = 4.26$, do not reject H_0. There is insufficient evidence to conclude that there is any difference in repair time among the three service centers.

(3) H_0: $\mu_A = \mu_B = \mu_C$ H_1: At least one mean differs.
Decision rule: If $F > 4.26$, reject H_0.
Test statistic: $F = 17.58$
Decision: Since $F_{calc} = 17.58$ is above the critical bound of $F = 4.26$, reject H_0. There is adequate evidence to conclude that there is a difference in repair time among the three brands of videocassette recorders (VCR).

(c) Management of the repair shop may consider charging for service by the minute to reflect differences in average repair time across brands of VCRs.

10.24 (a) (1) H_0: There is no interaction between aisle and shelf location.
H_1: There is an interaction between aisle and shelf location.

24	Source of Variation	SS	df	MS	F	P-value	F crit
25	Sample (Aisle)	2178	1	2178	33	0.004551	7.70865
26	Columns (Shelves)	882	1	882	13.36364	0.021664	7.70865
27	Interaction	98	1	98	1.484848	0.289969	7.70865
28	Within	264	4	66			
29							
30	Total	3422	7				

Decision: Since $F_{calc} = 1.48$ is below the critical bound of $F = 7.71$, do not reject H_0. There is insufficient evidence to conclude that there is any interaction between aisle and shelf location.

(2) H_0: $\mu_{Front} = \mu_{Rear}$ H_1: The two means differ.
Decision rule: If $F > 7.71$, reject H_0.
Test statistic: $F = 33.00$
Decision: Since $F_{calc} = 33$ is above the critical bound of $F = 7.71$, reject H_0.
There is sufficient evidence to conclude that the average sales of packaged candy bars differs by location in the aisle.

(3) H_0: $\mu_{Top} = \mu_{Bottom}$ H_1: The two means differ.
Decision rule: If $F > 7.71$, reject H_0.
Test statistic: $F = 13.36$
Decision: Since $F_{calc} = 13.36$ is above the critical bound of $F = 7.71$, reject H_0.
There is adequate evidence to conclude that the average sales of packaged candy bars differs by location in the shelf.

(c) Management should consider the profit margin from packaged candy bar sales and compare with that of items currently stocked in the prime locations.

10.26 (a) (1) H_0: There is no interaction between detergent brand and length of washing cycle.
H_1: There is an interaction between detergent brand and length of washing cycle.
Decision rule: If $F > 2.54$, reject H_0.
Test statistic: $F = 1.49$
Decision: Since $F_{calc} = 1.49$ is below the critical bound of $F = 2.54$, do not reject H_0.
There is not enough evidence to conclude that there is an interaction between detergent brand and length of washing cycle.

(2) H_0: $\mu_A = \mu_B = \mu_C = \mu_D$ H_1: At least one mean differs.
Decision rule: If $F > 3.24$, reject H_0.
Test statistic: $F = 0.79$
Decision: Since $F_{calc} = 0.79$ is below the critical bound of $F = 3.24$, do not reject H_0. There is insufficient evidence to conclude that there is any difference in the average amount of dirt removed from standard household laundry loads across the four detergent brands.

10.26 (3) H_0: $\mu_{18} = \mu_{20} = \mu_{22} = \mu_{24}$ H_1: At least one mean differs.
Cont.   Decision rule: If $F > 3.24$, reject H_0.
            Test statistic: $F = 52.07$
            Decision: Since $F_{calc} = 52.07$ is above the critical bound of $F = 3.24$, reject H_0.
            There is adequate evidence to conclude the average amount of dirt removed from
            standard household laundry loads does differ across the four lengths of washing
            cycle (18, 20, 22, and 24 minutes).

(c) It appears that washing cycles for 22 and 24 minutes are not different with respect to dirt
     removal, but both of these cycles are superior to 18 or 20 minute cycles with respect to
     dirt removal.

•10.28 (a) Decision rule: If $H > \chi_U^2 = 15.086$, reject H_0.

(b) Decision: Since $H_{calc} = 13.77$ is below the critical bound of 15.086, do not reject H_0.

10.30 (a) H_0: $M_{Low} = M_{Normal} = M_{High} = M_{Very\ High}$
            H_1: At least one of the medians differs.

	A	B
1	Kruskal Wallis Rank Test	
2		
3	Level of Significance	0.05
4	Group 1	
5	Sum of Ranks	73
6	Sample Size	5
7	Group 2	
8	Sum of Ranks	76
9	Sample Size	5
10	Group 3	
11	Sum of Ranks	39
12	Sample Size	5
13	Group 4	
14	Sum of Ranks	22
15	Sample Size	5
16	Sum of Squared Ranks/Sample Size	2622
17	Sum of Sample Sizes	20
18	Number of groups	4
19	H Test Statistic	11.91429
20	Critical Value	7.814725
21	p-Value	0.007683
22	Reject the null hypothesis	

Test statistic: $H = 11.91$
Decision: Since $H_{calc} = 11.91$ is above the critical bound of 7.815, reject H_0. There is
sufficient evidence to show there is a significant difference in the four pressure levels
with respect to median battery life. The p value is 0.008.

10.32 (a) H_0: $M_P = M_{NN} = M_{SA} = M_{Mr.S}$
H_1: At least one of the medians differs.
Decision rule: If $H > \chi_U^2 = 7.815$, reject H_0.
Test statistic: $H = 12.16$
Decision: Since $H_{calc} = 12.16$ is above the critical bound of 7.815, reject H_0. There is sufficient evidence to show there is a significant difference in the median hours of sleep based on sleep medication prescribed. The p value is 0.007.

10.34 (a) H_0: $M_{Front} = M_{Middle} = M_{Rear}$ H_1: At least one of the medians differs.

	A	B
1	Kruskal Wallis Rank Test	
2		
3	Level of Significance	0.05
4	Group 1	
5	Sum of Ranks	88.5
6	Sample Size	6
7	Group 2	
8	Sum of Ranks	25
9	Sample Size	6
10	Group 3	
11	Sum of Ranks	57.5
12	Sample Size	6
13	Sum of Squared Ranks/Sample Size	1960.583
14	Sum of Sample Sizes	18
15	Number of groups	3
16	H Test Statistic	11.7924
17	Critical Value	5.991476
18	p-Value	0.00275
19	Reject the null hypothesis	

Test statistic: $H = 11.79$
Decision: Since $H_{calc} = 11.79$ is above the critical bound of 5.991, reject H_0. There is sufficient evidence to show there is a difference in the median sales (in thousands of dollars) of pet toys among the three store aisle locations. The p value is 0.003.

(c)   In problem 10.11, we concluded that there was a difference in average sales volumes in thousands of dollars across the three store aisle locations. The results of problems 10.11 and 10.34 are consistent.

10.36 (a) H_0: $M_{Prof} = M_{Grad} = M_{Sales} = M_{Broker}$
H_1: At least one of the medians differs.
Decision rule: If $H > \chi_U^2 = 7.815$, reject H_0.
Test statistic: $H = 17.53$
Decision: Since $H_{calc} = 17.53$ is above the critical bound of 7.815, reject H_0. There is sufficient evidence to show there is a difference in the median performance scores across the various employee backgrounds. The p value is 0.001.

(c)   In problem 10.13, we concluded that average performance scores differed across employee backgrounds. The results of problems 10.13 and 10.36 are consistent.

•10.48 Part I

(a) To perform ANOVA, we must assume that the underlying populations have equal variances (H_0: $\sigma_1^2 = \sigma_2^2 = \sigma_3^2$).

(b) H_0: $\mu_1 = \mu_2 = \mu_3$ H_1: At least one of the means differs.
Decision rule: If $F > 3.68$, reject H_0.
Test statistic: $F = 4.09$
Decision: Since $F_{calc} = 4.09$ is above the critical bound of $F = 3.68$, reject H_0. There is enough evidence to conclude that the average breaking strengths differ for the three air-jet pressures.

(c) $Q_{(c, n-c)} = Q_{U(3, 15)} = 3.67$

$$\text{critical range} = Q_{U(c, n-c)}\sqrt{\frac{MSW}{2}\left(\frac{1}{n_j} + \frac{1}{n_{j'}}\right)} = 3.67\sqrt{\frac{0.988}{2}\left(\frac{1}{6} + \frac{1}{6}\right)} = 1.489$$

The pair of means that differs at the 0.05 level is marked with * below.
$|\overline{X}_{30} - \overline{X}_{40}| = 1.30$ $|\overline{X}_{30} - \overline{X}_{50}| = 1.516*$ $|\overline{X}_{40} - \overline{X}_{50}| = 0.216$

Breaking strength scores under 30 psi are significantly higher than those under 50 psi.

(d) Other things being equal, use 30 psi.

•10.48 Part II

(e) (1) H_0: There is no interaction between side-to-side aspect and air-jet pressure.
H_1: There is an interaction between side-to-side aspect and air-jet pressure.
Decision rule: If $F > 3.89$, reject H_0.
Test statistic: $F = 1.9719$
Decision: Since $F_{calc} = 1.9719$ is below the critical bound of 3.89, do not reject H_0. There is insufficient evidence to conclude there is an interaction between side-to-side aspect and air-jet pressure.

(2) H_0: $\mu_1 = \mu_2$ H_1: $\mu_1 \neq \mu_2$
Decision rule: If $F > 4.75$, reject H_0.
Test statistic: $F = 4.8694$
Decision: Since $F_{calc} = 4.8694$ is above the critical bound of 4.75, reject H_0. There is sufficient evidence to conclude that average breaking strength does differ between the two levels of side-to-side aspect.

(3) H_0: $\mu_1 = \mu_2 = \mu_3$ H_1: At least one of the means differs.
Decision rule: If $F > 3.89$, reject H_0.
Test statistic: $F = 5.6699$
Decision: Since $F_{calc} = 5.6699$ is above the critical bound of 3.89, reject H_0. There is enough evidence to conclude that the average breaking strengths differ for the three air-jet pressures.

•10.48   Part II
cont.

(f)   Fig A:Side-by-Side Aspect: Nozzle   Fig B: Side-by-Side Aspect: Opposite

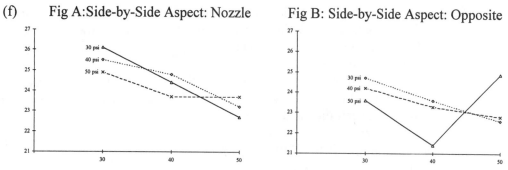

While the three sets of lines intersect in both graphs, they do not show any significant
pattern in doing so, certainly in Figure A on the left. The average breaking strength at 50
psi begins to show a more pronounced pattern in Figure B on the right, but not enough to
make any interaction statistically significant.

(g)   The average breaking strength is highest under 30 psi.

(h)   The two-factor experiment gave a more complete, refined set of results than the one-
factor experiment.

10.50 Part I
(a)   To perform ANOVA, we must assume that the underlying populations have equal variances
(H_0: $\sigma^2_{Acct} = \sigma^2_{Finc} = \sigma^2_{Mgt} = \sigma^2_{Mrk}$).

(b) H_0: $\mu_{Acct} = \mu_{Finc} = \mu_{Mgt} = \mu_{Mrk}$ H_1: At least one of the means differs.
Decision rule: If $F > 3.10$, reject H_0.
Test statistic: $F = 6.57$
Decision: Since $F_{calc} = 6.57$ is above the critical bound of $F = 3.10$, reject H_0. There is
enough evidence to conclude that the average starting salary package, including benefits,
for recent MBA graduates differs across the four areas of content concentration.

(c) $Q_{(c,n-c)} = Q_{U(4, 20)} = 3.96$

$$\text{critical range} = Q_{U(c,\ n-c)}\sqrt{\frac{MSW}{2}\left(\frac{1}{n_j} + \frac{1}{n_{j'}}\right)} = 3.96\sqrt{\frac{74.8}{2}\left(\frac{1}{6} + \frac{1}{6}\right)} = 13.982$$

The pair of means that differs at the 0.05 level is marked with * below.

$\left|\overline{X}_{Acct} - \overline{X}_{Finc}\right| = 1.20$ $\left|\overline{X}_{Acct} - \overline{X}_{Mgt}\right| = 15.95*$ $\left|\overline{X}_{Acct} - \overline{X}_{Mrk}\right| = 14.033*$

$\left|\overline{X}_{Finc} - \overline{X}_{Mgt}\right| = 17.15*$ $\left|\overline{X}_{Finc} - \overline{X}_{Mrk}\right| = 15.233*$ $\left|\overline{X}_{Mgt} - \overline{X}_{Mrk}\right| = 1.917$

(d)   Recent MBA graduates who had area concentrations in Accounting or Finance had
higher starting salary packages than graduates who had area concentrations in
Management or Marketing. Recent MBA graduates in Accounting and in Finance did not
have statistically different starting salary packages.

10.50 Part II

    (e)   (1) H_0: There is no interaction between area of major concentration and gender.
    H_1: There is an interaction between area of major concentration and gender.
    Decision rule: If $F > 3.24$, reject H_0.
    Test statistic: $F = 3.2655$
    Decision: Since $F_{calc} = 3.2655$ is above the critical bound of 3.24, reject H_0.
    There is sufficient evidence to conclude there is an interaction between area of major concentration and gender.

    (2) H_0: $\mu_1 = \mu_2$ H_1: $\mu_1 \neq \mu_2$
    Decision rule: If $F > 4.49$, reject H_0.
    Test statistic: $F = 13.6743$
    Decision: Since $F_{calc} = 13.6743$ is above the critical bound of 4.49, reject H_0. There is sufficient evidence to conclude that average starting salary does differ between recent male and female MBA graduates.

    (3) H_0: $\mu_{Acct} = \mu_{Finc} = \mu_{Mgt} = \mu_{Mrk}$ H_1: At least one of the means differs.
    Decision rule: If $F > 3.24$, reject H_0.
    Test statistic: $F = 12.9695$
    Decision: Since $F_{calc} = 12.9695$ is above the critical bound of 3.24, reject H_0. There is enough evidence to conclude that the average starting salary packages, including benefits, for recent MBA graduates differs across the four areas of content concentration.

    (f)   Given the interaction effect was significant, male and female graduates tend to distribute differently over the four areas of major content concentration. We cannot directly conclude that there is a significant difference in average starting salary due to gender or areas of major concentration (main effects) because the average salaries for different major concentrations are different for men and for women.

    (g)   Conclusions about the relative average starting salaries of recent MBA graduates cannot be drawn because major concentrations and gender interact.

    (h)   Because the two factors interact significantly, the completely randomized design model is superior to the factorial design model because the presence of their interaction prohibits us from being able to look at the individual effects of each factor separately.

CHAPTER 11

11.2 $p_{S_1} = \dfrac{X_1}{n_1} = \dfrac{45}{100} = 0.45, \; p_{S_2} = \dfrac{X_2}{n_2} = \dfrac{25}{50} = 0.50,$

and $\bar{p} = \dfrac{X_1 + X_2}{n_1 + n_2} = \dfrac{45 + 25}{100 + 50} = 0.467$

$H_0: p_1 = p_2 \quad H_1: p_1 \neq p_2$
Decision rule: If $Z < -2.58$ or $Z > 2.58$, reject H_0.

Test statistic: $Z = \dfrac{(p_{S_1} - p_{S_2}) - (p_1 - p_2)}{\sqrt{\bar{p} \cdot (1 - \bar{p}) \left(\dfrac{1}{n_1} + \dfrac{1}{n_2} \right)}} = \dfrac{0.45 - 0.50}{\sqrt{0.467 \cdot 0.533 \left(\dfrac{1}{100} + \dfrac{1}{50} \right)}} = 0.58$

Decision: Since $Z_{\text{calc}} = 0.58$ is between the critical bound of $Z = \pm 2.58$, do not reject H_0. There is insufficient evidence to conclude that the population proportion of successes differs for group 1 and group 2.

•11.4   (a)

	A	B
1	Performance Evaluation Methods	
2		
3	Hypothesized Difference	0
4	Level of Significance	0.05
5	Group 1	
6	Number of Successes	63
7	Sample Size	78
8	Group 2	
9	Number of Successes	49
10	Sample Size	82
11	Group 1 Proportion	0.807692308
12	Group 2 Proportion	0.597560976
13	Difference in Two Proportions	0.210131332
14	Average Proportion	0.7
15	Z Test Statistic	2.899181485
16		
17	Two-Tailed Test	
18	Lower Critical Value	-1.95996108
19	Upper Critical Value	1.959961082
20	p-Value	0.003741516
21	Reject the null hypothesis	

    (b) p value $= 2[P(Z > 2.90)] = 2[0.5 - 0.4981] = 0.0038$.
The probability of obtaining a difference in two sample proportions as large as 0.21 or more when the null hypothesis is true is 0.0038.

•11.6　(a)

	A	B
1	Laundry Temperature Comparison	
2		
3	Hypothesized Difference	0
4	Level of Significance	0.05
5	Group 1	
6	Number of Successes	280
7	Sample Size	500
8	Group 2	
9	Number of Successes	320
10	Sample Size	500
11	Group 1 Proportion	0.56
12	Group 2 Proportion	0.64
13	Difference in Two Proportions	-0.08
14	Average Proportion	0.6
15	Z Test Statistic	-2.5819889
16		
17	Lower-Tail Test	
18	Lower Critical Value	-1.644853
19	p-Value	0.004911668
20	Reject the null hypothesis	

Decision: Since $Z_{calc} = -2.58$ is below the critical bound of -1.645, reject H_0. There is sufficient evidence to conclude that a significantly higher proportion of individuals preferred the laundry results when used with the high-temperature setting than with the low-temperature setting.

(b)　p value $= P(Z < -2.58) = 0.5 - 0.4951 = 0.0049$.
The probability of obtaining a difference in two sample proportions as large as 0.08 or more when the null hypothesis is true is 0.0049.

•11.8　(a)-(b)

Observed Freq　Expected Freq	Observed Freq　Expected Freq	Total Obs, Row 1
20　　　　　　　　20 chi-sq contrib= 0	30　　　　　　　　30 chi-sq contrib= 0	50
Observed Freq　Expected Freq	Observed Freq　Expected Freq	Total Obs, Row 2
30　　　　　　　　30 chi-sq contrib= 0	45　　　　　　　　45 chi-sq contrib= 0	75
Total Obs, Col 1 50	Total Obs, Col 2 75	GRAND TOTAL 125

(c)　$\chi^2 = \sum \dfrac{(f_0 - f_e)^2}{f_e} = 0 + 0 + 0 + 0 = 0$

112

•11.10 (a)

	A	B	C	D	E	F
1	Enjoy Shopping for Clothing					
2						
3	Observed Frequencies:			Gender		
4			Enjoy Shopping	Male	Female	Total
5			Yes	136	224	360
6			No	104	36	140
7			Total	240	260	500
8						
9	Expected Frequencies:			Gender		
10			Enjoy Shopping	Male	Female	Total
11			Yes	172.8	187.2	360
12			No	67.2	72.8	140
13			Total	240	260	500
14						
15						
16	Level of Significance	0.01				
17	Number of Rows	2				
18	Number of Columns	2				
19	Degrees of Freedom	1				
20	Critical Value	6.634891				
21	Chi-Square Test Statistic	#NUM!				
22	p-Value	2.19E-13				
23	Reject the null hypothesis					

(b) p value = virtually zero.
The probability of obtaining a difference in two sample proportions as large as 0.295 or more when the null hypothesis is true is virtually zero.

(c) (a) $H_0: p_1 = p_2$ $H_1: p_1 \neq p_2$ where Populations: 1 = males, 2 = females
Decision rule: $df = 1$. If $\chi^2 > 6.635$, reject H_0.
Test statistic: $\chi^2 = 0.011$
Decision: Since $\chi^2_{calc} = 0.011$ is below the upper critical bound of 6.635, do not reject H_0. There is not enough evidence to conclude that the proportion of males and females who enjoy shopping for clothing are different.

(b) p value = 0.9180
The probability of obtaining a difference in two sample proportions as large as 0.004 or more when the null hypothesis is true is 0.9180.

113

•11.12 (a)

	A	B	C	D	E	F
1	Readability of Annual Reports					
2						
3	Observed Frequencies:			Company		
4			Understandable	A	B	Total
5			Yes	17	23	40
6			No	33	27	60
7			Total	50	50	100
8						
9	Expected Frequencies:			Company		
10			Understandable	A	B	Total
11			Yes	20	20	40
12			No	30	30	60
13			Total	50	50	100
14						
15						
16	Level of Significance	0.1				
17	Number of Rows	2				
18	Number of Columns	2				
19	Degrees of Freedom	1				
20	Critical Value	2.705541				
21	Chi-Square Test Statistic	1.499998				
22	p-Value	0.220671				
23	Do not reject the null hypothesis					

Decision: Since $\chi^2_{calc} = 1.500$ is below the upper critical bound of 2.706, do not reject H_0. There is inadequate evidence to conclude that there is a difference in the proportion of CPAs who find the annual reports understandable.

(b) p value = 0.221.
     The probability of obtaining a difference in two sample proportions as large as 0.12 or more when the null hypothesis is true is 0.221.

(c)   (a) $H_0: p_1 = p_2$ $H_1: p_1 \neq p_2$
         Decision rule: $df = 1$. If $\chi^2 > 2.706$, reject H_0.
         Test statistic: $\chi^2 = 10.240$
         Decision: Since $\chi^2_{calc} = 10.240$ is above the upper critical bound of 2.706, reject H_0. There is adequate evidence to conclude that there is a difference in the proportion of CPAs who find the annual reports understandable.

       (b) p value = 0.001.
         The probability of obtaining a difference in two sample proportions as large as 0.32 or more when the null hypothesis is true is 0.001.

11.14   (a) $H_0: p_1 = p_2$ $H_1: p_1 \neq p_2$
         Decision rule: $df = 1$. If $\chi^2 > 6.635$, reject H_0.
         Test statistic: $\chi^2 = 6.526$
         Decision: Since $\chi^2_{calc} = 6.526$ is below the upper critical bound of 6.635, do not reject H_0. There is inadequate evidence to conclude that the two medical approaches differ in the proportion of deaths or heart attacks within 6 months of treatment.

11.14 (b) p value = 0.011.
cont.   The probability of obtaining a difference in two sample proportions as large as 0.04 or more when the null hypothesis is true is 0.011.

(c)(a) H_0: $p_1 = p_2$ H_1: $p_1 \neq p_2$
Decision rule: $df = 1$. If $\chi^2 > 6.635$, reject H_0.
Test statistic: $\chi^2 = 1.982$
Decision: Since $\chi^2_{calc} = 1.982$ is below the upper critical bound of 6.635, do not reject H_0. There is inadequate evidence to conclude that the two medical approaches differ in the proportion of deaths or heart attacks within 6 months of treatment.

(b) p value = 0.16.
The probability of obtaining a difference in two sample proportions as large as 0.0204 or more when the null hypothesis is true is 0.16.

•11.16 (a)-(b) The expected frequencies in the first row are 20, 30, and 40.
The expected frequencies in the second row are 30, 45, and 60.
$\chi^2 = 12.500$. The critical value with 2 degrees of freedom and an $\alpha = .05$ level of significance is 5.991. The result is deemed significant.

•11.18 H_0: $p_1 = \ldots = p_7$ H_1: At least one proportion differs.
Decision rule: $df = (c - 1) = (7 - 1) = 6$. If $\chi^2 > 12.592$, reject H_0.
Test statistic: $\chi^2 = 73.467$
Decision: Since $\chi^2_{calc} = 73.467$ is above the upper critical bound of 12.592, reject H_0. There is adequate evidence to conclude that the proportion of males and females differ across the seven occupational titles.

11.20 (a)

	A	B	C	D	E	F	G	H	I
1	Quality of Auto parts								
2									
3	Observed Frequencies:						Day		
4			Result	Mon	Tues	Wed	Thurs	Fri	Total
5			Defective	12	7	7	10	14	50
6			Acceptable	88	93	93	90	86	450
7			Total	100	100	100	100	100	500
8									
9	Expected Frequencies:						Day		
10			Result	Mon	Tues	Wed	Thurs	Fri	Total
11			Defective	10	10	10	10	10	50
12			Acceptable	90	90	90	90	90	450
13			Total	100	100	100	100	100	500
14									
15									
16	Level of Significance	0.05							
17	Number of Rows	2							
18	Number of Columns	5							
19	Degrees of Freedom	4							
20	Critical Value	9.48773							
21	Chi-Square Test Statistic	4.22222							
22	p-Value	0.37677							
23	Do not reject the null hypothesis								
24									
25	NOTE:								
26	As p-value approaches zero,								
27	the Chi-square test statistic								
28	may appear as #NUM! due to								
29	a Microsoft Excel bug.								

Decision: Since $\chi^2_{calc} = 4.222$ is below the upper critical bound of 9.488, do not reject H_0. There is not enough evidence to show any difference in the proportion of defective parts produced on the various days of the week.

(b) $H_0: p_M = p_{Tu} = p_W = p_{Th} = p_F$ H_1: At least one proportion differs.
Decision rule: $df = (c - 1) = (5 - 1) = 4$. If $\chi^2 > 9.488$, reject H_0.
Test statistic: $\chi^2 = 18.750$

Decision: Since $\chi^2_{calc} = 18.750$ is below the upper critical bound of 9.488, reject H_0. There is enough evidence to show a difference in the proportion of defective parts produced on the various days of the week.

•11.22 (a)

	A	B	C	D	E	F	G
1	Cable Television						
2							
3	Observed Frequencies:				Type of Residence		
4			Purchase	C1	C2	C3	Total
5			Yes	94	39	77	210
6			No	56	36	98	190
7			Total	150	75	175	400
8							
9	Expected Frequencies:				Type of Residence		
10			Purchase	C1	C2	C3	Total
11			Yes	78.75	39.375	91.875	210
12			No	71.25	35.625	83.125	190
13			Total	150	75	175	400
14							
15							
16	Level of Significance	0.01					
17	Number of Rows	2					
18	Number of Columns	3					
19	Degrees of Freedom	2					
20	Critical Value	9.210351					
21	Chi-Square Test Statistic	11.29485					
22	p-Value	0.003526					
23	Reject the null hypothesis						

Decision: Since $\chi^2_{calc} = 11.295$ is above the upper critical bound of 9.210, reject H_0. There is enough evidence to show a difference in the proportion of households that adopt a cable TV service based on the type of residence.

•11.24   (a) $\chi^2 = 21.026$ (d) $\chi^2 = 23.209$
        (b) $\chi^2 = 26.217$ (e) $\chi^2 = 23.209$
        (c) $\chi^2 = 30.578$

11.26 (a) H_0: There is no relationship between men's ages and their preferences in sports.
H_1: There is a relationship between men's ages and their preferences in sports.
Decision rule: If $\chi^2 > 26.217$, reject H_0.

Test statistic: $\chi^2 = 186.8$

Decision: Since the $\chi^2_{calc} = 186.8$ is above the critical bound of 26.217,
reject H_0. There is sufficient evidence to show that a relationship does exist between
between men's ages and their preferences in sports.

(b) H_0: There is no relationship between men's ages and their preferences in sports.
H_1: There is a relationship between men's ages and their preferences in sports.
Decision rule: If $\chi^2 > 26.217$, reject H_0.

Test statistic: $\chi^2 = 157.738$

Decision: Since the $\chi^2_{calc} = 157.738$ is above the critical bound of 26.217,
reject H_0. There is sufficient evidence to show that a relationship does exist between
between men's ages and their preferences in sports.

11.28 (a)

	A	B	C	D	E	F	G	H
1	Lottery Fairness							
2								
3	Observed Frequencies:				Quarter of Year			
4			Number Set	Jan-Mar	Apr-June	Jul-Sept	Oct-Dec	Total
5			Low	21	28	35	38	122
6			Medium	34	22	29	37	122
7			High	36	41	28	17	122
8			Total	91	91	92	92	366
9								
10	Expected Frequencies:				Quarter of Year			
11			Number Set	Jan-Mar	Apr-June	Jul-Sept	Oct-Dec	Total
12			Low	30.333333	30.333333	30.666667	30.666667	122
13			Medium	30.333333	30.333333	30.666667	30.666667	122
14			High	30.333333	30.333333	30.666667	30.666667	122
15			Total	91	91	92	92	366
16								
17								
18	Level of Significance	0.05						
19	Number of Rows	3						
20	Number of Columns	4						
21	Degrees of Freedom	6						
22	Critical Value	12.5916						
23	Chi-Square Test Statistic	20.6802						
24	p-Value	0.00209						
25	Reject the null hypothesis							

Decision: Since the $\chi^2_{calc} = 20.680$ is above the critical bound of 12.592, reject H_0. There is
evidence of a relationship between the quarter of the year in which draftable-aged men were
born and the numbers assigned as their draft eligibilities during the Vietnam War.

(b) It appears that the results of the lottery drawing are different from what would be
expected if the lottery were random.

11.28 (c) H_0: There is no relationship between the quarter of the year in which draftable aged men were born and the numbers assigned as their draft eligibilities during the Vietnam War.
cont. H_1: There is a relationship between the quarter of the year in which draftable-aged men were born and the numbers assigned as their draft eligibilities.

Decision rule: If $\chi^2 > 12.592$, reject H_0.

Test statistic: $\chi^2 = 9.207$

Decision: Since the $\chi^2_{calc} = 9.207$ is below the critical bound of 12.592, do not reject H_0. There is not enough evidence to conclude there is any relationship between the quarter of the year in which draftable-aged men were born and the numbers assigned as their draft eligibilities during the Vietnam War.

11.36 (a) $H_0: p_1 \geq p_2$ $H_1: p_1 < p_2$ where Populations: 1 = aspirin, 2 = placebo

Decision rule: If $Z < -2.33$, reject H_0.

Test statistic:

$$Z = \frac{(p_{S_1} - p_{S_2}) - (p_1 - p_2)}{\sqrt{\bar{p}(1-\bar{p})\left(\frac{1}{n_1} + \frac{1}{n_2}\right)}} = \frac{(0.0094 - 0.0171)}{\sqrt{0.0133(0.9867)\left(\frac{1}{11,037} + \frac{1}{11,034}\right)}} = -5.00$$

Decision: Since $Z_{calc} = -5.00$ is below the critical bound of -2.33, reject H_0. There is enough evidence to conclude that the proportion having heart attacks is significantly lower for the male medical doctors in the United States who received the buffered aspirin every other day than for those who received the placebo.

(b) p value = virtually zero. The probability of obtaining a difference in two sample proportions as large as 0.0077 or more when the null hypothesis is true is virtually zero. There is a very small probability that the difference in heart attacks was higher in the group taking aspirin than in the group receiving the placebo. This is strong evidence of the effectiveness of the aspirin therapy.

(c) The χ^2-test should not be used because the alternative hypothesis required a directional test.

(d) $H_0: p_1 \geq p_2$ $H_1: p_1 < p_2$ where Populations: 1 = aspirin, 2 = placebo

Decision rule: If $Z < -2.33$, reject H_0.

Test statistic:

$$Z = \frac{(p_{S_1} - p_{S_2}) - (p_1 - p_2)}{\sqrt{\bar{p}(1-\bar{p})\left(\frac{1}{n_1} + \frac{1}{n_2}\right)}} = \frac{(0.0094 - 0.0135)}{\sqrt{0.0115(0.9885)\left(\frac{1}{11,037} + \frac{1}{11,034}\right)}} = -2.85$$

Decision: Since $Z_{calc} = -2.85$ is below the critical bound of -2.33, reject H_0. There is enough evidence to conclude that the proportion having heart attacks is significantly lower for the male medical doctors in the United States who received the buffered aspirin every other day than for those who received the placebo.

p value = $P(Z < -2.85) = 0.5 - 0.4978 = 0.0022$. The probability of obtaining a difference in two sample proportions as large as 0.0041 or more when the null hypothesis is true is 0.0022.

•11.38 H_0: There is no relationship between education level and individual assessment of personal
financial condition.

H_1: There is a relationship between education level and individual assessment of personal
financial condition.

Decision rule: If $\chi^2 > 9.488$, reject H_0.

Test statistic: $\chi^2 = 86.023$

Decision: Since $\chi^2_{calc} = 86.023$ is above the critical bound 9.488, reject H_0. There is enough evidence to conclude that there is a relationship between education level and individual assessment of personal financial condition.

11.40 (a) H_0: There is no relationship between the attitudes of employees toward the use of self-managed work teams and employee job classification.

H_1: There is a relationship between the attitudes of employees toward the use of self-managed work teams and employee job classification.

Decision rule: If $\chi^2 > 12.592$, reject H_0.

Test statistic: $\chi^2 = 11.895$

Decision: Since $\chi^2_{calc} = 11.895$ is below the critical bound 12.592, do not reject H_0. There is not enough evidence to conclude that there is a relationship between the attitudes of employees toward the use of self-managed work teams and employee job classification.

(b) H_0: There is no relationship between the attitudes of employees toward vacation time without pay and employee job classification.

H_1: There is a relationship between the attitudes of employees toward vacation time without pay and employee job classification.

Decision rule: If $\chi^2 > 12.592$, reject H_0.

Test statistic: $\chi^2 = 3.294$

Decision: Since $\chi^2_{calc} = 3.294$ is below the critical bound 12.592, do not reject H_0. There is not enough evidence to conclude that there is a relationship between the attitudes of employees toward vacation time without pay and employee job classification.

CHAPTER 12

12.2 (a) Proportion of nonconformances largest on Day 4, smallest on Day 3.

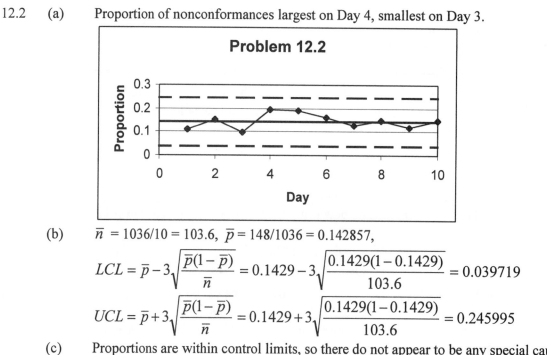

(b) $\bar{n} = 1036/10 = 103.6$, $\bar{p} = 148/1036 = 0.142857$,

$$LCL = \bar{p} - 3\sqrt{\frac{\bar{p}(1-\bar{p})}{\bar{n}}} = 0.1429 - 3\sqrt{\frac{0.1429(1-0.1429)}{103.6}} = 0.039719$$

$$UCL = \bar{p} + 3\sqrt{\frac{\bar{p}(1-\bar{p})}{\bar{n}}} = 0.1429 + 3\sqrt{\frac{0.1429(1-0.1429)}{103.6}} = 0.245995$$

(c) Proportions are within control limits, so there do not appear to be any special causes of variation.

•12.4 (a)

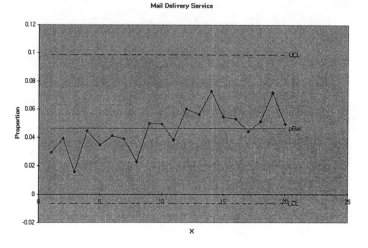

(b) Although none of the points are outside the control limits, there is evidence of a pattern over time, since the first eight points are all below the center line and most of the later points are above the center line. Thus, the special causes that might be contributing to this pattern should be investigated before any change in the system of operation is contemplated.

•12.6 (a) $\bar{n} = 113345/22 = 5152.0455$, $\bar{p} = 1460/113345 = 0.01288$,

$$LCL = \bar{p} - 3\sqrt{\frac{\bar{p}(1-\bar{p})}{\bar{n}}} = 0.01288 - 3\sqrt{\frac{0.01288(1-0.01288)}{5152.0455}} = 0.00817$$

$$UCL = \bar{p} + 3\sqrt{\frac{\bar{p}(1-\bar{p})}{\bar{n}}} = 0.01288 - 3\sqrt{\frac{0.01288(1-0.01288)}{5152.0455}} = 0.01759$$

The proportion of unacceptable cans is below the LCL on Day 4. There is evidence of a pattern over time, since the last eight points are all above the mean and most of the earlier points are below the mean. Thus, the special causes that might be contributing to this pattern should be investigated before any change in the system of operation is contemplated.

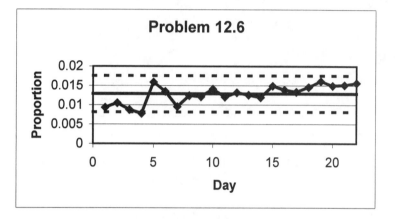

(b) Once special causes have been eliminated and the process is stable, process flow and fishbone diagrams of the process should be developed to increase process knowledge. Then implement Deming's fourteen points to improve the system.

12.8 (a) $\bar{p} = 0.1091$, $LCL = 0.0752$, $UCL = 0.1431$. Points 9, 26, and 30 are above the UCL.
   (b) First, the reasons for the special cause variation would need to be determined and local corrective action taken. Once special causes have been eliminated and the process is stable, process flow and fishbone diagrams of the process should be developed to increase process knowledge. Then implement Deming's fourteen points to improve the system.

12.12 (a) $\bar{R} = 3.97$
   $LCL = D_3 \bar{R} = 0\,(3.97) = 0$. LCL does not exist.
   $UCL = D_4 \bar{R} = (2.282)\,(3.97) = 9.05954$
   (b) There are no sample ranges outside the control limits and there does not appear to be a pattern.
   (c) $\bar{\bar{X}} = 13.95$
   $LCL = \bar{\bar{X}} - A_2 \bar{R} = 13.95 - (0.729)\,(3.97) = 11.05587$
   $UCL = \bar{\bar{X}} + A_2 \bar{R} = 13.95 + (0.729)\,(3.97) = 16.84413$
   (d) The sample mean on Day 7 is above the UCL, which is an indication there is evidence of special cause variation.

12.14 (a) $\overline{R}$ = 5.916, $\overline{\overline{X}}$ = 3.176. *R* chart: *UCL* = 7.249; *LCL* does not exist.

$\overline{\overline{X}}$ chart: *UCL* = 8.191; *LCL* = 3.641

(b)   There are no points outside the control limits and no evidence of a pattern.

•12.16 (a)

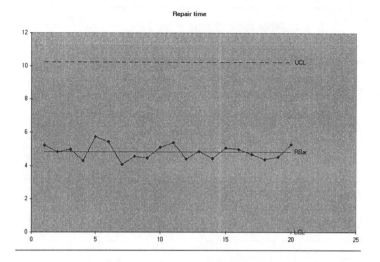

The process appears to be in control since there are no points outside the lower and upper control limits and there is no pattern in the results over time.

(b)   Since the process is in control, it is up to management to reduce the common cause variation by application of the 14 points of the Deming theory of management by process. In addition, process knowledge would be enhanced by the development of process flow and fishbone diagrams.

12.18 (a) $\overline{R}$ = .17286; *UCL* = .30296; *LCL* = .04276; The range chart does not appear to be giving an out of control signal since none of the points are above the *UCL* or below the *LCL* and there is no pattern to the values over time.

(b) $\overline{\overline{X}}$ = 7.3624; *LCL* = 7.3126; *UCL* = 7.4122.

(c) There appears to be some evidence of special cause variation in the average *pH* level. There is a cluster of four consecutive points that are below the *LCL* and two additional points that are above the *UCL*. Thus atmospheric and other conditions should be investigated in order to try to explain this special cause variation.

12.28 (a) $\overline{p}$ = 0.391, *LCL* = 0.302, *UCL* = 0.480.

(b)   The process is out of statistical control. The proportion of investigations that are closed is below the *LCL* on Days 2 and 16 and are above the *UCL* on Days 22 and 23.

(c)   Special causes of variation should be investigated and eliminated. Next, process knowledge should be improved to increase the proportion of investigations closed the same day.

12.30   Processing time:

$\overline{\overline{X}} = 2.2653$, $\overline{R} = 3.597$

Control chart for the range:

$LCL = .803$, $UCL = 6.391$

Control chart for the mean:

$LCL = 1.1567$, $UCL = 3.3749$

Processing time can be considered to be in control in terms of the mean and the range since there is no strong pattern in either chart and there are no points that are outside the control limits.

Proportion of rework in the laboratory:

$\overline{p} = .04737$, $LCL = .02722$, $UCL = .06752$

Days 6 and 29 are above the *UCL*. Thus, the special causes that might be contributing to these values should be investigated before any change in the system of operation is contemplated. Once special causes have been eliminated and the process is stable, process flow and fishbone diagrams of the process should be developed to increase process knowledge. Then Deming's fourteen points can be applied to improve the system.

CHAPTER 13

13.2 (a) When $X = 0$, the expected value of Y is 16.

(b) For increase in the value X by 1 unit, we can expect a decrease in 0.5 units in the value of Y.

(c) $\hat{Y} = 16 - 0.5X = 16 - 0.5(6) = 13$

13.4 (a)

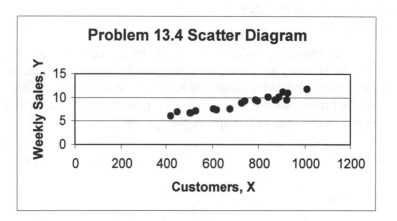

(c)

	A	B	C	D	E	F	G
1	Package Delivery Stores						
2							
3	*Regression Statistics*						
4	Multiple R	0.9549132					
5	R Square	0.91185922					
6	Adjusted R Square	0.90696251					
7	Standard Error	0.501495215					
8	Observations	20					
9							
10	ANOVA						
11		*df*	*SS*	*MS*	*F*	*Significance F*	
12	Regression	1	46.8335409	46.8335409	186.2187504	6.20621E-11	
13	Residual	18	4.526954104	0.25149745			
14	Total	19	51.360495				
15							
16		*Coefficients*	*Standard Error*	*t Stat*	*P-value*	*Lower 95%*	*Upper 95%*
17	Intercept	2.423044396	0.480964609	5.037885009	8.55388E-05	1.412574465	3.433514326
18	Customers	0.008729338	0.00063969	13.64619912	6.20621E-11	0.007385398	0.010073278

For each increase of one additional customer, there is an expected increase in weekly sales of 0.00873 thousands of dollars, or $8.73.

(d) $\hat{Y} = 2.423 + 0.00873X = 2.423 + 0.00873(600) = 7.661$, or $7661

(e) $b_0 = 1.578$, $b_1 = 0.01009$

For each increase in shelf space of an additional foot, there is an expected increase in weekly sales of 0.01009 thousands of dollars, or $10.09.

$\hat{Y} = 1.578 + 0.01009X = 1.578 + 0.01009(600) = 7.632$, or $7632

13.6

	A	B	C	D	E	F	G
1	Predicting Videos Sales						
2							
3	*Regression Statistics*						
4	Multiple R	0.853088695					
5	R Square	0.727760321					
6	Adjusted R Square	0.718037476					
7	Standard Error	47.8667885					
8	Observations	30					
9							
10	ANOVA						
11		*df*	*SS*	*MS*	*F*	*Significance F*	
12	Regression	1	171499.778	171499.778	74.85054744	2.1259E-09	
13	Residual	28	64154.42435	2291.229441			
14	Total	29	235654.2023				
15							
16		*Coefficients*	*Standard Error*	*t Stat*	*P-value*	*Lower 95%*	*Upper 95%*
17	Intercept	76.53514239	11.83184172	6.468573886	5.23655E-07	52.29868609	100.7715987
18	Gross	4.333108105	0.500843491	8.651621088	2.1259E-09	3.30717557	5.359040641

(c) $\hat{Y} = 76.54 + 4.3331X$

(d) For each increase of 1 million dollars in box office gross, expected home video units sold are estimated to increase by 4.3331 thousand, or 4333.1 units. 76.54 represents the portion of thousands of home video units that are not affected by box office gross.

(e) $\hat{Y} = 76.54 + 4.3331X = 76.54 + 4.3331(20) = 163.202$ or 163,202 units.

13.8

	A	B	C	D	E	F	G
1	Predicting Travel Time						
2							
3	*Regression Statistics*						
4	Multiple R	0.95793809					
5	R Square	0.917645385					
6	Adjusted R Square	0.909409923					
7	Standard Error	2.579237234					
8	Observations	12					
9							
10	ANOVA						
11		*df*	*SS*	*MS*	*F*	*Significance F*	
12	Regression	1	741.2582196	741.2582196	111.4261033	9.66059E-07	
13	Residual	10	66.52464708	6.652464708			
14	Total	11	807.7828667				
15							
16		*Coefficients*	*Standard Error*	*t Stat*	*P-value*	*Lower 95%*	*Upper 95%*
17	Intercept	3.374947947	2.610523714	1.292824091	0.225142125	-2.441662371	9.191558265
18	Distance	1.461229251	0.1384283	10.55585635	9.66059E-07	1.152791724	1.769666779

(c) For each increase of one mile in distance, the expected travel time is estimated to increase by 1.46 minutes. The Y-intercept 3.375 represents the portion of the travel time that is not affected by distance.

(d) $\hat{Y} = 3.375 + 1.46X = 3.375 + 1.46(21) = 34.035$ minutes

(e) $b_0 = 11.497$, $b_1 = 0.9673$

For each increase of one mile in distance, the expected travel time is estimated to increase by 0.9673 minutes. The Y-intercept 11.497 represents the portion of the travel time that is not affected by distance.

$\hat{Y} = 11.497 + 0.9673X = 11.497 + 0.9673(21) = 31.81$ minutes

•13.10 $SST = 40$ and $r^2 = 0.90$. So, 90% of the variation in the dependent variable can be explained by the variation in the independent variable.

13.12 $r^2 = 0.333$. So, 33.3% of the variation in the dependent variable can be explained by the variation in the independent variable.

•13.14 (a) $r^2 = 0.684$. So, 68.4% of the variation in the dependent variable can be explained by the variation in the independent variable.

      (b) $s_{YX} = 0.308$

      (c)   Based on (a) and (b), the model should be very useful for predicting sales.

•13.16 (a) $r^2 = 0.988$. So, 98.8% of the variation in the dependent variable can be explained by the variation in the independent variable.

      (b) $s_{YX} = 4.71$

      (c)   Based on (a) and (b), the model should be very useful for predicting sales.

13.18 (a) $r^2 = 0.723$. So, 72.3% of the variation in the dependent variable can be explained by the variation in the independent variable.

      (b) $s_{YX} = 194.6$

      (c)   Based on (a) and (b), the model should be very useful for predicting monthly rent.

•13.20   A residual analysis of the data indicates no apparent pattern. The assumptions of regression appear to be met.

•13.22 (a)-(b)   Based on a residual analysis, the model appears to be adequate.

•13.24 (a)-(b)   Based on a residual analysis, the model appears to be adequate.

13.26 (a)-(b)   Based on a residual analysis of the studentized residuals versus size, the model appears to be adequate.

•13.28 (a)   An increasing linear relationship exists.

      (b) $D = 0.109$

      (c)   There is strong positive autocorrelation among the residuals.

•13.30 (a)   No, since the data have been collected for a single period for a set of stores.

      (b)   If a single store was studied over a period of time and the amount of shelf space varied over time, computation of the Durbin-Watson statistic would be necessary.

13.32

	A	B	C	D	E	F
1	Regression Analysis		Durbin-Watson Calculations			
2						
3	*Regression Statistics*		Sum of Squared Difference of Residuals	1243.22442		
4	Multiple R	0.91880399	Sum of Squared Residuals	599.068347		
5	R Square	0.844200772	Durbin-Watson Statistic	2.07526308		
6	Adjusted R Square	0.837118989				
7	Standard Error	5.218273602				
8	Observations	24				
9						
10	ANOVA					
11		*df*	*SS*	*MS*	*F*	*Significance F*
12	Regression	1	3246.062049	3246.062049	119.2073751	2.38511E-10
13	Residual	22	599.0683465	27.23037939		
14	Total	23	3845.130396			
15						
16		*Coefficients*	*Standard Error*	*t Stat*	*P-value*	
17	Intercept	0.457625305	6.571882688	0.069633821	0.945114194	
18	Orders	0.016117564	0.001476209	10.918213	2.38511E-10	

(b) $b_0 = 0.458$, $b_1 = 0.0161$

(c)   For each increase of one order, the expected distribution cost is estimated to increase by 0.0161 thousand dollars, or \$16.10.

(d) $\hat{Y} = 0.458 + 0.0161X = 0.458 + 0.0161(4500) = 72.908$ or \$72,908

(e) $r^2 = 0.844$. So, 84.4% of the variation in distribution cost can be explained by the variation in the number of orders.

(f) $s_{YX} = 5.218$

(i) $D = 2.08 > 1.45$. There is no evidence of positive autocorrelation among the residuals.

(j)   Based on a residual analysis, the model appears to be adequate.

•13.34 (a) $t = b_1 / s_{b_1} = 4.5 / 1.5 = 3.00$

(b)   With n = 18, df = 18 − 2 = 16. $t_{16} = \pm 2.1199$

(c)   Reject H_0. There is evidence that the fitted linear regression model is useful.

(d) $b_0 - t_{16} s_{b_1} \le \beta_1 \le b_0 + t_{16} s_{b_1}$, $4.5 - 2.1199(1.5) \le \beta_1 \le 4.5 + 2.1199(1.5)$,
$1.32 \le \beta_1 \le 7.68$

•13.36 (a) $t = 4.65 > t_{10} = 2.2281$ with 10 degrees of freedom for $\alpha = 0.05$. Reject H_0. There is evidence that the fitted linear regression model is useful.

(b) $0.0386 \le \beta_1 \le 0.1094$

•13.38 (a) $t = 31.15 > t_{12} = 2.1788$ with 12 degrees of freedom for $\alpha = 0.05$. Reject H_0. There is evidence that the fitted linear regression model is useful.

(b) $1.8236 \le \beta_1 \le 2.0978$

13.40 (a) $t = 7.74 > t_{23} = 2.0687$ with 23 degrees of freedom for $\alpha = 0.05$. Reject H_0. There is evidence that the fitted linear regression model is useful.

(b) $0.7805 \le \beta_1 \le 1.3497$

13.42 (a) When $X = 2$, $\hat{Y} = 5 + 3X = 5 + 3(2) = 11$

$$h = \frac{1}{n} + \frac{(X_i - \bar{X})^2}{\sum_{i=1}^{n}(X_i - \bar{X})^2} = \frac{1}{20} + \frac{(2-2)^2}{20} = 0.05$$

95% confidence interval: $\hat{Y} \pm t_{18} s_{YX} \sqrt{h} = 11 \pm 2.1009 \cdot 1 \cdot \sqrt{0.05}$

$10.53 \le \mu_{YX} \le 11.47$

(b) 95% prediction interval: $\hat{Y} \pm t_{18} s_{YX} \sqrt{1+h} = 11 \pm 2.1009 \cdot 1 \cdot \sqrt{1.05}$

$8.847 \le Y_I \le 13.153$

•13.44 (a) $1.7867 \le \mu_{YX} \le 2.2964$

(b) $1.3100 \le Y_I \le 2.7740$

(c) Part (b) provides an estimate for an individual response and Part (a) provides an estimate for an average predicted value.

•13.46 (a) $98.08 \le \mu_{YX} \le 103.74$

(b) $90.27 \le Y_I \le 111.56$

(c) Part (b) provides an estimate for an individual response and Part (a) provides an estimate for an average predicted value.

13.48 (a) $1153.0 \le \mu_{YX} \le 1331.5$

(b) $829.9 \le Y_I \le 1654.6$

(c) Part (b) provides an estimate for an individual response and Part (a) provides an estimate for an average predicted value.

•13.50 $r = +\sqrt{r^2} = +\sqrt{81} = +0.9$

13.52 $r^2 = \text{SSR/SST} = 1.\ r = -\sqrt{r^2} = -\sqrt{1} = -1$

13.54 (a) $SSX = 217.64$, $SSY = 1958.73$, $SSXY = 652.91$.

$$r = \frac{SSXY}{\sqrt{SSX}\sqrt{SSY}} = \frac{652.91}{\sqrt{217.64}\sqrt{1958.73}} = +1.0$$

(b) $H_0 : \rho = 0, H_1 : \rho \ne 0$.

The test statistic t is positive infinity since $SSE = 0$ and $r = 1$. Reject H_0. There is evidence of an association between X and Y.

•13.56 (a) $r = -0.666$

(b) $H_0 : \rho = 0, H_1 : \rho \neq 0$.

    $t = -3.78 < -t_{18} = -2.1009$. Reject H_0. There is evidence of an association between average charge per minute and minutes expended.

(c)   Yes. As suspected, the correlation in the data is negative.

•13.58 (a) $r = +0.827$

(b) $t = 4.65 > t_{10} = 2.2281$. Reject H_0. There is evidence of an association between the two variables.

(c)   Except for possible rounding error, the results of the two t tests are identical.

•13.60 (a) $r = +0.994$

(b) $t = 31.15 > t_{12} = 2.1788$. Reject H_0. There is evidence of an association between the two variables.

(c)   Except for possible rounding error, the results of the two t tests are identical.

13.62 (a) $r = +0.850$

(b) $t = 7.74 > t_{23} = 2.0687$. Reject H_0. There is evidence of an association between the two variables.

(c)   Except for possible rounding error, the results of the two t tests are identical.

13.74

	Predicting Trade Executions		Durbin-Watson Calculations				
2							
3	*Regression Statistics*		Sum of Squared Difference of Res	56000.13401			
4	Multiple R	0.793770534	Sum of Squared Residuals	28560.83537			
5	R Square	0.63007166	Durbin-Watson Statistic	1.960731655			
6	Adjusted R Square	0.618861711					
7	Standard Error	29.41903907					
8	Observations	35					
9							
10	ANOVA						
11		*df*		*SS*	*MS*	*F*	*Significance F*
12	Regression	1		48645.56463	48645.56463	56.20646637	1.27826E-08
13	Residual	33		28560.83537	865.4798597		
14	Total	34		77206.4			
15							
16		*Coefficients*		*Standard Error*	*t Stat*	*P-value*	
17	Intercept	-63.02045762		54.59736729	-1.154276493	0.256677777	
18	Calls	0.189005684		0.025210515	7.497097196	1.27826E-08	

(b) $b_0 = -63.02, b_1 = 0.189$

(c) $\hat{Y} = -63.02 + 0.189X$, where X is the number of incoming calls and $\hat{Y}$ is the estimated number of trade executions.

(d)   For each additional incoming call, the estimated number of trade executions increases by 0.189 minutes. -63.02 is the portion of the estimated delivery time that is not affected by the number of incoming calls.

(e) $\hat{Y} = -63.02 + 0.189X = -63.02 + 0.189(2000) = 314.99$

(f)   No, 5000 incoming calls is outside the relevant range of the data used to fit the regression equation.

(g) $r^2 = 0.630$. So, 63.0% of the variation in trade executions can be explained by the variation in the number of incoming calls.

13.74 (h)   Since b_1 is positive, $r = +\sqrt{r^2} = +\sqrt{0.63} = +0.794$

cont. (i) $s_{YX} = 29.42$

      (j)   Based on a visual inspection of the graphs of the distribution of studentized residuals and the residuals versus the number of cases, there is no pattern. The model appears to be adequate.

      (k) $D = 1.96$

      (l) $D = 1.96 > 1.52$. There is no evidence of positive autocorrelation. The model appears to be adequate.

      (m) $t = 7.50 > t_{33} = 2.0345$ with 33 degrees of freedom for $\alpha = 0.05$. Reject H_0. There is evidence that the fitted linear regression model is useful.

(n), (o)

	A	B
1	Confidence Interval Estimate	
2		
3	X Value	2000
4	Confidence Level	95%
5	Sample Size	35
6	Degrees of Freedom	33
7	t Value	2.03451691
8	Sample Mean	2156.657143
9	Sum of Squared Difference	1361737.89
10	Standard Error of the Estimate	29.41903907
11	h Statistic	0.04659359
12	Average Predicted Y (YHat)	314.9909096
13		
14		
15	For Average Predicted Y (YHat)	
16	Interval Half Width	12.91971327
17	Confidence Interval Lower Limit	302.0711964
18	Confidence Interval Upper Limit	327.9106229
19		
20	For Individual Response Y	
21	Interval Half Width	61.23205321
22	Prediction Interval Lower Limit	253.7588564
23	Prediction Interval Upper Limit	376.2229628

      (p) $0.1377 \le \beta_1 \le 0.2403$

•13.76

	A	B	C	D	E	F	G
1	Predicting Assessed Value						
2							
3	Regression Statistics						
4	Multiple R	0.811995685					
5	R Square	0.659336993					
6	Adjusted R Square	0.633132146					
7	Standard Error	2.918927722					
8	Observations	15					
9							
10	ANOVA						
11		df	SS	MS	F	Significance F	
12	Regression	1	214.3741924	214.3741924	25.16087956	0.00023616	
13	Residual	13	110.7618076	8.520139046			
14	Total	14	325.136				
15							
16		Coefficients	Standard Error	t Stat	P-value	Lower 95%	Upper 95%
17	Intercept	51.91533994	5.562520886	9.333059777	3.98327E-07	39.89824648	63.9324334
18	Heating Area	16.63336947	3.316021403	5.016062157	0.00023616	9.469542149	23.79719679

•13.76
cont. (a) $b_0 = 51.915$, $b_1 = 16.633$

(b)   For each additional 1000 square feet in heating area, the estimated assessed value increases by \$16,633. \$51,915 is the portion of the estimated assessed value that is not affected by heating area.

(c) $\hat{Y} = 51.915 + 16.633X = 51.915 + 16.633(1.75) = 81.024$ or \$81,024

(d) $S_{YX} = 2.919$

(e) $r^2 = 0.659$. 65.9% of the variation in assessed value can be explained by the variation in heating area.

(f)   Since b_1 is positive, $r = +\sqrt{r^2} = +\sqrt{0.659} = +0.812$

(g)   Based on a visual inspection of the graphs of the distribution of studentized residuals and the residuals versus the heating area, there is no pattern. The model appears to be adequate.

(h) $t = 5.02 > t_{13} = 2.1604$ with 13 degrees of freedom for $\alpha = 0.05$. Reject H_0. There is evidence that the fitted linear regression model is useful.

(i) $79.279 \le \mu_{YX} \le 82.769$

(j) $74.479 \le Y_I \le 87.569$

(k) $9.469 \le \beta_1 \le 23.797$

(l) $b_0 = 52.805$, $b_1 = 15.849$
For each additional 1000 square feet in heating area, the estimated assessed value increases by \$15,849. \$52,805 is the portion of the estimated assessed value that is not affected by heating area.

$\hat{Y} = 52.805 + 15.849X = 52.805 + 15.849(1.75) = 80.541$ or \$80,541

$S_{YX} = 2.598$

$r^2 = 0.689$. 68.9% of the variation in assessed value can be explained by the variation in heating area.

Since b_1 is positive, $r = +\sqrt{r^2} = +\sqrt{0.689} = +0.83$

Based on a visual inspection of the graphs of the distribution of studentized residuals and the residuals versus the heating area, there is no pattern. The model appears to be adequate.

$t = 5.37 > t_{13} = 2.1604$ with 13 degrees of freedom for $\alpha = 0.05$. Reject H_0. There is evidence that the fitted linear regression model is useful.

$78.987 \le \mu_{YX} \le 82.096$

$74.716 \le Y_I \le 86.367$

$9.471 \le \beta_1 \le 22.227$

13.78 (a)

	A	B	C	D	E	F
1	Predicting Invoice Completion Time		Durbin-Watson Calculations			
2						
3	Regression Statistics		Sum of Squared Difference of Residuals	5.57539132		
4	Multiple R	0.944668576	Sum of Squared Residuals	3.12818443		
5	R Square	0.892398719	Durbin-Watson Statistic	1.78230902		
6	Adjusted R Square	0.888555816				
7	Standard Error	0.334246724				
8	Observations	30				
9						
10	ANOVA					
11		df	SS		MS	F	Significance F
12	Regression	1	25.94381557	25.94381557	232.2199511	4.3946E-15
13	Residual	28	3.128184432	0.111720873		
14	Total	29	29.072			
15						
16		Coefficients	Standard Error		t Stat	P-value	
17	Intercept	0.402374805	0.123582495	3.255920694	0.002954616	
18	Invoices Processed	0.012606814	0.000827286	15.23876475	4.3946E-15	

(b) $b_0 = 0.4024$, $b_1 = 0.012608$

(c) For each additional invoice processed, the estimated completion time increases by 0.012608 hours. 0.4024 is the portion of the estimated completion time that is not affected by the number of invoices processed.

(d) $\hat{Y} = 0.4024 + 0.012608X = 0.4024 + 0.012608(150) = 2.2934$

(e) $s_{YX} = 0.3342$

(f) $r^2 = 0.892$. 89.2% of the variation in completion time can be explained by the variation in the number of invoices processed.

(g) Since b_1 is positive, $r = +\sqrt{r^2} = +\sqrt{0.892} = +0.945$

(i) Based on a visual inspection of the graphs of the distribution of studentized residuals and the residuals versus the number of invoices, there is no pattern. The model appears to be adequate.

(j) $D = 1.78$

(k) $D = 1.78 > 1.49$. There is no evidence of positive autocorrelation. The model appears to be adequate.

(l) $t = 15.24 > t_{28} = 2.0484$ with 28 degrees of freedom for $\alpha = 0.05$. Reject H_0. There is evidence that the fitted linear regression model is useful.

(m), (n)

	A	B
1	Confidence Interval Estimate	
2		
3	X Value	150
4	Confidence Level	95%
5	Sample Size	30
6	Degrees of Freedom	28
7	t Value	2.048409442
8	Sample Mean	129.9
9	Sum of Squared Difference	163238.70
10	Standard Error of the Estimate	0.334246724
11	h Statistic	0.035808298
12	Average Predicted Y (YHat)	2.29339697
13		
14		
15	For Average Predicted Y (YHat)	
16	Interval Half Width	0.12956144
17	Confidence Interval Lower Limit	2.16383553
18	Confidence Interval Upper Limit	2.422958411
19		
20	For Individual Response Y	
21	Interval Half Width	0.696824836
22	Prediction Interval Lower Limit	1.596572134
23	Prediction Interval Upper Limit	2.990221807

CHAPTER 14

14.2 (a) Holding constant the effect of X_2, for each additional unit of X_1 the response variable Y is expected to decrease on average by 2 units. Holding constant the effect of X_1, for each additional unit of X_2 the response variable Y is expected to increase on average by 7 units.

(b) The Y-intercept 50 represents the portion of the measurement of Y that is not affected by the factors measured by X_1 and X_2.

(c) 40% of the variation in Y can be explained or accounted for by the variation in X_1 and the variation in X_2.

14.4

	A	B	C	D	E	F	G
1	Regression Analysis						
2							
3	*Regression Statistics*						
4	Multiple R	0.93591442					
5	R Square	0.875935802					
6	Adjusted R Square	0.864120164					
7	Standard Error	4.766165573					
8	Observations	24					
9							
10	ANOVA						
11		*df*	*SS*	*MS*	*F*	*Significance F*	
12	Regression	2	3368.087376	1684.043688	74.1336022	3.0429E-10	
13	Residual	21	477.0430196	22.71633427			
14	Total	23	3845.130396				
15							
16		*Coefficients*	*Standard Error*	*t Stat*	*P-value*	*Lower 95%*	*Upper 95%*
17	Intercept	-2.728246583	6.157879754	-0.443049668	0.662260247	-15.53426079	10.07776763
18	Sales	0.047113872	0.02032792	2.317692762	0.030643769	0.004839642	0.089388103
19	Orders	0.011946926	0.002248569	5.313123092	2.87239E-05	0.007270769	0.016623083

(a) $\hat{Y} = -2.72825 + 0.47114X_1 + 0.011947X_2$

(b) For a given number of orders, each increase of $1000 in sales is expected to result in an average increase in distribution cost by $471.14. For a given amount of sales, each increase of one order is expected to result in the average increase in distribution cost by $11.95.

(c) $\hat{Y}_i = -2.72825 + 0.47114(400) + 0.011947(4500) = 69.878$ or $69,878

(d) $r_{Y.12}^2 = SSR / SST = 3368.087 / 3845.13 = 0.8759$. So, 87.59% of the variation in distribution cost can be explained by variation in sales and variation in number of orders.

(e) $r_{adj}^2 = 1 - \left[(1 - r_{Y.12}^2) \dfrac{n-1}{n-p-1} \right] = 1 - \left[(1 - 0.8759) \dfrac{24-1}{24-2-1} \right] = 0.8641$

•14.6

	A	B	C	D	E	F	G
1	Regression Analysis of Sales						
2							
3	Regression Statistics						
4	Multiple R	0.899273236					
5	R Square	0.808692352					
6	Adjusted R Square	0.788554705					
7	Standard Error	158.9041256					
8	Observations	22					
9							
10	ANOVA						
11		df	SS	MS	F	Significance F	
12	Regression	2	2028032.69	1014016.345	40.15823435	1.50126E-07	
13	Residual	19	479759.9014	25250.52112			
14	Total	21	2507792.591				
15							
16		Coefficients	Standard Error	t Stat	P-value	Lower 95%	Upper 95%
17	Intercept	156.4304345	126.7578563	1.234088672	0.232217275	-108.8768901	421.7377592
18	RadioTV	13.08068096	1.759373685	7.434850861	4.88861E-07	9.398268369	16.76309354
19	Newspaper	16.79527808	2.963377915	5.667612623	1.83069E-05	10.59285489	22.99770127

(a) $\hat{Y} = 156.4 + 13.081X_1 + 16.795X_2$

(b)   For a given amount of newspaper advertising, each increase by $1000 in radio and television advertising is expected to result in an average increase in sales by $13,081. For a given amount of radio and television advertising, each increase by $1000 in newspaper advertising is expected to result in the average increase in sales by $16,795.

(c) $\hat{Y}_i = 156.4 + 13.081(20) + 16.795(20) = 753.95$ or $753,950

(d) $r^2_{Y.12} = SSR/SST = 2028033/2507793 = 0.8087$. So, 80.87% of the variation in sales can be explained by variation in radio and television advertising and variation in newspaper advertising.

(e) $r^2_{adj} = 1 - \left[(1 - r^2_{Y.12})\dfrac{n-1}{n-p-1}\right] = 1 - \left[(1 - 0.0.8087)\dfrac{22-1}{22-2-1}\right] = 0.7886$

14.8

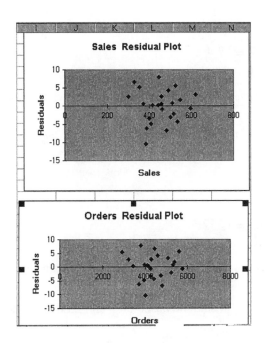

(a) Based upon a residual analysis the model appears adequate.

(b) There is no evidence of a pattern in the residuals versus time.

(c) $D = 2.26$

(d) $D = 2.26 > 1.55$. There is no evidence of positive autocorrelation in the residuals.

•14.10 There appears to be a curvilinear relationship in the plot of the residuals against both radio and television advertising. Thus, curvilinear terms for each of these explanatory models should be considered for inclusion in the model.

•14.12 (a) $MSR = SSR / p = 60 / 2 = 30$

$MSE = SSE / (n - p - 1) = 120 / 18 = 6.67$

(b) $F = MSR / MSE = 30 / 6.67 = 4.5$

(c) $F = 4.5 > F_{U(2,21-2-1)} = 3.555$. Reject H_0. There is evidence of a significant linear relationship.

•14.14 (a) $F = 97.69 > F_{U(2,15-2-1)} = 3.89$. Reject H_0. There is evidence of a significant linear relationship with at least one of the independent variables.

(b) The p value or probability of obtaining an F test statistic based on 2 and 12 degrees when H_0 is true is 0.0001.

14.16 (a) $MSR = SSR / p = 2451.974 / 2 = 1226.0$
$MSE = SSE / (n - p - 1) = 819.8681 / 47 = 17.4$
$F = MSR / MSE = 1226.0 / 17.4 = 70.28$
$F = 70.28 > F_{U(2, 50-2-1)} = 3.195$. Reject H_0. There is evidence of a significant linear relationship.

(b) The p value or probability of obtaining an F test statistic based on 2 and 47 degrees when H_0 is true is less than 0.001.

14.18 (a) $MSR = SSR / p = 27662.54 / 2 = 13831$
$MSE = SSE / (n - p - 1) = 28802.07 / 23 = 1252$
$F = MSR / MSE = 13831 / 1252 = 11.05$
$F = 11.05 > F_{U(2, 26-2-1)} = 3.422$. Reject H_0. There is evidence of a significant linear relationship.

(b) The p value or probability of obtaining an F test statistic based on 2 and 23 degrees when H_0 is true is less than 0.001.

14.20 (a) Variable X_1 has a larger slope than variable X_2.
(b) 95% confidence interval on $\beta_1 : b_1 \pm t_{n-p-1} s_{b_1}$, $4 \pm 2.1098 \cdot 1.2$
$1.46824 \le \beta_1 \le 6.53176$
(c) For X_1: $t = b_1 / s_{b_1} = 4 / 1.2 = 3.33 > t_{17} = 2.1098$ with 17 degrees of freedom for $\alpha = 0.05$. Reject H_0. There is evidence that the variable X_1 contributes to a model already containing X_2.
For X_2: $t = b_2 / s_{b_2} = 3 / 0.8 = 3.75 > t_{17} = 2.1098$ with 17 degrees of freedom for $\alpha = 0.05$. Reject H_0. There is evidence that the variable X_2 contributes to a model already containing X_1.
Both variables X_1 and X_2 should be included in the model.

14.22 (a) 95% confidence interval on $\beta_1 : b_1 \pm t_{n-p-1} s_{b_1}$, $0.471 \pm 2.0796 \cdot 0.0203$
$0.00488 \le \beta_1 \le 0.08932$
(b) For X_1: $t = b_1 / s_{b_1} = 0.0471 / 0.0203 = 2.32 > t_{21} = 2.0796$ with 21 degrees of freedom for $\alpha = 0.05$. Reject H_0. There is evidence that the variable X_1 contributes to a model already containing X_2.
For X_2: $t = b_2 / s_{b_2} = 0.01195 / 0.00225 = 5.31 > t_{21} = 2.0796$ with 21 degrees of freedom for $\alpha = 0.05$. Reject H_0. There is evidence that the variable X_2 contributes to a model already containing X_1.
Both variables X_1 and X_2 should be included in the model.

•14.24 (a)   95% confidence interval on β_1 : $b_1 \pm t_{n-p-1}s_{b_1}$, $13.0807 \pm 2.093 \cdot 1.7594$

$9.399 \le \beta_1 \le 16.763$

(b)   For X_1: $t = b_1 / s_{b_1} = 13.0807/1.7594 = 7.43 > t_{19} = 2.093$ with 19 degrees of freedom for $\alpha = 0.05$. Reject H_0. There is evidence that the variable X_1 contributes to a model already containing X_2.

For X_2: $t = b_2 / s_{b_2} = 16.7953/2.9634 = 5.67 > t_{19} = 2.093$ with 19 degrees of freedom for $\alpha = 0.05$. Reject H_0. There is evidence that the variable X_2 contributes to a model already containing X_1.

Both variables X_1 and X_2 should be included in the model.

•14.26 (a)   For X_1: $SSR(X_1|X_2) = SSR(X_1 \text{ and } X_2) - SSR(X_2) = 60 - 25 = 35$

$$F = \frac{SSR(X_1|X_2)}{MSE} = \frac{35}{120/18} = 5.25 > F_{U(1,18)} = 4.41 \text{ with 1 and 18 degrees of freedom}$$

and $\alpha = 0.05$. Reject H_0. There is evidence that the variable X_1 contributes to a model already containing X_2.

For X_2: $SSR(X_2|X_1) = SSR(X_1 \text{ and } X_2) - SSR(X_1) = 60 - 45 = 15$

$$F = \frac{SSR(X_2|X_1)}{MSE} = \frac{15}{120/18} = 2.25 < F_{U(1,18)} = 4.41 \text{ with 1 and 18 degrees of freedom}$$

and $\alpha = 0.05$. Do not reject H_0. There is not sufficient evidence that the variable X_2 contributes to a model already containing X_1.

Since variable X_2 does not significantly contribute to the model in the presence of X_1, only variable X_1 should be included and a simple linear regression model should be developed.

(b) $$r_{Y1.2} = \frac{SSR(X_1|X_2)}{SST - SSR(X_1 \text{ and } X_2) + SSR(X_1|X_2)} = \frac{35}{180 - 60 + 35}$$

$= 0.2258$. Holding constant the effect of variable X_2, 22.58% of the variation in Y can be explained by the variation in variable X_1.

$$r_{Y2.1} = \frac{SSR(X_2|X_1)}{SST - SSR(X_1 \text{ and } X_2) + SSR(X_2|X_1)} = \frac{15}{180 - 60 + 15}$$

$= 0.1111$. Holding constant the effect of variable X_1, 11.11% of the variation in Y can be explained by the variation in variable X_2.

14.28 (a)   For X_1:

$$SSR(X_1|X_2) = SSR(X_1 \text{ and } X_2) - SSR(X_2) = 3368.087 - 3246.062 = 122.025$$

$$F = \frac{SSR(X_1|X_2)}{MSE} = \frac{122.025}{477.043/21} = 5.37 > F_{U(1,21)} = 4.325 \text{ with 1 and 21 degrees of freedom}$$

and $\alpha = 0.05$. Reject H_0. There is evidence that the variable X_1 contributes to a model already containing X_2.

14.28 (a)
cont.

For X_2:

$$SSR(X_2|X_1) = SSR(X_1 \text{ and } X_2) - SSR(X_1) = 3368.087 - 2726.822 = 641.265$$

$$F = \frac{SSR(X_2|X_1)}{MSE} = \frac{641.265}{477.043/21} = 28.23 > F_{U(1,21)} = 4.325 \text{ with 1 and 21 degrees of freedom and}$$

$\alpha = 0.05$. Reject H_0. There is evidence that the variable X_2 contributes to a model already containing X_1.

Since each independent variable X_1 and X_2 makes a significant contribution to the model in the presence of the other variable, both variables should be included in the model.

(b)

$$r_{Y1.2} = \frac{SSR(X_1|X_2)}{SST - SSR(X_1 \text{ and } X_2) + SSR(X_1|X_2)}$$

$$= \frac{122.025}{3845.13 - 3368.087 + 122.025} = 0.2037. \text{ Holding constant the effect of the number of}$$

orders, 20.37% of the variation in Y can be explained by the variation in sales.

$$r_{Y2.1} = \frac{SSR(X_2|X_1)}{SST - SSR(X_1 \text{ and } X_2) + SSR(X_2|X_1)}$$

$$= \frac{641.265}{3845.13 - 3368.087 + 641.265} = 0.5734. \text{ Holding constant the effect of sales, 57.34\%}$$

of the variation in Y can be explained by the variation in the number of orders.

•14.30 (a)   For X_1:

$$SSR(X_1|X_2) = SSR(X_1 \text{ and } X_2) - SSR(X_2) = 2028033 - 632259.4 = 1395773.6$$

$$F = \frac{SSR(X_1|X_2)}{MSE} = \frac{1395773.6}{479759.9/19} = 55.28 > F_{U(1,19)} = 4.381 \text{ with 1 and 19 degrees of}$$

freedom and $\alpha = 0.05$. Reject H_0. There is evidence that the variable X_1 contributes to a model already containing X_2.

For X_2:

$$SSR(X_2|X_1) = SSR(X_1 \text{ and } X_2) - SSR(X_1) = 2028033 - 1216940 = 811093$$

$$F = \frac{SSR(X_2|X_1)}{MSE} = \frac{811093}{479759.9/19} = 32.12 > F_{U(1,19)} = 4.381 \text{ with 1 and 19 degrees of freedom}$$

and $\alpha = 0.05$. Reject H_0. There is evidence that the variable X_2 contributes to a model already containing X_1.

Since each independent variable X_1 and X_2 makes a significant contribution to the model in the presence of the other variable, both variables should be included in the model.

•14.30 (b)

	A	B	C	D
1	Regression Analysis			
2	Coefficients of Partial Determination			
3				
4	SSR(X1,X2)	2028032.69		
5	SST	2507792.591		
6	SSR(X2)	632259.4483	SSR(X1 | X2)	1395773.241
7	SSR(X1)	1216939.671	SSR(X2 | X1)	811093.0188
8				
9	r2 Y1.2	0.744200787		
10	r2 Y2.1	0.628338834		

Holding constant the effect of newspaper advertising, 74.42% of the variation in Y can be explained by the variation in radio and television advertising.

Holding constant the effect of radio and television advertising, 62.83% of the variation in Y can be explained by the variation in newspaper advertising.

•14.32 (a) $\hat{Y} = 5 + 3X + 1.5X^2 = 5 + 3(2) + 1.5(2^2) = 17$

(b) $t = 2.35 > t_{22} = 2.0739$ with 22 degrees of freedom. Reject H_0. The curvilinear term is significant.

(c) $t = 1.17 < t_{22} = 2.0739$ with 22 degrees of freedom. Do not reject H_0. The curvilinear term is not significant.

(d) $\hat{Y} = 5 - 3X + 1.5X^2 = 5 - 3(2) + 1.5(2^2) = 5$

14.34 (b) $\hat{Y} = 4.181 + 0.438X + 1.1905X^2$

(c) $\hat{Y} = 4.181 + 0.438(2.5) + 1.1905(2.5^2) = 12.72$

(d)   A residual analysis indicates no strong patterns.

(e) $F = 62.44 > F_{2,12} = 3.89$. Reject H_0. The overall model is significant. The p-value < 0.001.

(f) $t = 2.92 > t_{12} = 2.1788$. Reject H_0. The curvilinear effect is significant. The p-value $= 0.013$.

(g) $r_{Y.12}^2 = 0.912$. So, 91.2% of the variation in number of errors can be explained by the curvilinear relationship between number of errors and alcohol consumption.

(h) $r_{adj}^2 = 0.898$

14.36

	A	B	C	D	E	F	G
1	Predicting County Taxes						
2							
3	Regression Statistics						
4	Multiple R	0.967237191					
5	R Square	0.935547783					
6	Adjusted R Square	0.927491256					
7	Standard Error	48.40760315					
8	Observations	19					
9							
10	ANOVA						
11		df	SS	MS	F	Significance F	
12	Regression	2	544220.9475	272110.4738	116.1229605	2.97785E-10	
13	Residual	16	37492.73668	2343.296042			
14	Total	18	581713.6842				
15							
16		Coefficients	Standard Error	t Stat	P-value	Lower 95%	Upper 95%
17	Intercept	857.5883743	25.18944815	34.04554039	2.33404E-16	804.1891418	910.9876069
18	Age	-24.72208658	2.623757479	-9.422397754	6.24459E-08	-30.28420271	-19.15997045
19	Agesquared	0.293538926	0.051216368	5.731349866	3.09249E-05	0.1849651	0.402112752

(b) $\hat{Y} = 857.59 - 24.722X + 0.2935X^2$

(c) $\hat{Y} = 857.59 - 24.722(20) + 0.2935(20^2) = 480.6$

(d)   A residual analysis reveals patterns in the residuals vs. age, vs. the curvilinear variable (age squared), and vs. the fitted values.

(e) $F = 116.12 > F_{2,17} = 3.59$. Reject H_0. The overall model is significant.

(f)   The p-value < 0.001 indicates that the probability of having an F-test statistic of at least 116.12 when $\beta_1 = 0$ and $\beta_2 = 0$ is less than 0.001.

(g) $t = 5.73 > t_{17} = 2.1098$. Reject H_0. The curvilinear effect is significant.

(h)   The p-value < 0.001 indicates that the probability of having a t-test statistic with an absolute value of at least 5.73 when $\beta_2 = 0$ is less than 0.001.

(i) $r^2_{Y.12} = 0.936$. So, 93.6% of the variation in taxes can be explained by the curvilinear relationship between taxes and age of the house.

(j) $r^2_{adj} = 0.927$

14.38   (a)   First develop a multiple regression model using X_1 as the variable for the SAT score and X_2 a dummy variable with $X_2 = 1$ if a student had a grade of B or better in the introductory statistics course. If the dummy variable coefficient is significantly different than zero, you need to develop a model with the interaction term $X_1 X_2$ to make sure that the coefficient of X_1 is not significantly different if $X_2 = 0$ or $X_2 = 1$.

      (b)   If a student received a grade of B or better in the introductory statistics course, the student would be expected to have a grade point average in accountancy that is 0.30 higher than a student who had the same SAT score, but did not get a grade of B or better in the introductory statistics course.

14.40   (a) $\hat{Y} = 2.9682 + 0.0393X_1 + 0.1228X_2$, where X_1 = median assessed value of homes and X_2 = ATM location.

      (b)   Holding constant the effect of ATM location, for each additional thousand dollars of median assessed value, withdrawal amounts are expected to increase on average by 0.0393 thousands of dollars, or $39.30. For a given median assessed value of homes, a shopping center location is expected to increase withdrawal amounts on average by 0.1228 thousands of dollars, or $122.80.

14.40   (c) $\hat{Y} = 2.9682 + 0.0393(200) + 0.1228(1) = 10.95$ or $10,950

      (d)   Based on a residual analysis, the model appears adequate.

(e) $F = 1642.59 > F_{2,12} = 3.89$. Reject H_0. There is evidence of a relationship between withdrawal amounts and the two dependent variables.

(f)   For X_1: $t = 53.52 > t_{12} = 2.1788$. Reject H_0. Median assessed value of homes makes a significant contribution and should be included in the model.

For X_2: $t = 2.25 > t_{12} = 2.1788$. Reject H_0. ATM location makes a significant contribution and should be included in the model.

(g) $0.0377 \le \beta_1 \le 0.0409$, $0.0039 \le \beta_2 \le 0.2418$

(h) $r^2_{Y.12} = 0.996$. So, 99.6% of the variation in withdrawal amounts can be explained by variation in median assessed value of homes and variation in ATM location.

(i) $r^2_{adj} = 0.996$

(j) $r^2_{Y1.2} = 0.996$. Holding constant the effect of ATM location, 99.6% of the variation in withdrawal amounts can be explained by variation in median assessed value of homes.

$r^2_{Y2.1} = 0.297$. Holding constant the effect of value of homes, 29.7% of the variation in withdrawal amounts can be explained by variation in ATM location.

(k)   The slope of withdrawal amount with median assessed value of home is the same regardless of whether the ATM is located in a shopping center or not.

(l) $\hat{Y} = 2.896 + 0.0392X_1 + 0.095X_2 + 0.00015X_1X_2$.

For $X_1 X_2$: the p-value is 0.926. Do not reject H_0. There is not evidence that the interaction term makes a contribution to the model.

(m)   The two-variable model in (a) should be used.

14.42

	A	B	C	D	E	F	G
1	Predicting Total Cost						
2							
3	*Regression Statistics*						
4	Multiple R	0.890548183					
5	R Square	0.793076067					
6	Adjusted R Square	0.787701419					
7	Standard Error	2.715390278					
8	Observations	80					
9							
10	ANOVA						
11		*df*	*SS*	*MS*	*F*	*Significance F*	
12	Regression	2	2176.002359	1088.001179	147.5587096	4.55736E-27	
13	Residual	77	567.747516	7.373344364			
14	Total	79	2743.749875				
15							
16		*Coefficients*	*Standard Error*	*t Stat*	*P-value*	*Lower 95%*	*Upper 95%*
17	Intercept	-3.467096383	3.083353539	-1.124456323	0.264312662	-9.60684507	2.672652303
18	Type of School	8.12843951	0.717002785	11.33669168	4.37476E-18	6.700702841	9.556176179
19	Average Total SAT	0.016080183	0.002776169	5.792219565	1.43648E-07	0.010552117	0.021608249

(a) $\hat{Y} = -3.467 + 0.01608X_1 + 8.12864X_2$, where X_1 = average total SAT score and X_2 = type of institution (public = 0, private = 1).

(b)   Holding constant the effect of type of institution, for each point increase on the average SAT, the total cost is expected to increase on average by 0.1608 thousands of dollars, or $160.80. For a given average SAT score, a private college or university is expected to increase total cost over a public institution by 8.12864 thousands of dollars, or $8,128.64.

14.42
cont. (c) $\hat{Y} = -3.467 + 0.01608(1000) + 8.12864(0) = 12.613$ or $12,613

(d) Based on a residual analysis, the model appears adequate.

(e) $F = 147.56 > F_{2,77} = 3.1154$. Reject H_0. There is evidence of a relationship between total cost and the two dependent variables.

(f) For X_1: $t = 5.79 > t_{77} = 1.9913$. Reject H_0. Average total SAT score makes a significant contribution and should be included in the model.

For X_2: $t = 11.34 > t_{77} = 1.9913$. Reject H_0. Type of institution makes a significant contribution and should be included in the model.

(g) $0.0106 \le \beta_1 \le 0.0216$, $6.7007 \le \beta_2 \le 9.5562$

(h) $r^2_{Y.12} = 0.793$. 79.3% of the variation in total cost can be explained by variation in average SAT score and variation in type of institution.

(i) $r^2_{adj} = 0.788$

(j)

	A	B	C	D
1	Predicting Total Cost			
2	Coefficients of Partial Determination			
3				
4	SSR(X1,X2)	2176.002359		
5	SST	2743.749875		
6	SSR(X2)	1228.375878	SSR(X1 | X2)	947.6264808
7	SSR(X1)	1928.628075	SSR(X2 | X1)	247.374284
8				
9	r2 Y1.2	0.625341653		
10	r2 Y2.1	0.303481374		

Holding constant the effect of average SAT score, 62.5% of the variation in total cost can be explained by variation in type of institution.

(k) The slope of total cost with average SAT score is the same regardless of whether the institution is public or private.

(l)

	A	B	C	D	E	F	G
1	Interation Model for Predicting Total Cost						
2							
3	Regression Statistics						
4	Multiple R	0.895002968					
5	R Square	0.801030313					
6	Adjusted R Square	0.793176246					
7	Standard Error	2.680148892					
8	Observations	80					
9							
10	ANOVA						
11		df	SS	MS	F	Significance F	
12	Regression	3	2197.82682	732.6089402	101.9892437	1.42462E-26	
13	Residual	76	545.9230545	7.183198086			
14	Total	79	2743.749875				
15							
16		Coefficients	Standard Error	t Stat	P-value	Lower 95%	Upper 95%
17	Intercept	5.546801449	6.000353953	0.924412375	0.3581975	-6.403954486	17.49755738
18	Type of School	-4.27400243	7.150426227	-0.597726946	0.551799088	-18.51532875	9.967323887
19	Average Total SAT	0.007857324	0.005455545	1.44024545	0.153904874	-0.00300835	0.018722998
20	Type*SAT	0.010997125	0.006309084	1.743062048	0.085367166	-0.001568521	0.023562771

$\hat{Y} = 5.547 + 0.0079X_1 - 4.274X_2 + 0.011X_1X_2$.

For X_1X_2: the p-value is 0.085. Do not reject H_0. There is not evidence that the interaction term makes a contribution to the model.

•14.44 (a) $\ln \hat{Y} = 4.62 + 0.5(8.5) + 0.7(5.2) = 12.51$

   $\hat{Y} = e^{12.51} = 271,034.12$

   (b) Holding constant the effects of X_2, for each additional unit of X_1 the natural logarithm of Y is expected to increase on average by 0.5. Holding constant the effects of X_1, for each additional unit of X_2 the natural logarithm of Y is expected to increase on average by 0.7.

•14.46 (a) $\ln \hat{Y} = 2.3882 + 0.004557 X_1$

   (b) $\ln \hat{Y} = 2.3882 + 0.004557(55) = 2.6388$

   $\hat{Y} = e^{2.6388} = 14.00$ miles per gallon.

   (c) The residual analysis indicates a clear curvilinear pattern. The model does not adequately fit the data.

   (d) $t = 1.10 < t_{26} = 2.0555$. Do not reject H_0. The model does not provide a significant relationship.

   (e) $r^2_{Y.12} = 0.045$. Only 4.5% of the variation in the natural logarithm of miles per gallon can be explained by variation in the highway speed.

   (f) $r^2_{adj} = 0.008$

   (g) The curvilinear model in Problem 14.33 is far superior to the inadequate models developed here and in Problem 14.45. The transformation of square root of highway speed or the natural logarithm of miles per gallon did virtually nothing to enhance the fit.

14.48 (a) $\hat{Y} = 4.666 + 5.0685\sqrt{X_1}$

   (b) $\hat{Y} = 4.666 + 5.0685\sqrt{55} = 42.255$ pounds

   (c) The residual analysis does not indicate clear patterns.

   (d) $t = 12.86 > t_{10} = 2.2281$. Reject H_0. The model provides a significant relationship.

   (e) $r^2_{Y.12} = 0.943$. So, 94.3% of the variation in yield can be explained by variation in the square root of the amount of fertilizer applied.

   (f) $r^2_{adj} = 0.937$

   (g) The curvilinear model in Problem 14.35 is slightly better than the model here. Both this model and the model in Problem 14.35 are better than the model in Problem 14.47.

14.50 $VIF = \dfrac{1}{1-0.5} = 2.0$

14.52 $R_1^2 = 0.008464$, $VIF_1 = \dfrac{1}{1-0.008464} = 1.009$

   $R_2^2 = 0.008464$, $VIF_2 = \dfrac{1}{1-0.008464} = 1.009$

   There is no reason to suspect the existence of collinearity.

•14.54 (a) $$C_p = \frac{(1-R_p^2)(n-T)}{1-R_T^2} - [n - 2(p+1)] = \frac{(1-0.274)(40-7)}{1-0.653} - [40 - 2(2+1)]$$
$$= 35.04$$

(b) C_p overwhelmingly exceeds $p + 1 = 3$, the number of parameters (including the Y-intercept), so this model does not meet the criterion for further consideration as a best model.

•14.56 Let Y = selling price, X_1 = assessed value, X_2 = time period, and X_3 = whether house was new (0 = no, 1 = yes).

Based on a full regression model involving all of the variables, all of the VIF values (1.3, 1.0, and 1.3, respectively) are less than 5. There is no reason to suspect the existence of collinearity.

	A	B	C	D	E	F	G
1	Predicting Assessed Value						
2							
3	R2T	0.944827					
4	1 - R2T	0.055173					
5	n	30					
6	T	4					
7	n - T	26					
8							Consider
9		Cp	p+1	R Square	Adj. R Square	Std. Error	This Model?
10	X1	9.058101	2	0.925606	0.922948943	3.474934	No
11	X1X2	9.306584	3	0.929323	0.924087276	3.449169	No
12	X1X2X3	4	4	0.944827	0.93846131	3.105498	Yes
13	X1X3	2.848067	3	0.943028	0.938807597	3.096749	Yes
14	X2	371.6988	2	0.156074	0.125933484	11.70387	No
15	X2X3	336.853	3	0.234261	0.177540021	11.3531	No
16	X3	415.2237	2	0.063713	0.030273923	12.32769	No

Based on a best subsets regression and examination of the resulting C_p values, the best models appear to be a model with variables X_1 and X_2, which has $C_p = 2.8$, and the full regression model, which has $C_p = 4.0$. Based on a regression analysis with all original variables, variable X_3 fails to make a significant contribution to the model at the 0.05 level. Thus, the best model is the model using assessed value (X_1) and time (X_2) as the independent variables.

A residual analysis shows no strong patterns.

The final model is: $\hat{Y} = -44.988 + 1.7506X_1 + 0.368X_2$
$r_{Y.12}^2 = 0.943$, $r_{adj}^2 = 0.939$
Overall significance of the model: $F = 223.46$, $p < 0.001$
Each independent variable is significant at the 0.05 level.

14.58   Let Y = gasoline mileage, X_1 = weight, X_2 = width, X_3 = length, and X_4 = type of drive.

Based on a full regression model involving all of the variables:
$VIF_1 = 8.1$, $VIF_2 = 4.9$, $VIF_3 = 8.6$, $VIF_4 = 1.6$
Variable X_3 dropped from the model.

Based on regression model for remaining variables, all VIF values are less than 5.

A residual analysis shows no strong patterns. However, the p-values for the t-test statistics Variables X_2 and X_4 are 0.445 and 0.126, respectively. X_2 dropped from the analysis since it is not significant at the 0.05 level.

Based on a regression model using X_1 and X_4, the t-test statistic for variable X_4 has a p-value of 0.123 and should be dropped from the analysis.

The resulting model: $\hat{Y} = 47.885 - 0.0078538X_1$
$r^2 = 0.820$

Overall significance of the model: $F = 396.35$, $p < 0.001$

14.70   (a) $\hat{Y} = -44.988 + 1.7506X_1 + 0.368X_2$,
                where X_1 = assessed value (in thousands of dollars) and X_2 = time period (in months).
        (b)   Holding constant the effects of time period, for each additional thousand dollars in assessed value the selling price of the house is expected to increase on the average by 1.7506 thousands of dollars, or $1,750.60. Holding constant the effects of assessed value, for each additional month the selling price of the house is expected to increase on the average by 0.368 thousands of dollars, or $368.
        (c) $\hat{Y} = -44.988 + 1.7506(70) + 0.368(12) = 81.969$ or $81,969
        (d)   All four residual plots indicate that the fitted model appears to be adequate.
        (e) $F = 301.27 > F_{U(2,26)} = 3.369$ with 2 and 26 degrees of freedom. Reject H_0. At least one of the independent variables is linearly related to the dependent variable.
        (f)   The p value is less than 0.001. This means that the probability of obtaining an F test statistic of 301.27 or greater if there were not relationship between the dependent variable and independent variables is less than 0.001.
        (g) $r^2_{Y.12} = 0.959$. So, 95.9% of the variation in selling price can be explained by the variation in assessed value and the variation in time period.
        (h) $r^2_{adj} = 0.955$
        (i)   For X_1: $t = 22.53 > t_{26} = 2.0555$ with 26 degrees of freedom. Reject H_0. There is evidence that X_1 significantly contributes to a model already containing X_2. For X_2:
                $t = 4.59 > t_{26} = 2.0555$ with 26 degrees of freedom. Reject H_0. There is evidence that X_2 significantly contributes to a model already containing X_1. Therefore, each independent variable makes a significant contribution in the presence of the other variable, and both variables should be included in the model.

14.70
cont.

(j) For X_1, the p value is less than 0.001. This means the probability of obtaining a t-test statistic which differs from zero by 22.53 or more (positively or negatively) when the null hypothesis that $\beta_1 = 0$ is true is less than 0.001. For X_2, the p value is less than 0.001. This means the probability of obtaining a t-test statistic which differs from zero by 4.59 or more (positively or negatively) when the null hypothesis that $\beta_2 = 0$ is true is less than 0.001.

(k) $1.509 \le \beta_1 \le 1.812$. This is a net regression coefficient. That is, taking into account the time period, this coefficient measures the expected average increase in selling price for each additional thousand dollars in assessed value. In Problem 13.75 the coefficient did not take into account (and hold constant) the effects of the time period.

(l) $r_{Y1.2} = 0.9513$. For a given time period, 95.13% of the variation in selling price can be explained by variation in assessed value. $r_{Y2.1} = 0.4481$. For a given assessed value, 44.81% of the variation in selling price can be explained by variation in time period.

14.72 (a) $\hat{Y} = -21.864 + 0.0239X_1 + 2.5191X_2$,
where X_1 = average SAT and X_2 = room and board expenses (in thousands of dollars).

(b) Holding constant the effects of room and board expenses, for each additional point of average SAT score the annual total cost is expected to increase on the average by 0.0239 thousands of dollars, or \$23.90. Holding constant the effects of average SAT score, for each additional thousand dollars of room and board expense the annual total cost is expected to increase on the average by 2.5191 thousands of dollars, or \$2519.10.

(c) $\hat{Y} = -21.864 + 0.0239(1100) + 2.5191(5.0) = 17.045$ or \$17,045

(d) All four residual plots indicate that the fitted model appears to be adequate.

(e) $F = 100.15 > F_{U(2,77)} = 3.1154$ with 2 and 77 degrees of freedom. Reject H_0. At least one of the independent variables is linearly related to the dependent variable.

(f) The p value is less than 0.001. This means that the probability of obtaining an F test statistic of 100.15 or greater if there were not relationship between the dependent variable and independent variables is less than 0.001.

(g) $r^2_{Y.12} = 0.722$. 72.2% of the variation in annual cost can be explained by the variation in average SAT score and the variation in room and board expense.

(h) $r^2_{adj} = 0.715$

(i) For X_1: $t = 8.14 > t_{77} = 1.9913$ with 77 degrees of freedom. Reject H_0. There is evidence that X_1 significantly contributes to a model already containing X_2. For X_2: $t = 8.73 > t_{77} = 1.9913$ with 77 degrees of freedom. Reject H_0. There is evidence that X_2 significantly contributes to a model already containing X_1. Therefore, each independent variable makes a significant contribution in the presence of the other variable, and both variables should be included in the model.

(j) For X_1, the p value is less than 0.001. This means the probability of obtaining a t-test statistic which differs from zero by 8.14 or more (positively or negatively) when the null hypothesis that $\beta_1 = 0$ is true is less than 0.001. For X_2, the p value is less than 0.001. This means the probability of obtaining a t-test statistic which differs from zero by 8.73 or more (positively or negatively) when the null hypothesis that $\beta_2 = 0$ is true is less than 0.001.

(k) $0.0181 \le \beta_1 \le 0.0298$. This is a net regression coefficient. That is, taking into account the room and board expense, this coefficient measures the expected average increase in annual total cost for each point in average SAT score.

(l) $r_{Y1.2} = 0.4626$. For a given room and board expense, 46.26% of the variation in annual total cost can be explained by variation in average SAT score. $r_{Y2.1} = 0.4972$. For a given average SAT score, 49.72% of the variation in annual total cost can be explained by variation in room and board expense.

(m) Room and board expense is a minor component of annual total cost of attending a college or university. The remaining components tend to rise when room and board expenses rise.

14.74 (a) $\hat{Y} = 74.067 - 13.895X_1 + 0.0879X_2$, where X_1 = team E.R.A. and X_2 = runs scored.

(b) Holding constant the effects of runs scored, for each additional point of team E.R.A. the number of wins is expected to decrease on the average by 13.895 wins. Holding constant the effects of team E.R.A., for each additional run scored the number of wins is expected to increase on the average by 0.879 wins.

(c) $\hat{Y} = 74.067 - 13.895(4.00) + 0.0879(750) = 84.417$ wins

(d) All four residual plots indicate that the fitted model appears to be adequate.

(e) $F = 54.78 > F_{U(2,25)} = 3.3852$ with 2 and 25 degrees of freedom. Reject H_0. At least one of the independent variables is linearly related to the dependent variable.

(f) The p value is less than 0.001. This means that the probability of obtaining an F test statistic of 54.78 or greater if there were not relationship between the dependent variable and independent variables is less than 0.001.

(g) $r_{Y.12}^2 = 0.814$. 81.4% of the variation in team wins can be explained by the variation in team E.R.A. and the variation in team runs scored.

(h) $r_{adj}^2 = 0.799$

(i) For X_1: $t = -8.80 < -t_{25} = -2.0595$ with 25 degrees of freedom. Reject H_0. There is evidence that X_1 significantly contributes to a model already containing X_2. For X_2: $t = 7.79 > t_{25} = 2.0595$ with 25 degrees of freedom. Reject H_0. There is evidence that X_2 significantly contributes to a model already containing X_1. Therefore, each independent variable makes a significant contribution in the presence of the other variable, and both variables should be included in the model.

(j) For X_1, the p value is less than 0.001. This means the probability of obtaining a t-test statistic which differs from zero by 8.80 or more (positively or negatively) when the null hypothesis that $\beta_1 = 0$ is true is less than 0.001. For X_2, the p value is less than 0.001. This means the probability of obtaining a t-test statistic which differs from zero by 7.79 or more (positively or negatively) when the null hypothesis that $\beta_2 = 0$ is true is less than 0.001.

(k) $-17.1484 \le \beta_1 \le -10.642$. This is a net regression coefficient. That is, taking into account the number of runs scored, this coefficient measures the expected average increase in team wins for each point in team E.R.A.

14.74 (l)
cont.
$r_{Y1.2} = 0.7558$. For a given number of team wins, 75.58% of the variation in team wins can be explained by variation in team E.R.A.. $r_{Y2.1} = 0.7082$. For a given team E.R.A., 70.82% of the variation in team wins can be explained by variation in runs scored.

(m) Pitching as measured by team E.R.A. is slightly more important in predicting wins, based on the t-test statistics and coefficients of partial determination. However, both measures are important in predicting wins.

14.76 (a) $\hat{Y} = 132.50 - 11.461X_1 - 2.563X_2$,
where X_1 = team E.R.A. and X_2 = league (American = 0, National = 1).

(b) Holding constant the effect of league, for each E.R.A. point, team wins are expected to decrease on average by 11.461. For a team E.R.A., being in the National League as opposed to the American League is expected to decrease team wins on average by 2.563.

(c) $\hat{Y} = 132.50 - 11.461(4.00) - 2.563(0) = 86.65$ wins

(d) Based on a residual analysis, the model appears adequate.

(e) $F = 7.64 > F_{2,25} = 3.39$. Reject H_0. There is evidence of a relationship between team wins and the two dependent variables.

(f) For X_1: $t = -3.87 < -t_{25} = -2.0595$. Reject H_0. Team E.R.A. makes a significant contribution and should be included in the model.
For X_2: $t = -0.81 > -t_{25} = -2.0595$. Do not reject H_0. League does not make a significant contribution and should not be included in the model.

(g) $-17.5548 \leq \beta_1 \leq -5.3679$, $-9.0676 \leq \beta_2 \leq 3.9419$

(h) The slope here takes into account the effect of the other predictor variable, league, while the solution for Problem 13.79 did not.

(i) $r^2_{Y.12} = 0.379$. 37.9% of the variation in team wins can be explained by variation in team E.R.A. and variation in league.

(j) $r^2_{adj} = 0.330$

(k) $r^2_{Y.12} = 0.379$ while $r^2 = 0.363$. The inclusion of the league variable has resulted in the increase.

(l) $r^2_{Y1.2} = 0.375$. Holding constant the effect of league, 37.5% of the variation in team wins can be explained by variation in team E.R.A..
$r^2_{Y2.1} = 0.026$. Holding constant the effect of team E.R.A., 2.6% of the variation in team wins can be explained by variation in league.

(m) The slope of team wins with team E.R.A. is the same regardless of which the league the team is in.

(n) $\hat{Y} = 145.34 - 14.274X_1 - 22.86X_2 + 4.583X_1X_2$.
For the X_1X_2 coefficient: the p-value is 0.462. Do not reject H_0. There is not evidence that the interaction term makes a contribution to the model.

(o) A simple regression model with team E.R.A. as the independent variable should be used.

14.78 An analysis of the linear regression model with all possible independent variables reveals that one of the variables, annual total cost, has a VIF value (6.9) in excess of 5.0. Based on the procedure recommended in the text, this variable should be deleted from the model.

An analysis of the linear regression model with the remaining independent variables indicates none of the remaining variables have a VIF value that is 5.0 or larger. A best subsets regression produces several subsets of variables with C_p values at or below $p + 1$. The following variables belong to most of the subsets with better C_p values:
X_2 = Type of institution (0=public, 1=private)
X_3 = Average total SAT Score
X_4 = TOEFL Criterion at least 550 (0=no, 1=yes)
For a linear regression model fit to these three variables, there is not sufficient evidence that β_3 is significantly different from zero ($t = -0.86$, $p=0.392$). Removing X_3 and fitting a new model, there is not sufficient evidence that β_4 is significantly different from zero ($t = -1.38$, $p=0.172$).

The best model using best subsets regression appears to be the simple regression model:
$\hat{Y} = 10.9368 + 3.592X_2$. There is sufficient evidence that β_2 is significantly different from zero
($t = 3.90$, $p < 0.001$) and
$r^2 = 0.163$. A residual analysis shows no strong patterns.

14.80-14.84
Based on best subsets regression, the following were the best models for predicting appraised value using six measures available for the homes in the sample for each community – lot size, number of bedrooms, number of bathrooms, age of house, presence of an eat-in-kitchen (EIK), and presence of central air conditioning (CAC):
East Meadow:
$\hat{Y} = 137.68 + 41.969$ Bath $+ 13.581$ CAC
$r^2 = 0.503$, $r^2_{adj} = 0.489$. The C_p value $= 3.0$.

Farmingdale:
$\hat{Y} = 142.61 - 1.0451$Lotsize $- 5.103$Bedrooms $+ 31.958$Bathrooms $+ 22.14$EIK $+ 49.37$CAC
$r^2 = 0.437$, $r^2_{adj} = 0.385$. The C_p value $= 6.0$.

Levittown:
$\hat{Y} = 174.99 + 1.1906$ Lotsize $+ 14.341$ Bathrooms $- 1.1408$ Age $+8.718$ EIK
$r^2 = 0.359$, $r^2_{adj} = 0.331$. The C_p value $= 3.6$.

Islip:
$\hat{Y} = 100.99 + 0.7436$ Lotsize $+ 4.784$ Bedrooms $+ 11.904$ Bathrooms
$- 0.1926$ Age $+ 15.09$ EIK $+ 27.09$ CAC
$r^2 = 0.366$, $r^2_{adj} = 0.317$. The C_p value $= 7.0$.

Islip Terrace:
$\hat{Y} = 98.87 + 11.141$ Bedrooms $- 0.7143$ Age $+ 35.70$ EIK $+ 16.811$ CAC
$r^2 = 0.590$, $r^2_{adj} = 0.549$. The C_p value $= 4.4$.

14.80-14.84
cont.

Based on best subsets regression, the following were the best models for predicting taxes using six measures available for the homes in the sample for each community – lot size, number of bedrooms, number of bathrooms, age of house, presence of an eat-in-kitchen (EIK), and presence of central air conditioning (CAC):

East Meadow:

$$\hat{Y} = 175.0 + 153.5 \text{ Lotsize} + 178.37 \text{Bedrooms} + 784.3 \text{ Bathrooms}$$

$r^2 = 0.598$, $r^2_{adj} = 0.581$. The C_p value = 4.0.

Farmingdale:

$$\hat{Y} = 3168.8 + 499.5 \text{ Bathrooms} - 28.003 \text{ Age} + 562.9 \text{ CAC}$$

$r^2 = 0.394$, $r^2_{adj} = 0.362$. The C_p value = 3.8.

Levittown:

$$\hat{Y} = 2904.8 + 58.65 \text{ Lotsize} + 492.53 \text{ Bathrooms} - 35.47 \text{ Age} + 541.0 \text{ CAC}$$

$r^2 = 0.504$, $r^2_{adj} = 0.483$. The C_p value = 4.7.

Islip:

$$\hat{Y} = 2859.5 + 260.11 \text{ Bedrooms} + 441.6 \text{ Bathrooms} - 10.652 \text{ Age} + 800.2 \text{ CAC}$$

$r^2 = 0.604$, $r^2_{adj} = 0.584$. The C_p value = 3.4.

Islip Terrace:

$$\hat{Y} = 2835.8 + 591.2 \text{ Bathrooms}$$

$r^2 = 0.257$, $r^2_{adj} = 0.240$. The C_p value = 1.0.

CHAPTER 15

•15.2 (a) Since you need data from four prior years to obtain the centered 9-year moving average for any given year and since the first recorded value is for 1955, the first centered moving average value you can calculate is for 1959.

(b) You would lose four years for the period 1955-1958 since you do not have enough past values to compute a centered moving average. You will also lose the final four years of recorded time series since you do not have enough later values to compute a centered moving average. Therefore, you will "lose" a total of eight years in computing a series of 9-year moving averages.

•15.4 (a),(b),(c),(e)

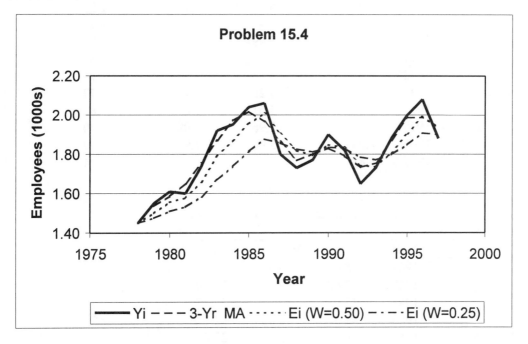

(d) $\hat{Y}_{1998} = E_{1997} = 1.94$ thousand employees

(f) $\hat{Y}_{1998} = E_{1997} = 1.90$ thousand employees

(g) The results are nearly the same.

•15.4 (b),(c),(e)
cont.

Year	Y_i	3-Yr Moving Total	3-Yr MA	$E_i(W=0.50)$	$E_i(W=0.25)$
1978	1.45			1.45	1.45
1979	1.55	4.61	1.54	1.50	1.48
1980	1.61	4.76	1.59	1.56	1.51
1981	1.60	4.95	1.65	1.58	1.53
1982	1.74	5.26	1.75	1.66	1.58
1983	1.92	5.61	1.87	1.79	1.67
1984	1.95	5.91	1.97	1.87	1.74
1985	2.04	6.05	2.02	1.95	1.81
1986	2.06	5.90	1.97	2.01	1.88
1987	1.80	5.59	1.86	1.90	1.86
1988	1.73	5.30	1.77	1.82	1.82
1989	1.77	5.40	1.80	1.79	1.81
1990	1.90	5.49	1.83	1.85	1.83
1991	1.82	5.37	1.79	1.83	1.83
1992	1.65	5.20	1.73	1.74	1.79
1993	1.73	5.26	1.75	1.74	1.77
1994	1.88	5.61	1.87	1.81	1.80
1995	2.00	5.96	1.99	1.90	1.85
1996	2.08	5.96	1.99	1.99	1.91
1997	1.88			1.94	1.90

15.6 (b) 3-Year Moving Averages:

Year	All Races	Whites	Blacks
1981	38.07	39.87	22.53
1982	37.63	39.47	22.10
1983	37.93	39.73	22.17
1984	38.57	40.43	22.87
1985	39.70	41.57	23.63
1986	40.60	42.50	24.33
1987	41.33	43.30	24.70
1988	41.67	43.77	24.80
1989	41.57	43.63	24.90
1990	41.13	43.17	24.63
1991	40.37	42.43	24.00
1992	39.63	41.90	23.23
1993	39.53	41.80	23.67
1994	39.83	42.00	24.70

15.6
cont.   (c), (e) Exponentially Smoothed Series, $W = 0.50$ and $W = 0.25$:

	Year	$W = 0.50$ All Races	Whites	Blacks	$W = 0.25$ All Races	Whites	Blacks
	1980	38.90	40.60	23.50	38.90	40.60	23.50
	1981	38.40	40.20	22.95	38.65	40.40	23.23
	1982	37.90	39.70	22.33	38.34	40.10	22.84
	1983	37.75	39.55	22.26	38.15	39.93	22.68
	1984	38.28	40.08	22.43	38.31	40.09	22.66
	1985	38.79	40.69	23.12	38.56	40.40	22.95
	1986	39.89	41.74	23.81	39.17	41.00	23.33
	1987	40.70	42.57	24.25	39.75	41.60	23.68
	1988	41.10	43.14	24.58	40.19	42.12	23.98
	1989	41.55	43.67	24.69	40.64	42.64	24.19
	1990	41.37	43.33	24.84	40.78	42.73	24.39
	1991	40.79	42.82	24.47	40.64	42.62	24.32
	1992	40.24	42.41	23.69	40.40	42.47	23.96
	1993	39.62	41.90	23.19	40.05	42.20	23.65
	1994	39.76	41.95	24.30	40.01	42.15	24.09
	1995	40.18	42.28	25.15	40.16	42.26	24.56

(d) $\hat{Y}_{1996} = E_{1995} = 40.18$ for all races, 42.28 for whites, 25.15 for blacks

(All values in thousands of constant 1995 dollars)

(f) $\hat{Y}_{1996} = E_{1995} = 40.16$ for all races, 42.26 for whites, 24.56 for blacks

(All values in thousands of constant 1995 dollars)

(g)   The results are nearly the same for all races and whites. The result is slightly lower for blacks when $W = 0.25$.

15.8   (b)   3-Year Moving Averages:

Year	Balance	Spending	Taxes
1982	2766.67	6016.00	3249.00
1983	2740.00	6048.33	3308.00
1984	2742.00	6192.00	3450.00
1985	3006.00	6464.33	3458.33
1986	3153.00	6573.00	3420.00
1987	3625.33	6922.00	3296.67
1988	3718.00	6891.33	3173.67
1989	3792.33	6897.33	3105.33
1990	3501.00	6656.67	3156.00
1991	3546.33	6823.67	3277.33
1992	3601.00	7030.00	3429.00
1993	3561.33	7088.67	3527.33
1994	3450.67	7040.67	3590.00

15.8
cont.
(c), (e) Exponentially Smoothed Series, $W = 0.50$ and $W = 0.25$:

		$W = 0.50$			$W = 0.25$	
Year	Balance	Spending	Taxes	Balance	Spending	Taxes
1981	2961.00	6212.00	3251.00	2961.00	6212.00	3251.00
1982	2937.00	6097.50	3160.00	2949.00	6154.75	3205.50
1983	2681.50	5975.25	3293.50	2818.25	6079.31	3260.88
1984	2781.25	6142.13	3360.75	2833.94	6136.73	3302.66
1985	2850.13	6278.06	3427.88	2855.20	6206.05	3350.74
1986	3034.06	6474.03	3439.94	2945.90	6322.04	3376.06
1987	3178.03	6554.52	3376.47	3039.93	6400.28	3360.29
1988	3757.02	7007.76	3250.73	3363.95	6665.46	3301.47
1989	3626.51	6792.88	3166.87	3396.96	6643.59	3246.85
1990	3585.75	6722.94	3137.43	3433.97	6645.95	3212.14
1991	3523.88	6730.97	3207.22	3440.98	6669.21	3228.35
1992	3577.94	6904.98	3327.11	3488.73	6771.66	3283.02
1993	3643.47	7088.49	3445.05	3543.80	6896.74	3353.01
1994	3493.23	7001.75	3508.53	3493.60	6901.31	3407.76
1995	3396.62	6968.37	3571.76	3445.20	6909.73	3464.57

(d) $\hat{Y}_{1996} = E_{1995} = \$3396.12$ for balance of payments per capita, $\$6968.37$ for federal spending per capita, and $\$3571.76$ for federal taxes per capita.
(All values in constant 1995 dollars)

(f) $\hat{Y}_{1996} = E_{1995} = \$3445.20$ for balance of payments per capita, $\$6909.73$ for federal spending per capita, and $\$3464.57$ for federal taxes per capita.
(All values in constant 1995 dollars)

(g)   The amounts are nearly the same. The federal taxes per capita forecast in part (d) is more sensitive to increases in the final years of the time series.

•15.10 (a)   The Y-intercept $b_0 = 4.0$ is the fitted trend value reflecting the real total revenues (in millions of real constant 1995 dollars) during the origin or base year 1978.

(b)   The slope $b_1 = 1.5$ indicates that the real total revenues are increasing at a rate of 1.5 million dollars per year.

(c)   Year is 1982, $X = 1982 - 1978 = 4$
$\hat{Y}_5 = 4.0 + 1.5(4) = 10.0$ million dollars

(d)   Year is 1997, $X = 1997 - 1978 = 19$,
$\hat{Y}_{20} = 4.0 + 1.5(19) = 32.5$ million dollars

(e)   Year is 2000, $X = 2000 - 1978 = 22$
$\hat{Y}_{23} = 4.0 + 1.5(22) = 37.0$ million dollars

•15.12 (b)   The series has been increasing continuously over the period.

15.14 (b) $\hat{Y} = 4804.64 + 152.248X$, where X = years relative to 1982

(c) $X = 1997 - 1982 = 15$, $\hat{Y} = 4804.64 + 152.248 (15) = \$7088.4$ billion

$X = 1998 - 1982 = 16$, $\hat{Y} = 4804.64 + 152.248 (16) = \$7240.6$ billion

$X = 1999 - 1982 = 17$, $\hat{Y} = 4804.64 + 152.248 (17) = \$7392.9$ billion

$X = 2000 - 1982 = 18$, $\hat{Y} = 4804.64 + 152.248 (18) = \$7545.1$ billion

•15.16 (a)

Year	Receipts	Year	Receipts	Year	Receipts
1978	612.9	1985	682.3	1992	777.8
1979	638.2	1986	701.9	1993	798.9
1980	627.5	1987	752.1	1994	849.3
1981	659.3	1988	768.6	1995	887.0
1982	640.2	1989	799.4	1996	909.4
1983	603.0	1990	789.6	1997	932.1
1984	641.5	1991	774.6		

(c)

	A	B	C	D	E	F	G
1	Predicting Real Federal Receipts						
2							
3	*Regression Statistics*						
4	Multiple R	0.957256968					
5	R Square	0.916340902					
6	Adjusted R Square	0.911693174					
7	Standard Error	30.563609					
8	Observations	20					
9							
10	ANOVA						
11		*df*	*SS*	*MS*	*F*	*Significance F*	
12	Regression	1	184172.8762	184172.8762	197.1589062	3.87171E-11	
13	Residual	18	16814.41552	934.1341953			
14	Total	19	200987.2917				
15							
16		*Coefficients*	*Standard Error*	*t Stat*	*P-value*	*Lower 95%*	*Upper 95%*
17	Intercept	584.1840666	13.17125905	44.35294033	7.71439E-20	556.5122567	611.8558764
18	Coded Year	16.64186569	1.185205921	14.04132851	3.87171E-11	14.15183852	19.13189286

$\hat{Y} = 584.18 + 16.642X$, where X = years relative to 1978

(d) $X = 1998 - 1978 = 20$, $\hat{Y} = 584.18 + 16.642 (20) = \$917.0$ billion

$X = 1999 - 1978 = 21$, $\hat{Y} = 584.18 + 16.642 (21) = \$933.7$ billion

$X = 2000 - 1978 = 22$, $\hat{Y} = 584.18 + 16.642 (22) = \$950.3$ billion

(f) $\hat{Y} = 373.26 + 55.435X$, where X = years relative to 1978

(g) $X = 1998 - 1978 = 20$, $\hat{Y} = 373.26 + 55.435 (20) = \$1482.0$ billion

$X = 1999 - 1978 = 21$, $\hat{Y} = 373.26 + 55.435 (21) = \$1537.4$ billion

$X = 2000 - 1978 = 22$, $\hat{Y} = 373.26 + 55.435 (22) = \$1592.8$ billion

(h) The forecasts in (g) are actual (current) dollars while the forecasts in (d) are adjusted real (constant) dollars. The forecasts in (g) are adjusted to remove the portion of illusory increase due to inflation.

(i) Both real and actual federal receipts have been generally increasing over the period.

15.18 (b) $\hat{Y} = 3.733 - 0.0099X + 0.0334X^2$, where X years relative to 1975

(c) 1997: $\hat{Y} = 3.733 - 0.0099(22) + 0.0334(22)^2 = \$19.7$ billion

1998: $\hat{Y} = 3.733 - 0.0099(23) + 0.0334(23)^2 = \$21.2$ billion

1999: $\hat{Y} = 3.733 - 0.0099(24) + 0.0334(24)^2 = \$22.7$ billion

2000: $\hat{Y} = 3.733 - 0.0099(25) + 0.0334(25)^2 = \$24.4$ billion

(d)

Year	Revenues	Year	Revenues	Year	Revenues
1975	5.4	1983	6.6	1990	7.8
1976	5.4	1984	6.9	1991	8.5
1977	5.9	1985	7.3	1992	9.3
1978	6.6	1986	6.4	1993	9.7
1979	6.2	1987	6.8	1994	10.9
1980	6.4	1988	7.0	1995	11.8
1981	6.1	1989	7.3	1996	11.8
1982	6.1				

(f)

	A	B	C	D	E	F
2						
3	Regression Statistics					
4	Multiple R	0.891760401				
5	R Square	0.795236612				
6	Adjusted R Square	0.784998443				
7	Standard Error	0.903091589				
8	Observations	22				
9						
10	ANOVA					
11		df	SS	MS	F	Significance F
12	Regression	1	63.34869184	63.34869184	77.67371118	2.53115E-08
13	Residual	20	16.31148837	0.815574419		
14	Total	21	79.66018021			
15						
16		Coefficients	Standard Error	t Stat	P-value	
17	Intercept	4.751348974	0.372310912	12.76177739	4.54777E-11	
18	Coded Year	0.267469671	0.03034852	8.81326904	2.53115E-08	

$\hat{Y} = 4.751 + 0.2675X$, where X = years relative to 1975

156

(g)

	A	B	C	D	E	F
1	Predicting Real Revenues					
2						
3	*Regression Statistics*					
4	Multiple R	0.967065062				
5	R Square	0.935214834				
6	Adjusted R Square	0.928395343				
7	Standard Error	0.521172666				
8	Observations	22				
9						
10	ANOVA					
11		*df*	*SS*	*MS*	*F*	*Significance F*
12	Regression	2	74.4993822	37.2496911	137.1385064	5.11703E-12
13	Residual	19	5.16079801	0.271620948		
14	Total	21	79.66018021			
15						
16		*Coefficients*	*Standard Error*	*t Stat*	*P-value*	
17	Intercept	6.139956921	0.30518003	20.11913073	2.85875E-14	
18	Coded Year	-0.149112713	0.06733532	-2.214479909	0.039217859	
19	YearSquared	0.019837256	0.003096081	6.407214271	3.82324E-06	

$$\hat{Y} = 6.14 - 0.1491X + 0.0198X^2, \text{ where } X = \text{years relative to } 1975$$

(h)

	A	B	C	D	E	F
1	Exponential Trend Model for Real Revenue					
2						
3	*Regression Statistics*					
4	Multiple R	0.920786691				
5	R Square	0.847848129				
6	Adjusted R Square	0.840240536				
7	Standard Error	0.040893941				
8	Observations	22				
9						
10	ANOVA					
11		*df*	*SS*	*MS*	*F*	*Significance F*
12	Regression	1	0.186375449	0.186375449	111.4476117	1.26221E-09
13	Residual	20	0.033446289	0.001672314		
14	Total	21	0.219821738			
15						
16		*Coefficients*	*Standard Error*	*t Stat*	*P-value*	
17	Intercept	0.713989024	0.016859044	42.35050566	4.71145E-21	
18	Coded Year	0.01450775	0.001374247	10.55687509	1.26221E-09	

$$\hat{Y} = 5.176(1.034)^X, \text{ where } X = \text{years relative to } 1975$$

(i)

	Forecasts of Real Net Revenues Based on Models		
Year	Linear	Quadratic	Exponential
1997	10.6	12.4	10.8
1998	10.9	13.2	11.2
1999	11.2	14.0	11.5
2000	11.4	14.8	11.9

(j)   The forecasts of actual net revenues increase more per year than do the forecasts of real net revenues, due to the fact that the real revenues have been adjusted to remove the increase that is explained by inflation.

(k)   Both actual and real net revenues generally increased over the period. The quadratic and exponential models appear to provide a better fit to the real net revenue data.

•15.20 (b) $\hat{Y} = 0.649(1.1129)^{X}$, where X = years relative to 1975

(c)   1997: $\hat{Y} = 0.649 (1.1129)^{22} = \$6.8$ billion
       1998: $\hat{Y} = 0.649 (1.1129)^{23} = \$7.6$ billion
       1999: $\hat{Y} = 0.649 (1.1129)^{24} = \$8.5$ billion
       2000: $\hat{Y} = 0.649 (1.1129)^{25} = \$9.4$ billion

(d)

Year	Revenues	Year	Revenues	Year	Revenues
1975	1.3	1983	1.2	1990	3.7
1976	1.2	1984	1.4	1991	3.5
1977	1.3	1985	1.6	1992	3.4
1978	1.5	1986	1.6	1993	3.4
1979	1.7	1987	1.7	1994	3.5
1980	1.5	1988	1.9	1995	3.1
1981	1.3	1989	2.6	1996	3.1
1982	1.2				

(f) $\hat{Y} = 0.827 + 0.1241X$, where X = years relative to 1975

(g) $\hat{Y} = 1.226 + 0.0042 + 0.0057X^{2}$, where X = years relative to 1975

(h) $\hat{Y} = 1.073(1.0586)^{X}$, where X = years relative to 1975

(i)

	Forecasts of Real Gross Revenues Based on Models		
Year	Linear	Quadratic	Exponential
1997	3.6	4.1	3.8
1998	3.7	4.3	4.0
1999	3.8	4.6	4.2
2000	3.9	4.9	4.5

(j)   The forecasts of actual gross revenues are higher and increase more per year than do the forecasts of real gross revenues, due to the fact that the real revenues have been adjusted to remove the increase that is explained by inflation since 1982-84.

(k)   Actual gross revenue climbed slowly during the early years of the period and increased to nearly 5 billion in the 1990s. Real gross revenue was stable through 1987, increased for a couple of years, and then declined slowly in the 1990s. The quadratic and exponential models appear to provide the best fits to the real gross revenue data.

15.22 (a)   For Time Series I, the graph of Y vs. X appears to be more linear than the graph of log Y vs. X, so a linear model appears to be more appropriate. For Time Series II, the graph of log Y vs. X appears to be more linear than the graph of Y vs. X, so an exponential model appears to be more appropriate.

15.22

cont. (b)   Time Series I: $\hat{Y} = 100.082 + 14.9752X$, X = years relative to 1988

Time Series II: $\hat{Y} = 99.704(1.1501)^X$, X = years relative to 1988

(c)   Time Series I: $\hat{Y} = 100.082 + 14.9752(12) = 279.8$

Time Series II: $\hat{Y} = 99.704(1.1501)^{12} = 534.0$

•15.24 (a)

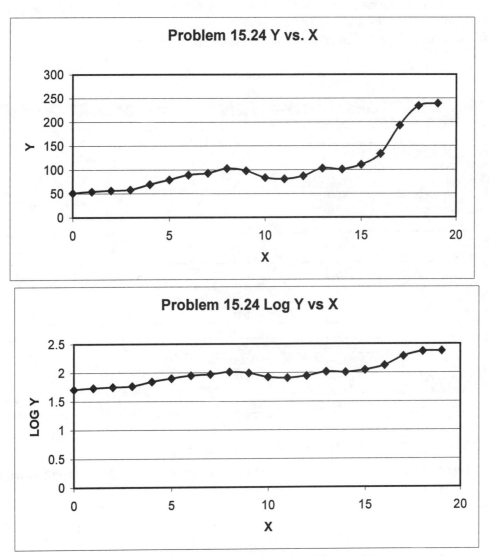

Since the second graph is more linear, an exponential model appears to be more appropriate.

(b) $\hat{Y} = 50.049(1.0705)^X$, where X = years relative to 1978

(c)   Annual growth has been 7.05% per year.

(d) $\hat{Y} = 50.049(1.0705)^{22} = 224.0$ millions of constant 1995 dollars

15.26 $t = \dfrac{a_3}{S_{a_2}} = \dfrac{0.24}{0.10} = 2.4 > t_{10,0.025} = 2.2281$. Reject H_0. There is sufficient evidence that the third-

order regression parameter is significantly different than zero. A third-order autoregressive model is appropriate.

15.28 (a) $t = \dfrac{a_3}{S_{a_2}} = \dfrac{0.24}{0.15} = 1.6 < t_{10,0.025} = 2.2281$. Do not reject H_0. . There is not sufficient evidence that

the third-order regression parameter is significantly different than zero. A third-order autoregressive model is not appropriate.

(b) Fit a second-order autoregressive model and test to see if it is appropriate.

15.30 (a)

	A	B	C	D	E	F
1	Third Order Autoregressive Model					
2						
3	Regression Statistics					
4	Multiple R	0.968439758				
5	R Square	0.937875565				
6	Adjusted R Square	0.925450678				
7	Standard Error	0.522987607				
8	Observations	19				
9						
10	ANOVA					
11		df	SS	MS	F	Significance F
12	Regression	3	61.93794976	20.64598325	75.48362966	2.80547E-09
13	Residual	15	4.102740557	0.273516037		
14	Total	18	66.04069031			
15						
16		Coefficients	Standard Error	t Stat	P-value	
17	Intercept	-0.655529424	0.82065946	-0.798783729	0.43688152	
18	X Variable 1	0.972910366	0.279347976	3.482790103	0.003339405	
19	X Variable 2	0.026242666	0.389558066	0.067365223	0.947180696	
20	X Variable 3	0.141097321	0.339846253	0.415179864	0.683887982	

$$\hat{Y}_i = -0.6555 + 0.9729Y_{i-1} + 0.262Y_{i-2} + 0.1411Y_{i-3}$$

Test of A_3: $t = 0.4152 < t_{15,0.025} = 2.1315$. Do not reject H_0 that $A_3 = 0$. Third-order term can be deleted.

15.30 (b)
cont.

	A	B	C	D	E	F
1	Second order Autoregressive Model					
2						
3	Regression Statistics					
4	Multiple R	0.968795006				
5	R Square	0.938563764				
6	Adjusted R Square	0.931335972				
7	Standard Error	0.501446814				
8	Observations	20				
9						
10	ANOVA					
11		df	SS	MS	F	Significance F
12	Regression	2	65.30371054	32.65185527	129.8548308	5.03048E-11
13	Residual	17	4.27463142	0.251448907		
14	Total	19	69.57834196			
15						
16		Coefficients	Standard Error	t Stat	P-value	
17	Intercept	-0.321162839	0.610514683	-0.526052604	0.605647099	
18	X Variable 1	0.993336011	0.26376464	3.765993853	0.001540487	
19	X Variable 2	0.096416299	0.314077543	0.306982466	0.762585181	

$$\hat{Y}_i = -0.3212 + 0.9933Y_{i-1} + 0.0964Y_{i-2}$$

Test of A_2: $t = 0.3070 < t_{17,0.025} = 2.1098$. Do not reject H_0 that $A_2 = 0$. Second-order term can be deleted.

(c)

	A	B	C	D	E	F
1	First order Autoregressive Model					
2						
3	Regression Statistics					
4	Multiple R	0.970739176				
5	R Square	0.942334548				
6	Adjusted R Square	0.939299525				
7	Standard Error	0.476241544				
8	Observations	21				
9						
10	ANOVA					
11		df	SS	MS	F	Significance F
12	Regression	1	70.42025152	70.42025152	310.4867116	3.14189E-13
13	Residual	19	4.309314148	0.226806008		
14	Total	20	74.72956567			
15						
16		Coefficients	Standard Error	t Stat	P-value	
17	Intercept	-0.249163087	0.460902556	-0.540598189	0.595065906	
18	X Variable 1	1.075282954	0.061024082	17.62063312	3.14189E-13	

$$\hat{Y}_i = -0.2492 + 1.0753Y_{i-1}$$

Test of A_1: $t = 17.621 > t_{19,0.025} = 2.093$. Reject H_0 that $A_1 = 0$. A first-order autoregressive model is appropriate.

15.30

cont. (d) 1997: $\hat{Y}_{22} = -0.2492 + 1.0753Y_{21} = -0.2492 + 1.0753(11.79) = \$12.43$ billion

1998: $\hat{Y}_{23} = -0.2492 + 1.0753\hat{Y}_{22} = -0.2492 + 1.0753(12.43) = \$13.12$ billion

1999: $\hat{Y}_{24} = -0.2492 + 1.0753\hat{Y}_{23} = -0.2492 + 1.0753(13.12) = \$13.85$ billion

2000: $\hat{Y}_{25} = -0.2492 + 1.0753\hat{Y}_{24} = -0.2492 + 1.0753(13.85) = \$14.65$ billion

•15.32 (a) $\hat{Y}_i = 0.2321 + 1.2526Y_{i-1} - 0.3708Y_{i-2} + 0.0417Y_{i-3}$

Test of A_3: $t = 0.146 < t_{15,0.025} = 2.1315$. Do not reject H_0 that $A_3 = 0$. Third-order term can be deleted.

(b) $\hat{Y}_i = 0.2353 + 1.2429Y_{i-1} - 0.3233Y_{i-2}$

Test of A_2: $t = -1.397 > -t_{17,0.025} = -2.1098$. Do not reject H_0 that $A_2 = 0$. Second-order term can be deleted.

(c) $\hat{Y}_i = 0.1840 + 0.9533Y_{i-1}$

Test of A_1: $t = 12.549 > t_{19,0.025} = 2.093$. Reject H_0 that $A_1 = 0$. A first-order autoregressive model is appropriate.

(d) 1997: $\hat{Y}_{22} = 0.1840 + 0.9533Y_{21} = 0.1840 + 0.9533(3.12) = \$3.16$ billion

1998: $\hat{Y}_{23} = 0.1840 + 0.9533\hat{Y}_{22} = 0.1840 + 0.9533(3.16) = \$3.20$ billion

1999: $\hat{Y}_{24} = 0.1840 + 0.9533\hat{Y}_{23} = 0.1840 + 0.9533(3.20) = \$3.23$ billion

2000: $\hat{Y}_{25} = 0.1840 + 0.9533\hat{Y}_{24} = 0.1840 + 0.9533(3.23) = \$3.27$ billion

•15.34 (a) $S_{YX} = \sqrt{\dfrac{\sum_{i=1}^{n}(Y_i - \hat{Y}_i)^2}{n - p - 1}} = \sqrt{\dfrac{305}{12 - 1 - 1}} = 5.523$. The standard error of the estimate is 5.523 billion constant 1995 dollars.

(b) $MAD = \dfrac{\sum_{i=1}^{n}|Y_i - \hat{Y}_i|}{n} = \dfrac{38}{12} = 3.167$. The mean absolute deviation is 3.167 billion constant 1995 dollars.

15.38 (a)-(c)

				Residuals by Model		
Year	Yearcode	Y_i	Linear	Quadratic	Exponent	Autoreg
1975	0	2.602	0.642	-0.372	0.440	
1976	1	2.636	0.569	-0.156	0.407	0.002
1977	2	2.640	0.466	0.002	0.342	-0.042
1978	3	2.607	0.325	0.093	0.237	-0.081
1979	4	2.755	0.366	0.337	0.311	0.113
1980	5	2.791	0.295	0.440	0.272	-0.058
1981	6	2.530	-0.074	0.216	-0.068	-0.371
1982	7	2.280	-0.432	-0.026	-0.399	-0.253
1983	8	2.209	-0.610	-0.117	-0.553	0.028
1984	9	2.214	-0.712	-0.162	-0.634	0.133
1985	10	2.230	-0.803	-0.223	-0.706	0.143
1986	11	2.555	-0.586	-0.006	-0.473	0.444
1987	12	2.817	-0.431	0.120	-0.305	0.249
1988	13	3.043	-0.313	0.180	-0.175	0.106
1989	14	3.065	-0.399	0.007	-0.254	-0.191
1990	15	3.290	-0.280	0.010	-0.132	0.004
1991	16	3.451	-0.227	-0.082	-0.077	-0.153
1992	17	3.706	-0.079	-0.108	0.069	-0.124
1993	18	3.737	-0.156	-0.388	-0.014	-0.453
1994	19	4.116	0.116	-0.348	0.249	-0.117
1995	20	4.462	0.355	-0.370	0.474	-0.306
1996	21	6.182	1.968	0.953	2.071	0.927
	SSE		7.954	1.996	7.088	1.784
	S_{YX}		0.631	0.324	0.595	0.306
	Abs Sum		10.203	4.715	8.660	4.300
	MAD		0.464	0.214	0.394	0.205

(d) The residuals in the first three models and the autoregressive model show strings of consecutive positive and negative values. The quadratic model provides a good fit and, using the principle of parsimony, would probably be a good model for forecasting.

15.40 (a) $\ln b_0 = 2$. $b_0 = e^2 = 7.389$. This is the fitted value for January 1993 prior to adjustment by the January multiplier.

(b) $\ln b_1 = 0.01$. $b_1 = e^{0.01} = 1.01005$. The estimated monthly compound growth rate is $(b_1 - 1)$ x 100% = 1.005%.

(c) $\ln b_2 = 0.1$. $b_2 = e^{0.1} = 1.1052$. The January values in the time series are estimated to require a 10.52% increase above the value determined based on the monthly compound growth rate.

•15.42 (a) $\ln b_0 = 3.0$. $b_0 = e^{3.0} = 20.086$. This is the fitted value for January 1993 prior to adjustment by the quarterly multiplier.

(b) $\ln b_1 = 0.1$. $b_1 = e^{0.1} = 1.1052$. The estimated quarterly compound growth rate is $(b_1 - 1)$ x 100% = 10.52%.

(c) $\ln b_3 = 0.2$. $b_3 = e^{0.2} = 1.2214$. The second quarter values in the time series are estimated to require a 22.14% increase above the value determined based on the quarterly compound growth rate.

•15.44 (a)

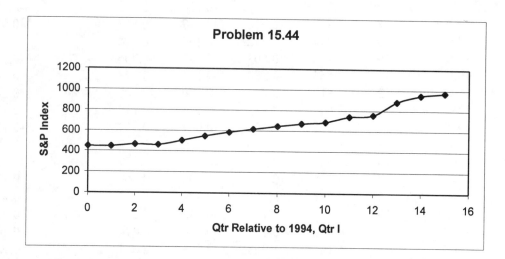

	A	B	C	D	E	F
2	Exponential Model for S&P Index					
3	Regression Statistics					
4	Multiple R	0.989936819				
5	R Square	0.979974906				
6	Adjusted R Square	0.972693054				
7	Standard Error	0.043867069				
8	Observations	16				
9						
10	ANOVA					
11		df	SS	MS	F	Significance F
12	Regression	4	1.03588206	0.258970515	134.5776962	2.91173E-09
13	Residual	11	0.021167517	0.00192432		
14	Total	15	1.057049577			
15						
16		Coefficients	Standard Error	t Stat	P-value	
17	Intercept	6.011187697	0.031115484	193.1895916	8.96553E-21	
18	Q1	0.010421639	0.031879168	0.326910637	0.749871743	
19	Q2	0.023885562	0.031404042	0.760588787	0.462894872	
20	Q3	0.019342411	0.031115484	0.621632977	0.546850376	
21	Coded Quarter	0.055372493	0.002452244	22.58033882	1.44859E-10	

(b) $\ln \hat{Y} = 6.01119 + X(0.05537) + Q_1(0.01042) + Q_2(0.02389) + Q_3(0.01934)$

(1) $Y_{15} = 903.02$

(2) $Y_{16} = 936.15$

(3)   1998: $Y_{17} = 999.81$, $Y_{18} = 1071.06$, $Y_{19} = 1126.91$, $Y_{20} = 1168.25$
        1999: $Y_{21} = 1247.70$, $Y_{22} = 1336.62$, $Y_{23} = 1406.31$, $Y_{24} = 1457.90$

164

•15.44 (b)
cont.

(4) $\ln b_1 = 0.055372$. $b_1 = e^{0.055372} = 1.0569$. The estimated quarterly compound growth rate is $(b_1 - 1)$ x $100\% = 5.69\%$.

(5) $\ln b_3 = 0.023886$. $b_3 = e^{0.023886} = 1.0242$. The second quarter values in the time series are estimated to require a 2.42% increase above the value determined based on the quarterly compound growth rate.

•15.46 (a)

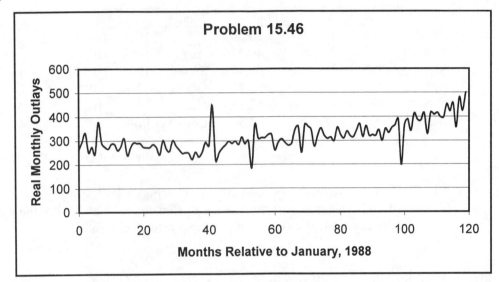

(b) Exponential trend equation:
        lnExpY = 5.52 + 0.00358 CodeMon - 0.0399 M1 - 0.0146 M2 + 0.0779 M3
        - 0.0882 M4- 0.0097 M5 + 0.0102 M6 + 0.0315 M7 + 0.0392 M8
        - 0.0434 M9+ 0.0052 M10 + 0.0353 M11

Month	Year	Code	Fitted Value
Nov	1997	118	396.44
Dec	1997	119	384.06

Month	Year	Code	Forecast	Month	Year	Code	Forecast
Jan	1998	120	370.36	Jul	1998	126	406.39
Feb	1998	121	381.20	Aug	1998	127	411.01
Mar	1998	122	419.66	Sep	1998	128	379.80
Apr	1998	123	356.69	Oct	1998	129	400.12
May	1998	124	387.22	Nov	1998	130	413.84
Jun	1998	125	396.43	Dec	1998	131	400.92

(4) $\ln b_1 = 0.003579$. $b_1 = e^{0.003579} = 1.0036$. The estimated monthly compound growth rate is $(b_1 - 1)$ x $100\% = 0.36\%$.

(5) $\ln b_7 = 0.010215$. $b_7 = e^{0.010215} = 1.0103$. The June values in the time series are estimated to require a 1.03% increase above the value determined based on the monthly compound growth rate.

15.48 (c), (e) Exponential trend equation:

$$\ln ExpY = 2.54 + 0.0158 \text{ CodeMon} - 0.031 \text{ M1} - 0.168 \text{ M2} - 0.055 \text{ M3} - 0.073 \text{ M4}$$
$$- 0.177 \text{ M5} - 0.165 \text{ M6} - 0.148 \text{ M7} - 0.150 \text{ M8} - 0.194 \text{ M9} - 0.187 \text{ M10}$$
$$- 0.225 \text{ M11}$$

Month	Year	Code	Fitted Value
Nov	1997	94	44.34
Dec	1997	95	56.42

Month	Year	Code	Forecast	Month	Year	Code	Forecast
Jan	1998	96	55.56	Jul	1998	102	54.35
Feb	1998	97	49.24	Aug	1998	103	55.06
Mar	1998	98	56.00	Sep	1998	104	53.56
Apr	1998	99	55.87	Oct	1998	105	54.79
May	1998	100	51.13	Nov	1998	106	53.57
Jun	1998	101	52.56	Dec	1998	107	68.16
				Dec	2000	131	99.49

(4) The estimated monthly compound growth rate is 1.59%.

(5) The July values in the time series are estimated to be 86.27% of the value determined based on the monthly compound growth rate.

15.60 (b) $\hat{Y} = 0.8267 + 0.4253X$, where X = years since 1915

(c) 1960: $\hat{Y} = 0.8267 + 0.4253(45) = 19.97$

1965: $\hat{Y} = 0.8267 + 0.4253(50) = 22.09$

1970: $\hat{Y} = 0.8267 + 0.4253(55) = 24.22$

(e) Mechanical trend extrapolations cannot account for structural changes that occur after the historical period, such as a polio vaccine in this situation.

15.62 (c) $\hat{Y} = 1.458 + 2.1492X$, where X = years relative to 1975

(d) $\hat{Y} = 5.120 + 1.0506X + 0.0523X^2$, where X = years relative to 1975

(e) $\hat{Y} = 6.856(1.1055)^X$, where X = years relative to 1975

(f) $\hat{Y}_i = 1.9973 + 1.1464Y_{i-1} - 0.162Y_{i-2} - 0.0023Y_{i-3}$

Test of A_3: $t = -0.008 > -t_{15,0.025} = -2.1315$. Do not reject H_0 that $A_3 = 0$. Third-order term can be deleted.

(g) $\hat{Y}_i = 1.8443 + 1.1537Y_{i-1} - 0.1673Y_{i-2}$

Test of A_2: $t = -0.685 > -t_{17,0.025} = -2.1098$. Do not reject H_0 that $A_2 = 0$. Second-order term can be deleted.

(h) $\hat{Y}_i = 1.848 + 0.9971Y_{i-1}$

Test of A_1: $t = 24.135 > t_{19,0.025} = 2.093$. Reject H_0 that $A_1 = 0$. A first-order autoregressive model is appropriate.

15.62   (i)-(k)
cont.

Year	Yearcode	Y_i	Residuals by Model Linear	Quadratic	Exponent	Autoreg
1975	0	6.691	5.234	1.572	-0.165	
1976	1	7.557	3.950	1.334	-0.022	-0.963
1977	2	8.581	2.825	1.151	0.201	-0.802
1978	3	10.123	2.217	1.380	0.859	-0.281
1979	4	11.157	1.102	0.998	0.916	-0.785
1980	5	11.650	-0.553	-0.030	0.328	-1.322
1981	6	11.771	-2.582	-1.536	-0.746	-1.694
1982	7	12.021	-4.482	-3.017	-1.817	-1.565
1983	8	13.052	-5.599	-3.821	-2.246	-0.782
1984	9	13.282	-7.519	-5.531	-3.630	-1.581
1985	10	14.870	-8.080	-5.988	-3.827	-0.222
1986	11	23.631	-1.468	0.625	2.961	6.956
1987	12	24.824	-2.425	-0.437	1.972	-0.587
1988	13	26.796	-2.602	-0.823	1.533	0.196
1989	14	36.129	4.582	6.047	8.200	7.562
1990	15	39.250	5.554	6.600	8.374	1.377
1991	16	41.483	5.638	6.161	7.348	0.498
1992	17	42.124	4.129	4.025	4.387	-1.088
1993	18	42.145	2.001	1.164	0.426	-1.705
1994	19	43.927	1.634	-0.040	-2.195	0.055
1995	20	43.373	-1.070	-3.686	-7.616	-2.276
1996	21	44.105	-2.487	-6.149	-12.265	-0.991
	SSE		366.821	289.266	477.547	130.848
	S_{YX}		4.283	3.902	4.886	2.624
	Abs Sum		77.733	62.112	72.037	33.289
	MAD		3.533	2.823	3.274	1.585

(l), (m)   The autoregressive model should be selected.

Year	Yearcode	Forecasts by Model Linear	Quadratic	Exponent	Autoreg
1997	22	48.74	53.55	62.32	45.83
1998	23	50.89	56.96	68.90	47.54
1999	24	53.04	60.47	76.17	49.25
2000	25	55.19	64.08	84.20	50.96

15.64 (c) $\hat{Y} = 32.89 + 0.193X$, where X = years relative to 1975

(d) $\hat{Y} = 24.374 + 2.7479X - 0.1217X^2$, where X = years relative to 1975

(e) $\hat{Y} = 32.786(1.0045)^X$, where X = years relative to 1975

(f) $\hat{Y}_i = 6.6876 + 0.8689Y_{i-1} + 0.2899Y_{i-2} - 0.3607Y_{i-3}$

Test of A_3: $t = -1.006 > -t_{15,0.025} = -2.1315$. Do not reject H_0 that $A_3 = 0$. Third-order term can be deleted.

(g) $\hat{Y}_i = 6.8777 + 0.8936Y_{i-1} - 0.0941Y_{i-2}$

Test of A_2: $t = -0.387 > -t_{17,0.025} = -2.1098$. Do not reject H_0 that $A_2 = 0$. Second-order term can be deleted.

(h) $\hat{Y}_i = 8.9617 + 0.747Y_{i-1}$

Test of A_1: $t = 4.90 > t_{19,0.025} = 2.093$. Reject H_0 that $A_1 = 0$. A first-order autoregressive model is appropriate.

(i)-(k)

Year	Yearcode	Y_i	Residuals by Model Linear	Quadratic	Exponent	Autoreg
1975	0	24.349	-8.541	-0.025	-8.436	
1976	1	31.107	-1.976	4.107	-1.826	3.957
1977	2	32.343	-0.933	2.960	-0.737	0.145
1978	3	35.123	1.653	3.600	1.894	2.001
1979	4	33.747	0.084	0.328	0.369	-1.451
1980	5	30.583	-3.273	-4.489	-2.945	-3.587
1981	6	30.143	-3.905	-6.338	-3.535	-1.663
1982	7	31.088	-3.153	-6.560	-2.741	-0.390
1983	8	36.044	1.610	-2.527	2.063	3.860
1984	9	37.344	2.716	-1.907	3.210	1.457
1985	10	37.825	3.005	-1.861	3.538	0.968
1986	11	38.595	3.582	-1.285	4.154	1.378
1987	12	42.606	7.399	2.776	8.010	4.814

Year	Yearcode	Y_i	Residuals by Model			
			Linear	Quadratic	Exponent	Autoreg
1988	13	42.519	7.120	2.983	7.769	1.732
1989	14	43.387	7.795	4.388	8.481	2.664
1990	15	42.846	7.061	4.628	7.783	1.475
1991	16	41.997	6.019	4.802	6.777	1.030
1992	17	37.277	1.106	1.349	1.899	-3.056
1993	18	35.156	-1.208	0.738	-0.381	-1.652
1994	19	36.842	0.285	4.178	1.146	1.620
1995	20	22.900	-13.850	-7.767	-12.956	-13.582
1996	21	24.347	-12.596	-4.080	-11.671	-1.721
	SSE		753.739	334.330	763.882	296.066
	S_{YX}		6.139	4.195	6.180	3.947
	Abs Sum		98.872	73.677	102.322	54.204
	MAD		4.494	3.349	4.651	2.581

(l),(m) The autoregressive model should be chosen.

Year	Yearcode	Forecasts by Model			
		Linear	Quadratic	Exponent	Autoreg
1997	22	37.14	25.94	36.18	27.15
1998	23	37.33	23.22	36.34	29.24
1999	24	37.52	20.25	36.50	30.80
2000	25	37.72	17.03	36.67	31.97

15.66 (b),(e) Exponential trend equation:

$$\ln ExpY = 3.72 + 0.000246\ CodeMon - 0.00702\ M1 - 0.00313\ M2 - 0.00180\ M3$$
$$- - 0.00082\ M4 - 0.00187\ M5 - 0.00291\ M6 - 0.00316\ M7$$
$$- 0.00220\ M8 - 0.00204\ M9 - 0.00110\ M10 - 0.00014\ M11$$

Month	Year	Code	Forecast	Month	Year	Code	Forecast
Jan	1998	72	41.74	Jul	1998	78	41.96
Feb	1998	73	41.91	Aug	1998	79	42.01
Mar	1998	74	41.98	Sep	1998	80	42.03
Apr	1998	75	42.03	Oct	1998	81	42.08
May	1998	76	42.00	Nov	1998	82	42.13
Jun	1998	77	41.96	Dec	1998	83	42.15
				Dec	2000	107	42.40

(c) The estimated monthly compound growth rate is 0.025%.
The June values in the time series are estimated to be 99.71% of the value determined based on the monthly compound growth rate.